Elisabeth Ann Bowles
Belongs to Margaret S. Rune

A GOOD BEGINNING

Charles Duncan McIver

Julius I. Foust

Walter Clinton Jackson

A GOOD BEGINNING

The First Four Decades of

The University of North Carolina

at Greensboro

∽

Elisabeth Ann Bowles

THE UNIVERSITY OF NORTH CAROLINA PRESS

CHAPEL HILL

PREFACE

"Of a good beginning cometh a good end."   John Heywood

This is the story of a good beginning—the beginning of the State
Normal and Industrial School for Girls in Greensboro, North Carolina, and of the strong liberal arts college for women which it became.
It is an inspiring story, for it illustrates how much can be achieved by
devotion and faith. It is a story of struggle—against a chronic lack
of money, a typhoid epidemic, a fire, World War I, and the Depression—and a story of the men like Charles Duncan McIver and Julius
I. Foust and their faculties and students who found a way through
all difficulties. From this good beginning there truly cometh a good
end—The University of North Carolina at Greensboro. Although the
school has already surpassed anything envisioned in those early years,
it has the foundation on which to build a future greatness of immense
height and breadth because its early builders were men and women of
integrity, sound scholarship, and unselfish service.

The extent to which the story of the school is rooted in its many
alumnae and many friends is indicated by the means of the persons to
whom I am indebted for assistance with this book. It was originally
prepared as a thesis at The University of North Carolina at Chapel
Hill, a brother institution, under the direction of Dr. J. Minor
Gwynn, whose wise counsel and encouragement were essential to me—
and whose wife and sisters are alumnae. Miss Jane Summerell, Class
of 1910, gave advice drawn from her experience as a student and as a
member of the faculty, loving advice drawn from her deep interest in
the institution. Mrs. Frank Bouknight (Martha Lineberger), Class
of 1958, assisted me with the research and prepared the manuscript
(even my typing needed deciphering) for my excellent typist, Miss
Elizabeth Booker, Class of 1941.

Mrs. Albert Lathrop (Virginia Terrell), Class of 1923, who edited
the thesis for publication, was, during her student days, editor of the
Carolinian and president of the Student Government Association.
Later she returned to the college to establish the News Bureau, and

since 1949 she has been a member of the Board of Trustees of The University of North Carolina. Her closeness to the school and her editorial skill have given her, the one a love of the subject, and the other an objectivity, which have made her a careful and discerning editor.

Many are the librarians, secretaries, teachers, and fellow alumnae who have supplied information in such a kindly manner that my work has been made the more pleasant by the need for turning to them. Of that great multitude I have space to mention only a few, and these from the staff of the Walter Clinton Jackson Library, itself my greatest single source of information: Miss Marjorie Hood, Class of 1925; Miss Mary Robert Seawell; and Mrs. Elizabeth J. Holder.

Most of all I am grateful to my parents, who encouraged, sustained, and endured—and who in the beginning sent me to school at what had been the State Normal and Industrial College for Girls and which has become The University of North Carolina at Greensboro.

Contents

Illustrations

A GOOD BEGINNING

∼ one ∼

The Foundation
of the School

Although Charles Duncan McIver is the recognized founder of the State Normal and Industrial School, he always traced its origin back to the North Carolina Constitution of 1776. In December of that year a convention met in Halifax to adopt a constitution to protect the newly declared independence. Section 41 called for the "instruction of youth . . . at low prices." It also stated that "all useful learning shall be encouraged at one or more universities." One such university for men was established soon afterward in Chapel Hill; it was chartered in 1789. The cornerstone of its first building was laid in 1793 and its doors opened to students in 1795. The College of Agriculture and Mechanic Arts was opened in Raleigh in 1889. Even as late as that, however, the state had not interpreted "youth" to mean young women as well as young men.

The establishment of a small normal school might appear unimportant to those accustomed to thinking in terms of mass education, but viewed against the background of 1891, it assumes its rightful place as a milestone in the educational development of North Carolina.

The educational advances made by Calvin H. Wiley in the 1850's and Archibald Murphey in the second decade of the century were swallowed up by the disaster of the Civil War and Reconstruction. In 1873 a group of educators called to Raleigh by the State Board of Education adopted resolutions which included the statement: "That the general educational interests of this State are deplorable and alarming in a high degree, and are such as to require the noblest and most self-sacrificing efforts of every true son of North Carolina to relieve her from such serious embarrassment."[1]

In 1877 normal schools were established for the two races, one, for

1. Edgar W. Knight, *Public School Education in North Carolina* (New York: Houghton Mifflin Company, 1916), p. 257.

whites, at the University of North Carolina in Chapel Hill and one, for Negroes, in Fayetteville. The school in Chapel Hill offered a summer program, one of the first to be provided by a college in the United States. Because other educational facilities for the Negro race were not adequate, the school in Fayetteville was established on an eight-months basis to provide work in subject matter as well as methods. In reporting on the success of these schools and the need for others, State Superintendent of Public Instruction John C. Scarborough said,

> The larger number of teachers of the public schools who did not attend the Normal Schools, were incompetent, wanting in habits of study and in a knowledge of how to study to an advantage and consequently non-progressive, knowing nothing of any studies except such as they had imperfectly learned at the ordinary schools and nothing of the improved methods of teaching. . . .
> They were simply school *keepers*, nothing more.[2]

During the decade that followed other normal schools were added for the different races, enrolling men and women. Then in 1889 the statute providing for the normal schools for the white race was repealed, establishing county teachers' institutes instead. Thus, in the area of higher education, the state provided for white men at the university and at the College of Agriculture and Mechanic Arts, for Negro men and women at six normal schools, and for Indians at one. There was no provision for white women.

Despite these efforts there was a great need for teachers. Men like Charles Duncan McIver, Edwin A. Alderman, M. C. S. Noble, J. Y. Joyner, E. P. Moses, Alexander Graham, John J. Blair, and E. L. Hughes worked throughout the state to improve the caliber of teachers, but the educational conditions of 1891 were still "deplorable and alarming."

When the United States commissioner of education made his report in 1891, it appeared that North Carolina had the poorest school system of any state or territory in the nation with the possible exception of South Carolina, which often vied with North Carolina for last place. On per pupil expenditure, the national average was $17.62; North Carolina spent $3.36, South Carolina $3.03. The average length of the school term in the United States was 135.7 days; in North Carolina it was 60.3, the lowest in the country. The expenditure per

2. *Biennial Report of the Superintendent of Public Instruction* (Raleigh: Ashe and Gatling, 1883), p. 22.

capita of the adult male population was also the lowest, $2.06. The national average for teachers' salaries was $44.89 a month; the lowest reported was North Carolina's $24 a month. Although the report contained no figures on the educational background of teachers, there can be no doubt that the majority of teachers were poorly prepared, many of them having no training beyond that offered in the schools in which they taught. In the percentage of school population enrolled in public schools, North Carolina led only four other states, having 57.12 per cent enrolled. The national average was 68.95 per cent. The illiteracy rate in North Carolina was 36 per cent; in the nation it was less than 14. In fairness it must be added that in valuation of real and personal property, the average for the United States was $1,036; in North Carolina it was $361.[3]

No one can deny that North Carolina was a poor state. Much energy had been spent in self-pity and recriminations after the war, but this was in the past. A new age was in the making. A new breed of men, born in the war and reared in its desolation, had determined that the South would have a renascence and that education must be the midwife.

Early Efforts and the Charter

Among the groups advocating state-supported education for women, the North Carolina Teachers' Assembly was perhaps the most articulate and persistent. In 1886 the assembly, meeting in Black Mountain, passed unanimously "a Memorial to the General Assembly of North Carolina from the State Teachers' Assembly, praying for the establishment of a North Carolina Normal College for Training the Men and Women of the State who Are Preparing to Teach together with the proposed 'Act to Establish a Normal College.' "[4] Similar resolutions were passed by each succeeding Teachers' Assembly, and in 1889 a bill presented by them passed the Senate by a large majority but failed in the House by only a few votes.[5]

As recognition of the need for higher education of women grew, support was forthcoming. Major Sidney M. Finger, superintendent of public instruction, in his biennial reports in 1886, 1888, and 1890, and Governor Daniel G. Fowle, in his message to the General As-

3. *Report of the Commissioner of Education for the Year 1890-'91* (Washington: Government Printing Office, 1894), pp. 1-32.

4. North Carolina Teachers' Assembly, *Memorial in Behalf of the North Carolina Teachers' Training School* (n.p., 1886).

5. "Prospectus of the Normal and Industrial School of North Carolina, 1892-'93," in *Report of the Board of Directors, 1892-1930*, p. 5.

sembly in 1891, advocated the establishment of a normal school, and the King's Daughters petitioned the legislature to establish an industrial school for girls.[6] In 1890 the North Carolina Farmers' State Alliance expressed a belief in the paramount importance of free and liberal education alike for males and females and passed a resolution favoring and recommending "that ample appropriations and provisions be made by the State for the training and higher education of females."[7]

When the General Assembly met in Raleigh in January of 1891, Charles Duncan McIver and Edwin A. Alderman were there to represent the Teachers' Assembly in its proposal for a normal school. Both men were well known throughout the state because of their work in the teachers' institutes, and they had spread abroad the gospel of the normal school. Taking advantage of the great support for female education, they decided to restrict the normal school to girls.[8] Powerful support came from Dr. J. L. M. Curry, executive secretary of the Peabody Fund, who addressed the General Assembly. His advocacy of the normal school carried weight because he could promise aid from the Peabody Fund, a powerful new educational foundation established in 1867.

On February 18, 1891, all the resolutions, recommendations, and proposals became law; the North Carolina State Normal and Industrial School was established. Its purpose is set forth in Section 5 of the act, which in effect may be said to serve as the charter of the school:

> The objects of the Institution shall be (1) to give to young women such education as shall fit them for teaching; (2) to give instruction to young women in drawing, telegraphy, typewriting, stenography, and such other industrial arts as may be suitable to their sex and conducive to their support and usefulness. Tuition shall be free to those who signify their intention to teach upon such conditions as may be prescribed by the Board of Directors.

There was much to be done, however, before the school became a reality. The legislature appropriated $10,000 for the first year and elected a Board of Directors, one member from each of the nine congressional districts. Major Finger, as superintendent of public

6. *Ibid.*

7. *Proceedings of the Fourth Annual Session of the North Carolina Farmers' State Alliance held in the city of Asheville, N. C.—August 12, 13, 14, and 15, 1890* (Raleigh: Edwards and Broughton, 1890).

8. Rose Howell Holder, *McIver of North Carolina* (Chapel Hill: The University of North Carolina Press, 1957), pp. 112-13.

instruction, was a member ex officio and president. The first members were R. D. Gilmer, Waynesville; Colonel A. C. McAlister, Asheboro; M. C. S. Noble, Wilmington; Dr. J. M. Spainhour, Lenoir; Dr. R. H. Stancill, Margarettsville, B. F. Aycock, Fremont; H. G. Chatham, Elkin; W. P. Shaw, Winston; and E. McK. Goodwin, Raleigh.

Location and Building of the School

Since the primary task of the board was to find a suitable location for the school, the first meeting, which was held on June 9, 1891, was devoted to hearing bids from towns offering to provide a site and suitable buildings. The first offer made was that of Floral College, in Maxton, which offered to turn all its buildings over to the state. Then Graham and Thomasville each offered $20,000 in bonds. After lunch the representative from Durham came forth with an offer of $20,000 in cash and a site valued at $10,000. Thereupon Dr. Spainhour made a motion that they visit the towns, and the board decided to visit Durham and Graham on the next day, to spend the night in Greensboro, and to visit Thomasville on the following day.[9]

The stopover in Greensboro proved decisive; while the board was at the Benbow House, they were visited by a committee of Greensboro citizens offering $25,000 in behalf of the city of Greensboro. Since this offer had not been officially voted on by the people, a mass meeting of citizens that day had provided personal pledges for the full amount. Telegrams from the board to Durham, Graham, and Thomasville brought offers of $30,000. Greensboro was then given an opportunity to raise its offer,[10] and another meeting brought pledges of $5,000 more.

When Dr. Benbow announced that Greensboro offered $30,000 and a site, Mr. Chatham moved to accept the offer and locate the school in Greensboro. The motion carried and the board went to Benbow Hall where Major Finger announced its decision to the citizens gathered there. He said,

> I believe it will grow into a great State School. Not for poor people alone but for both rich and poor. I congratulate Greensboro on the result. I believe this is the proper place for it. Piedmont is the coming part of the State. I believe in co-education of the sexes, and believe and hope that the institution today located here may grow into a school for both sexes. There will be

9. Board of Directors, Proceedings, I (June 9, 1891), 1.
10. Greensboro *Patriot*, June 18, 1891.

two other similar schools, one in the east and one in the west, but they will come hereafter. Yours is first.[11]

With this announcement, the people set the bells ringing and the whistles to blowing. The town was happy.[12]

The competing towns were, of course, not pleased by the decision. The Graham *Gleaner* accused Benbow and Finger of being sly and cunning and criticized Greensboro as an appropriate site because board there would not be inexpensive and the students at Greensboro Female College would look down on the girls from ''The Institute.''[13] The *Carolina Watchman* of Salisbury concurred in these objections and added that Greensboro's bid was too late.[14] The Durham *Weekly Globe*, however, conceded defeat gracefully: ''Greensboro was a winner sure enough. She had the boodle and she got the school. Greensboro will please shake.''[15]

At the meeting in Greensboro, the board made another important decision: Charles Duncan McIver was unanimously elected president of the school at a salary of $2,250. Edwin A. Alderman was selected as professor of English and history at a salary of $2,000. Having transacted its business, the board adjourned, leaving Greensboro to raise the money and to provide a suitable location.[16]

Raising the money was not difficult; the bond issue was passed on July 28, 1891, by a vote of 771 to 0, and during the first six months $6,000 in bonds were sold. The remaining $24,000 in bonds were sold in New York through the efforts of Thomas Woodroffe, who was on commission. Selecting a site did not prove to be so easy. Aycock, McAlister, and Chatham composed the Committee on a Site, and on August 20 the board, meeting in Greensboro, notified the mayor that the sites offered were not suitable. After considering several locations, they finally approved the one donated by R. S. Pullen and R. T. Gray of Raleigh. Located in the southwestern section of town near Moore's Mineral Springs and the railroad, it ''promised to be more healthful, to have better surroundings, and be more conspicuous to the traveling public.''[17] When the need for more space became apparent, the board purchased from Pullen and Gray three and a half acres adjoining the original ten-acre lot.

11. *The Daily Workman* (Greensboro, N. C.), June 13, 1891.
12. *News and Observer* (Raleigh, N. C.), June 13, 1891.
13. June 18, 1891.
14. July 9, 1891.
15. June 12, 1891.
16. Board of Directors, Proceedings, I (June 19, 1891), 4.
17. *Ibid.*, p. 25.

The Building Committee, composed of Goodwin, Noble, and Stan-cill, recommended that the board accept the plans submitted by Epps and Hackett of Greensboro and that Thomas Woodroffe be commissioned to erect the buildings. The architects charged $500, and Woodroffe agreed to do the work and supply the materials for the cost plus 10 per cent. The principal buildings were Main Building (later called Administration Building and then officially named in honor of Dr. Julius I. Foust in 1960) and Brick Dormitory. These were built of brick, trimmed with granite, covered with metal shingles, and plastered with Acme cement. The school building had two stories. On the first there were the president's office, six large recitation rooms with necessary cloak rooms, and retiring rooms for teachers and pupils. On the second floor there were five large recitation rooms, a chapel equipped with desks, and two rooms with bay windows. The dormitory was three stories high. In the basement was the kitchen, and on the first floor there was a dining room seating 150. There were fourteen rooms on the first floor and twenty-two on the second. There was space for twenty-two rooms on the third floor, but there was not enough money to complete it. Both buildings had hot-water heat.

On the property purchased from Pullen and Gray, the board erected two frame buildings, one a ten-room house for the president, the other a twenty-two room dormitory, Midway, so called for the famous section of the Chicago World's Fair and later named Guilford Hall. Since these buildings were not included in the agreement made with Greensboro, the board mortgaged them and the property for $9,000. When the wells proved insufficient for the water supply, the board connected the buildings with the city water works.

The First Faculty

On May 20, 1892, the Board of Directors met in Greensboro to inspect the buildings and to approve plans for the opening of the school. They voted at that time that their meetings were to be private and that neither the president of the school nor any other person should be present except by invitation. After approving the purchase of furniture and the appointment of a treasurer, they invited President McIver to join them, and then the appointment of the faculty was considered. McIver, in addition to being president, was to occupy the Chair of Science, Art, and History of Education, and Alderman the Chair of English Literature and History. McIver had been graduated from the University of North Carolina in 1881; Alderman in 1882. Noble moved to establish other chairs: mathematics, natural science, ancient and modern languages, physical training, vocal music, freehand and industrial art (drawing), and stenography, typewriting, telegraphy, and bookkeeping.

After several testimonials were heard, the following appointments and salaries were approved:

Mathematics	Miss Gertrude Mendenhall	$ 750.00
Natural Sciences	Miss Dixie Lee Bryant	900.00
Ancient Languages	Miss Viola Boddie	750.00
Domestic Science	Miss Edith McIntyre	600.00
Physical Training	Dr. Marian Bitting	1,000.00
Art	Miss Melville Fort	450.00
Vocal Music	Miss Bessie Worthington	600.00

Newspapers throughout the state praised the qualifications of the staff. A native of Guilford County, Miss Mendenhall had attended Guilford College and had received her A.B. degree from Wellesley. She had taught three years at Peace Institute and three at Guilford. Miss Bryant had taught in elementary and preparatory schools before going to Massachusetts Institute of Technology, where she was graduated with high rank, receiving a B.S. degree. Miss Boddie, another native North Carolinian, was graduated from Peabody Normal College with the degree of Licentiate of Instruction. She had taught both before and after college. Dr. Bitting was the daughter of a well-known clergyman, Dr. C. C. Bitting of the American Baptist Publication Board. She had received her medical degree from the Woman's Medical College, located in Philadelphia, where she had subsequently practiced. Miss Fort was a graduate, with honors, from the Mississippi Industrial Institute and College. She had received additional training in New York and had taught at a college in Kentucky. Miss McIntyre had studied and taught at the New York College for the Training of Teachers.

At later meetings of the board other appointments were made. Edward J. Forney was appointed to serve as bursar and as instructor in commercial subjects, and Mrs. Fannie Cox Bell was to assist him in his teaching. Upon the resignation of Miss Worthington, Clarence R. Brown was selected to teach voice culture. Mrs. W. P. Carraway was to be the matron or housekeeper, and Miss Sue May Kirkland was lady principal and "referee in matters social and domestic." These appointments completed the staff which was to serve with McIver during that important first year.

Organization of the College

In the *Prospectus* McIver said, "The State wants this institution to be good enough for anybody, and the expenses low enough for anybody; and that is what it will strive to become."[18] Since it incorporated the plans of the Teachers' Assembly, the King's Daughters, and the Farmers' Alliance, the school was to be both a normal college and an industrial school; but from the beginning, the normal function was the more important. The general purpose of the institution was to provide education that would increase "the efficiency of a woman's work in whatever walk of life her lot may be cast."[19] There were to be three departments: Normal, Business, and Domestic Science.

The Normal Department was designed to provide work in English, history, mathematics, natural science, ancient and modern languages, art, vocal music, and physical culture. In addition, there were the courses in pedagogy taught by McIver: the principles and history of education and the science and art of teaching. As was the practice in most normal schools and colleges, the program had to meet the needs of students of widely varying backgrounds. Some had already graduated from other institutions such as Peace Institute in Raleigh and Greensboro Female College; many already had some teaching experience; some had a less adequate background than was desirable. McIver believed that the ideal normal college would accept only those students who had completed their "literary education," but at that time there was no need for such a school in North Carolina. Therefore, he determined to continue the project he and Alderman had begun in the teachers' institutes, that of raising the standards of the teaching profession.

The Business Department taught stenography, typewriting, telegraphy, and bookkeeping. One of the purposes of the school was to provide vocational training for those women who were forced to be self-supporting, and since teaching would not appeal to everyone, the business courses were offered.

Students in the Domestic Science Department were to include in their program some work in the Normal and Business departments because Dr. McIver believed that "a model woman, as the mistress of a model home, ought to know something of business, and, above all things, ought to be an intelligent teacher." In addition, the Domestic Science Department offered courses in theory and practice in cooking

18. *Prospectus*, p. 7.
19. *Ibid.*, p. 8.

and sewing, cutting and fitting, care of the sick, and general household economy. This was designed to prepare a woman for her "natural and proper position in life . . . at the head of her own household."[20]

There was also work available in special departments: Vocal Culture, Physical Culture, and Industrial Art. The vocal culture included vocal music and reading and elocution. The resident physician supervised the physical culture, which included gymnastics, calisthenics, and lectures on physical culture and on personal and public hygiene. The Industrial Art Department provided instruction "in form study and freehand drawing," architectural and mechanical drawing, modeling in clay, designing and decorative art, and the history of art. Some work in all these departments was required for the normal school students because every teacher had to be able to teach all of them.[21]

There were two courses of study leading to certification. The full course required four years and entitled the graduate to a diploma, which was to be a life-license to teach in North Carolina. This was the only school at that time authorized to award such diplomas and was the envy of its rival institutions.[22] Applicants might be admitted to any class for which they were qualified. The two-year course was made up of most of the freshman and sophomore work and some of the junior and senior courses. Completion of this program qualified the student for a five-year teaching license. One important requirement for both programs was a course in practice teaching. In addition to the undergraduate programs, the college offered postgraduate courses in any area.[23]

Admission Regulations

Regulations concerning admission of students were based on county representation. Each county was to have representation in proportion to its white school population. If there were too many applicants from one county, the county superintendent of public instruction was to administer an examination prepared by the president of the college, who later graded the papers and made the appointment on the basis of scholarship. If a county did not fill its quota, the vacancies could be filled by applicants from counties already having

20. *Ibid.*, p. 10.
21. *Ibid.*, p. 11.
22. *Ibid.*, p. 12.
23. *Ibid.*, p. 21. Although postgraduate courses were not described in the catalogue, some were offered. Of the first 118 graduates, 20 had returned for postgraduate work by 1899. Greensboro *Record*, Jan. 28, 1899.

their number of applicants. After the school was in operation, these vacancies were filled by other applicants, in this order: (1) graduates of colleges for young women, (2) students who had formerly boarded with private families and who had been recommended by the faculty, and (3) the most qualified of the new applicants.[24] The advantage of being included in the quota was that it qualified a student for a place in the dormitory at eight dollars a month. Those who lived in private homes paid ten or twelve dollars. Seventy-three of the counties were allotted one student; twenty-two were entitled to two; and one, Buncombe, to three.

Graduates of the "best country public schools" who had been industrious students were supposed to be able to meet the entrance requirements listed in the *Prospectus*:

1. They must be able
   a. to analyze any ordinary arithmetical problem
   b. to read any English page fluently at sight
   c. to express thoughts accurately in writing
   d. to answer fairly well questions on English Grammar, Geography, History of the United States, and the History of North Carolina.
2. They should be sixteen years old and in good health.
3. They should send with their applications, which they themselves should write, statements from their last teachers as to scholarship and character.[25]

Expenses

The list of expenses was in keeping with the stipulation by the Board of Directors and the philosophy of President McIver that the cost be "low enough for anybody."

Tuition for the entire course	$ 40
Board in dormitories (not to exceed)	64
Laundry (not to exceed)	12
Physician's fee	5
Book fee	5
Contingent fee	2
	$128[26]

Tuition, board, and laundry were paid for quarterly, in advance, and the other charges were payable upon entering. Tuition was free to

24. *First Annual Catalogue of The State Normal and Industrial School* (Greensboro, N. C.: C. F. Thomas Printer, 1892-1893), p. 38.

25. *Prospectus*, p. 16.

26. *Ibid.*, p. 18.

those who planned to teach. There were a few other expenses—for medicine actually used, materials for art and science, and a gymnasium suit—but there was only one luxury offered. If a student wished a single bed, she was charged an additional four dollars.[27]

Each student was instructed to bring a pillow and a pair of pillow cases, one pair of sheets, one pair of blankets, one counterpane, towels, and table napkins.

During the summer McIver continued his work with the teachers' institutes while making the final arrangements for the opening of the school. Throughout the state competitive examinations were given for the scholarships. So eager for an education were the young women of North Carolina that McIver had to turn down more applicants than he could accept.[28]

27. *Ibid.*, p. 19.
28. Holder, *McIver*, p. 124.

two

The First Year

The State Normal and Industrial School opened on October 5, 1892. President McIver, who was at the depot to meet the students, helped them into carriages and sent them to the school. When one train arrived, McIver went aboard and found one student, Phoebe Pegram of Surry County, sitting in a corner by herself. She was at first reluctant to let him help with her bag, but she was quickly won over by his winning smile. Meeting the students at the depot was a custom which he continued for years.

When the girls reached the campus, they were met by Miss Kirkland, the dignified lady principal, who assigned them to their rooms. The first student to register was Mary Dail of Snow Hill, and hers was the first check registered in the treasurer's book. Miss Dail later explained, "Dr. McIver said, 'Now Mary, when the door opens, I expect you to be there.' I took him at his word, you see, and was the first to register." All day they came until there were 198 of them. By the end of the year the number had grown to 223, and McIver reported that there would have been 300 if room had been available. Of the total, 70 of the students lived in private homes, 10 were local students, and the others were crowded into the dormitories.[1]

The First Students

According to McIver, these girls represented socially, financially, and educationally every respectable class of North Carolina people.[2] For years he listed in the catalogue the occupations of the fathers to show the wide range of backgrounds of students. Their educational backgrounds also varied. A few were graduates of the leading institutions for girls; others had been graduated from graded schools or

1. *First Annual Catalogue of The State Normal and Industrial School* (Greensboro, N. C.: C. F. Thomas Printer, 1892-1893), p. 47.
2. *Ibid.*, p. 46.

private academies; some came with more limited preparation. From the mountains, from the coast—from all over the state they came.

The average age of the students the first year was nineteen and two-thirds years. Eighty of them had already taught, and ninety-five of them were paying their own expenses. President McIver saw in them "an earnestness and dignity of purpose which challenged admiration, and gave promise of good results in the future."[3]

The Opening of the College

The two main buildings which welcomed the students stood bleak and bare on a red clay hill with only one tree to break the monotony of the landscape. To the students, however, these gaunt structures were beautiful, for they represented the dream of higher education which had been denied its women by the state of North Carolina for so many years. Although the cost of an education at the Normal was not great, many students and their families had to make sacrifices. One such student, Fodie Buie of Robeson County, had borrowed a pacing horse and had driven seventeen miles to take the examination. When she succeeded in winning a scholarship, her father sold part of his farm to pay the remainder of her expenses. In addition to the freshman course, Fodie took physiology, shorthand, and typewriting. As a result of her part-time work in McIver's office, she was given a permanent position the following year. In a later tribute to McIver, she described her first day at the Normal:

> In the front of the building was a cornfield. I remember those forsaken-looking cornstalks yet. We were assigned rooms. We sat on our trunks in the hall and visited with each other, while we waited for our trunks to be carried to our rooms. While we waited for our beds to be put up for us, we had to sweep the shavings out, for the rooms were not even finished. Nobody knew anybody; even the faculty did not know each other. Everybody was homesick.[4]

This feeling did not persist, for there was too much to do, too much to learn. The students were without books for a while,[5] but all of

3. Charles Duncan McIver, "Report of the President," in *Report of the Board of Directors, 1892-1930*, Dec. 20, 1892, p. 33.

4. E. J. Forney, Fodie Buie, and Emily Semple Austin, *Leaves from The Stenographer's Notebook* (Greensboro: Harrison Printing Co., n.d.), p. 15.

5. McIver had ordered directly from the publisher to save money for the students and in so doing had antagonized one of the state's prominent book salesmen and editor of *The North Carolina Teacher*, whose attacks were soon to plague McIver and the school. *Webster's Weekly* (Reidsville, N. C.), May 4, 1893, and Greensboro *Record*, May 22, 1893.

them made the best of everything. They swept floors, made beds, and washed dishes. They met together and established rules for study and bedtime. In his report to the Board of Directors, McIver said that his policy was "to trust the students and appeal to their honor and pride, and to their interest in the success of the Institution."[6] Although the Student Government Association was not formally organized until 1914, it can trace its spiritual beginning to the faithfulness and responsibility that the students gave in return for McIver's trust.

President McIver was very pleased that the students repaid his confidence with a dedication to their work. Only two went home early for Christmas, one because of sickness in her family, the other because of the wedding of a close relative. Although many letters came from parents requesting that others come home early too, the students did not "consider it business-like to quit before their work was done."[7]

When students failed in their responsibilities, McIver could be very severe. Emily Semple Austin,[8] who succeeded Fodie Buie as stenographer, and her sister Eliza once over-stayed by one day their Christmas vacation with their uncle. Their excuse that they had written permission from their parents was not accepted, and they were required to write the "Contract" fifty times. Eliza wrote hers as directed, but Emily went to work for McIver and did not have time to finish.[9] The "Contract" referred to reads as follows:

I do hereby contract with the State Normal and Industrial College, that so long as I shall remain a student of the institution, I will endeavor to comply cheerfully with all its regulations in all particulars, and I agree not to deface or injure, by writing or otherwise, any of its furniture, books, or other property. Moreover, if I should accidently do damage to any property of the institution, I hereby agree to report it promptly to the President of the institution, or in case it should be dormitory property, I agree to report it to the lady in charge of the building where the damage is done, in order that it may be properly assessed, and that I may pay for the same.

The sterner side of McIver's character was not often in evidence. He carried a list of students in his pocket and made a point of talking with each of them at least once during the year so that he would be

6. *Report of the Board of Directors—December 20, 1892*, p. 35.

7. *Ibid.*

8. Miss Austin was President McIver's secretary until 1904. This incident probably occurred in 1900.

9. Forney, *et al., Stenographer's Notebook*, p. 21.

able to talk about them with their parents.[10] They knew him well, for whenever he was on campus he presided over the required daily assembly program. All the faculty were required to sit with him on the stage, but the students felt that their teachers did so with pride. McIver would read a bit of Scripture, often the fifth chapter of Matthew or the thirteenth chapter of First Corinthians. He then gave them news from the paper he always brought with him and sometimes gave specific instructions for the day. There might be a rebuke for some misdemeanor or an amusing illustration pointing out that some young lady should lengthen her skirt.[11]

E. J. Forney, who was to be treasurer of the college for many years, recalled McIver's custom of providing speakers for the girls.[12] Whenever an important person was visiting in the area or perhaps on the campus, he was usually persuaded to speak to the girls. When such an occasion arose, McIver would ring the bell[13] for a long time and the girls would assemble in the auditorium. One time they heard President E. Benjamin Andrews of Brown University; on another occasion, Vice-President Charles W. Fairbanks. Theodore Roosevelt talked about the dogwood blossoms, and Ambassador James Bryce of England spoke on college friendships. William Jennings Bryan chose as his topic "Women of the East," and Charles B. Aycock followed his familiar theme of "education for every country boy and girl." One Chautauqua lecturer gave the same impromptu talk on two different occasions twenty years apart.[14]

In addition to daily chapel programs, the students attended church on Sunday, each going to the church of her choice. Because it was not practical for them to attend Sunday night services in town, ministers often visited the school and conducted evening services in the auditorium. There were some small organizations among the students of a religious and benevolent character, but the first important

10. Miss Emma McKinney recalled that McIver once summoned her to his office to tell her that he had met her father at a meeting in Danville. Personal interview, Nov. 8, 1964.

11. Forney, *et al., Stenographer's Notebook*, p. 20.

12. *Ibid.*, p. 8.

13. This bell, known as ''Prep,'' was used to warn students to prepare for breakfast and to announce meals, classes, and walking period. It first stood behind the Administration Building, but as the campus expanded, it was moved to more central locations, first between the bridge and the library and later between Woman's and Spencer. In 1921 it was replaced by an electric bell system. It was then used for special occasions, such as election night, until it was taken down and stored. Later the Class of 1923 donated funds to have it mounted on a brick pillar on the site of the McIver House. It is still there.

14. Forney, *et al., Stenographer's Notebook*, p. 8.

student organization was the Young Women's Christian Association. On December 6, 1892, seventy-five students held an organizational meeting at which Bertha Lee of Davie County was elected president. This group was responsible for most of the religious work on the campus.

Literary Societies

Literary societies were popular at all colleges, and the girls wasted no time in organizing two at the Normal. The first plan to name the societies for McIver and Alderman and to have each student join one was abandoned because one name was drawing more people. It was decided that each student would be a member of one of the societies and that the voluntary plan for choosing members would not be satisfactory. Two student leaders, Mary Arrington of Nashville and Alice Green of Wilmington, were chosen to prepare lists of students. When the two lists were as equal as they could make them, the two students drew for them. After Miss Green drew Miss Arrington's list, the two girls exchanged groups and the societies were known by their initials, A and G, for the first year. During the second year the names "Cornelian" and "Adelphian" were adopted, and the Cornelian Society framed a formal constitution with the help of their honorary member, Mr. Forney. Two or three years later the Adelphians solicited Mr. Forney's help in writing theirs.[15]

The other organization which President McIver advocated was the Woman's Education Club. Membership was not limited to the students. Any women of the state who were interested in education could belong. Each member promised that for five years she would pay two dollars on the first of December to provide a scholarship fund at the school.

Students were encouraged but not required to join these organizations. All dues together were not over five dollars.

Social Life

The social life of the college was under the aegis of Miss Kirkland. One of the reasons for bringing her to the school was to establish a proper social atmosphere, for the administration wanted to provide opportunities for the students to "mingle with and accustom themselves to the requirements of cultured society."[16] In the evenings between study hour and lights-out they sat on the steps in Brick

15. *Ibid.*, p. 18.
16. *First Annual Catalogue*, p. 44.

Dormitory singing songs and telling jokes. Shopping, visiting, and receiving friends were among the activities encouraged by the school. Receiving gentlemen friends was evidently not encouraged with much enthusiasm because the first catalogue made the following statement: "Visits from gentlemen must be restricted to holiday occasions and those stated times when the young ladies will announce that they are 'At Home' to their friends generally."[17]

Miss Kirkland had somewhat rigid standards of dress and conduct. Since no lady would appear on the street without hat and gloves, the girls who lived in the small dormitory never came to the dining hall in Brick Dormitory without being hatted and gloved. Students were not allowed to wear trousers when playing men's roles in the plays. Miss Kirkland thought long black skirts were a satisfactory substitute. Many girls had their first training in the social amenities under the tutelage of this "referee in matters social and domestic."

Curriculum[18]

The other members of the faculty had been selected for the prestige they might contribute to academic affairs because of their background and ability. They were dedicated to making this institution one of the best normal schools in the country. They developed a course of study designed to meet the needs of the young women of North Carolina; the emphasis was on teacher preparation.

The Department of Pedagogy, the special province of President McIver, based its course of study on the following: (1) the history of education and of educational reformers, (2) the science of education, or educational principles, and (3) the art of education, or methods of teaching. In addition to the basic texts, Page's *Theory and Practice of Teaching* and Compayre's *History of Education*, the students studied Rousseau's *Emile*, Pestalozzi's *Leonard and Gertrude*, a critical study of Spencer's essay on education, essays on Bacon and his philosophy, *Evolution of Dodd*, and the lives and theories of the great educational reformers. The students were required to read these works critically, to express in their own language the views of the authors, and to make criticisms on the theories studied.

This department offered work in the sophomore, junior, and senior years. Each of the other departments supplemented this program by giving instruction in the teaching of its particular subject. Department heads also supervised the seniors in their practice teaching.

17. *Ibid.*
18. All information on the course of study was obtained from *ibid.*

Before the practice school was established in 1893, seniors taught underclassmen. Eleven students were classified as assistants or tutors in the *First Annual Catalogue*: Maude F. Broadaway, Minnie R. Hampton, Lina J. McDonald, Lizzie Lee Williams, Mary K. Applewhite, Georgia McLeod, Annie M. Page, Zella McCulloch, Carrie Mullins, Mattie Bolton, and Maggie Burke.

Edwin A. Alderman, professor of English and history, was such a popular lecturer that a rule was made limiting the number of spectators to those who could find seats, so numerous were the townspeople who crowded in to hear him.[19] The *First Annual Catalogue* outlined his course of study:

COURSE I. Clark's Briefer Rhetoric, Exercises in Composition, Letter Writing, Language Work, Readings in Nineteenth Century American Literature, Parallel Readings.
COURSE II. Morgan's *History of English and American Literature*, Critical Readings in Eighteenth Century Literature, Essays in Exposition, Parallel Readings, Trench on Words.
COURSE III. History of English Language, Shakespeare: Merchant of Venice, Macbeth, Julius Caesar, Tennyson's Idylls of the King.
COURSE IV. Critical Essays, Lectures, Practice in Writing, Practice in Methods of Teaching Language.

This course of study was arranged to achieve the purposes of the department: the ability to use the language with simplicity and force by means of composition in its simpler forms; a knowledge of the ground work of rhetoric, figurative language, and versification; a taste for good reading; and a knowledge of the rational methods of teaching these subjects.

This was Alderman's course of studies in history:

COURSE I. Studies in Civil Government, Constitutional History of the United States, Biographical Studies.
COURSE II. History of Greece and Rome, with lectures on the beginnings of history: Beginnings of Modern History.
COURSE III. English History, French Revolution, Studies in Colonial Records.

The purpose set forth by the History Department was to inculcate "a love and enthusiasm for historical study; a clear notion of the course of human events and the evolution of certain nations, communities and institutions; and aptitude and skill in handling books in historical research; and appreciation of the fact that history, like

19. Rose Howell Holder, *McIver of North Carolina* (Chapel Hill: The University of North Carolina Press, 1957), p. 133.

charity begins at home; and correct notions of teaching this great subject.''[20] During the third year Alderman gave the students opportunity for research on a subject in colonial records.

Students were required to take three years of mathematics and were offered a fourth as an elective. The required courses were elementary algebra; plane, solid, and spherical geometry; higher algebra; and plane trigonometry. The fourth year included spherical trigonometry and analytical geometry. Although a knowledge of arithmetic was required for admission to college, some attention was paid to arithmetic and to the methods of teaching it. Miss Gertrude Mendenhall was assisted by two tutors, Zella McCulloch and Carrie Mullins.[21]

The Department of Science was headed by Miss Dixie Lee Bryant, assisted by Minnie R. Hampton. Tutors were Mattie Bolton and Maggie Burke, also members of the graduating class.

In the freshman year the students studied physical geography one semester and botany the other. Both courses were developed through recitations, lectures, and observations. The next course was chemistry, which was taught for a year. Through lectures, recitations, problems, and laboratory work, students were encouraged to develop a scientific habit of thought. They were given the opportunity ''to do, to see, and to conclude.'' Physics was offered the junior year and was organized in much the same manner as chemistry, with more individual and independent laboratory work. In the senior year students might choose betwen zoology and geology, each a full year's work.

The chemical laboratory which Miss Bryant set up in the Main Building was the first such laboratory for women in the state. When funds were exhausted in the purchase of equipment, Miss Bryant designed the tables, which were made locally.[22] Until microscopes could be bought in the second year, students used hand lenses. Some specimens, both preserved in alcohol and fresh, were available for the study of comparative anatomy. Although equipment was limited, every effort was made to give the students opportunities to observe and to express their observations in recitations, in writing, and in sketches.

In the Department of Ancient and Modern Languages, Miss Viola Boddie taught Latin and French and Miss Mendenhall taught Ger-

20. *First Annual Catalogue*, p. 23.

21. All tutors and assistants were in the first graduating class except Mary Applewhite, who graduated in 1894.

22. Virginia Terrell Lathrop, *Educate a Woman* (Chapel Hill: The University of North Carolina Press, 1942), p. 13.

man. Lizzie Lee Williams was an assistant and Annie M. Page, a tutor. Each student was required to take three years of Latin and two years of either French or German. Fourth-year Latin and third-year French and German were offered as electives.

Although Latin was not required for admission, the students were advised to have at least one year's training so that they could do the more advanced work of the department. During the first course in Latin, grammar, composition, and vocabulary were stressed. In the second year students read Caesar's *Gallic Wars* and did work in prose composition. The third course included Cicero and Vergil, and the fourth, Livy and Horace or comparable Latin authors.

The first year's work in French included conversation and composition. Rougemont's *Drill Book "B"* was used with anecdotes, nouvelles, and other easy stories in French. During the second year, reading, conversation, and composition were continued. The third year was devoted to the study of the history of French literature and to the work of the best French authors. Grammar was taught through the literature, and dictation exercises and conversation were used to develop the student's ear for French.

In German the first year was spent in the study of grammar, which was continued in the second year and augmented by a study of the life and works of Schiller. During the third year the students read *Iphigenia in Tauris* and studied Goethe's life.

The work of the Department of Physiology and Health had two main objectives: instruction in hygiene and an individualized program of exercise. As resident physician, Dr. Bitting not only taught physiology in the classroom but on her morning and evening rounds made suggestions about ventilation, clothing, bathing, dressing, and other points of personal hygiene. She was assisted by Maude F. Broadaway, a student, who acted as director of the gymnasium. A small room in the northeast section of the Main Building was equipped with eleven bars, chest weights, Indian clubs, and a weighing machine.[23] Although the gymnasium was in use only for four and one-half months during the first year, "many chests increased in girth, shoulders straightened, arms became stronger, and the general bearing much improved."[24] Dr. T. H. Pritchard, former president of Wake Forest College, who delivered the first commencement

23. Marion O'Neill, "A History of the Physical Education Department at The Woman's College of The University of North Carolina" (Master's thesis, Department of Physical Education, Woman's College of The University of North Carolina, Greensboro, 1955), p. 92.

24. *First Annual Catalogue*, p. 30.

address at the Normal, observed other evidence of the work of this department. He said that there were three ways by which a Normal girl might be recognized: "she doesn't flirt with the boys, she walks erect and throws her shoulders back well, and she has a large waist." Dr. Bitting had taught the girls that lacing was not conducive to health, and two-thirds of them had been persuaded to discard their corsets.[25]

The Department of Vocal Music emphasized the function of a normal school in developing its program. Its purpose was to enable each student "to become a fairly good singer, to know sufficient of the rudiments of music to enable her to read at sight all ordinary music, and to be able to teach the first principles of singing and sightreading to the pupils of her school." The department also recognized its obligation to the talented student by making provision for more specialized training. In this department, Clarence R. Brown was assisted by Lina McDonald.[26]

Miss Melville Fort was in charge of the Department of Art, which was to provide part of the "industrial" work of the school. Classes met twice each week, and one year's work was required for certificate or diploma. The first course consisted of freehand drawing and work in plaster casts and bas-relief. The second continued the work with casts and added principles of design, mechanical drawing, and modeling in clay. Students might also take up wood carving and china painting. The third course included applied design, principles of architectural drawing, and the history of art. The department sought to provide aesthetic and vocational training for the students and confidently stated that "should no immediate use be made of the study, from an educational point of view, the habits of promptness, neatness, and accuracy that are acquired by this training are of inestimable value."

The Department of Domestic Science formed another part of the industrial training and taught cooking and sewing as "means of mental culture." There were two courses in sewing; the first was hand sewing and the study of textiles, and the second included instruction in dress cutting, fitting, and making as well as the study of color. In the third year instruction was given in cooking through lectures, laboratories, and reading, with special lessons on cooking for the

25. *Journal* (New Bern, N. C.), June 22, 1893.
26. Miss McDonald was fatally injured when struck by a train as she walked along the tracks west of the campus on January 16, 1893. Her mother, Mrs. J. A. McDonald, had been on the committee appointed by the North Carolina Teachers' Assembly in 1886 to petition the legislature for a normal school.

sick. The fourth course was the study of general household economy. Miss Edith A. McIntyre taught the domestic science courses.

E. J. Forney, bursar of the school, supervised the work of the Commercial Department with the assistance of Mrs. Fannie Cox Bell. They taught shorthand, typewriting, bookkeeping, commercial law, and telegraphy. The department offered correspondence work in shorthand and recommended that students currently enrolled as well as prospective students learn the elementary work in this way so that they could take more of the advanced work. The average time required to complete the commercial courses was eight months. If other subjects were taken, the time would of course be longer. Certificates were awarded to those students who could take dictation at 80, 100, and 125 words per minute. These certificates were awarded at commencement; although they were only sheets of Mr. Forney's letterhead tied with yellow ribbon, it was considered a great honor to be allowed to walk up to the rostrum and receive one from President McIver.

The Attacks of Critics

The State Normal and Industrial School became so popular that some religious denominations began to fear the competition it gave their female schools. When the bill to increase the Normal's appropriation to $15,000 was presented to the legislature in 1893, the presidents of some of the denominational schools asked that their rival be restricted to the normal and industrial function for which it was established and that it cease its operation as a female seminary. Music and art were not considered appropriate subjects and the life license, which only the Normal could give, should be eliminated. They wanted to make the school an institution primarily for the needy.[27]

This attack was reinforced by E. G. Harrell, editor of the *North Carolina Teacher*. One of the original supporters of the school, Harrell now questioned the December financial report, objected to the state's paying for the additional buildings, and charged that the school was not serving its industrial and normal purpose. "If the president of the institution cannot realize this perhaps a competent man can be easily found who will do the work that the state intended should be done for North Carolina girls."[28]

When word reached Greensboro that the appropriation had been passed, the girls were attending an indignation meeting over Colonel

27. *State Chronicle* (Raleigh, N. C.), Feb. 21, 1893.
28. *North Carolina Teacher*, X (April, 1893), 312.

Harrell's attack. They adjourned the meeting, but Harrell had not conceded. On May 10, 1893, an article signed "Observer" appeared in the *Biblical Recorder* attacking McIver as "totally unfit" to be president and accusing him of misappropriating funds and turning the normal and industrial school into another female seminary.

McIver had ignored other criticisms, but this time he wrote to the editor, the Reverend C. T. Bailey, and asked the identity of the author. Dr. Bailey replied that the article was handed him by a boy and was in the handwriting of Colonel E. G. Harrell. Harrell explained that the article was sent him by a gentleman with a note, "Please read the enclosed, re-write it, and hand to the *Recorder* for publication if you have no objection."[29] Harrell was generally acknowledged as the orginal author, and he was ridiculed by the newspapers for inventing his own endorsements since he could get them no other way. He wrote to prominent educators over the state sending stamped envelopes for their replies, hoping to win their support. Although he promised his readers to report on his findings, he never did. However, J. Y. Joyner, superintendent of Goldsboro's graded schools, and George A. Grimsley, superintendent of Greensboro's graded schools, both announced that they had been approached by him and had written in support of McIver and the school.[30]

McIver found many other supporters. At a meeting late in May the Board of Directors passed unanimously a vote of confidence in President McIver. Each signed his name in the minutes following the resolution which stated that the books and vouchers had been thoroughly examined and approved. Dr. Spainhour was not at the meeting, but he later added his name to the minutes: "I was not present but concur." Some of the newspapers that defended McIver were the Greensboro *Patriot*, the Charlotte *Observer*, *Webster's Weekly* (Reidsville), the Greensboro *Record*, the Wilmington *Messenger*, the *Patron and Gleaner* (Lasker), the *Caucasian* (Goldsboro), the Durham *Recorder*, and the Burlington *Herald*. In June, Harrell announced in the *Teacher*: "We have closed our discussion of the Normal and Industrial School for the present."[31]

The First Commencement

In the meantime the school year had come to a close, and invitations had been issued to the first commencement. This was such a

29. *Biblical Recorder*, May 10, 1893.
30. Greensboro *Record*, May 23, 1893.
31. X (June, 1893), 460.

special occasion that the Richmond and Danville Railroad set special rates for the trip. The auditorium was decorated in the school colors, yellow and white, and despite bad weather, large crowds came.

Tuesday, May 23, was Dedication Day. The main address was given by the Honorable Thomas M. Holt, former governor of North Carolina, and short addresses were presented by Alex Q. Holladay, president of the North Carolina College of Agriculture and Mechanic Arts, and the Honorable S. M. Finger, former superintendent of public instruction. Governor Holt traced the history of the education of women and pointed out the need which had existed for a normal and industrial school. He expressed a hope that the school would "stand forever, a monument to the mothers, and an inspiration to the daughters. And whatever its pupils may acquire in science or art let them preserve always the exquisite modesty and rare grace, which, like its own blushing wild rose, is the heritage of their land."[32]

Class exercises were held Tuesday night. Miss Annie M. Page gave the president's address; Miss Maude F. Broadaway, the class history; Miss Minnie R. Hampton, the class essay ("Woman's Work Today"); and Miss Maggie C. Burke, the class prophecy.

Two exhibitions by a physical culture class were presented to which lady visitors were admitted upon presentation of cards.[33]

Commencement day followed with speeches by Dr. Thomas H. Pritchard; Dr. George T. Winston, president of the University of North Carolina; Governor Elias Carr; and the Honorable John C. Scarborough, state superintendent of public instruction. President McIver presented the diplomas[34] and certificates. These diplomas were life licenses to teach in the public schools of North Carolina.

Ten young ladies received diplomas. All but one had previously graduated from other institutions: Mattie Lou Bolton (Louisburg Female College), Franklin County; Maude Fuller Broadaway (Salem Female Academy), Forsyth County; Margaret Clement Burke (Peace Institute), Davie County; Mary Rebekah Hampton (Statesville Female College), Iredell County; Bertha Marvin Lee (Greensboro Female College), Davie County; Zella McCulloch, Alamance County; Margaret Rockwell McIver (Greensboro Female College), Chatham County; Carrie Melinda Mullins (Peace Institute), Wake County;

32. *Dedication Address by The Honorable Thomas M. Holt at The State Normal and Industrial School. Greensboro, N. C., May 23, 1893.* (Greensboro: Reece and Elam, Power Printers, 1893), p. 23.
33. *News and Observer* (Raleigh, N. C.), May 25, 1893.
34. The first degrees were conferred in 1903.

Annie May Page (Greensboro Female College), Burke County; Lizzie Lee Williams (Murfreesboro Female College), Gates County.

Six girls received certificates in the Normal Department, which entitled them to a five-year license to teach: Allie Mary Bell, Transylvania County; Elise Callier Fulghum, Wayne County; Mary Elizabeth Holt, Wayne County; Maria Davis Loftin, Duplin County; Georgia Hulse McLeod, New Hanover County; Jennie Taylor, Guilford County.

Five certificates were given in the Business Department: Rachel Cuthbert Brown, Craven County; Fodie Margaret Buie, Robeson County; Ella Mauvers Reeks, Vance County; Fannie Smith, Guilford County; Blanche Alline Tuch, Person County.

In making the presentation President McIver said,

> This diploma comes from the first public institution established and supported by the State into which it was possible for you to gain admission unless you had become criminal or insane or were otherwise afflicted. . . . The State does not consider that it has given you anything. State education is not charity. North Carolina has simply invested in you and other students of this institution. . . . North Carolina has a right to a return for her investment, and she desires it to come in the form of womanhood, patriotic citizenship, and your very best professional service in the field of education.[35]

When people considered the work of the State Normal and Industrial School during its first year, many of them agreed with the man who said, "It certainly was not a normal school, for it had developed abnormally."[36]

35. *News and Observer* (Charlotte, N. C.), May 25, 1893.
36. *Patron and Gleaner* (Lasker, N. C.), June 15, 1893.

∾ three ∾

The Faculty

From the beginning the college was strengthened and sustained by a competent, dedicated faculty. When the Normal School was established, McIver gathered round him men and women who shared his resolve to make this an outstanding college. Later, his successor, Julius I. Foust, added people who worked with him to achieve accreditation and to make the college a part of the consolidated university. More important than any other factor contributing to the success of the college was the faculty, whose standards of excellence became traditional.

The faculty has been divided here into five groups: those who were charter members or came before 1900; those who came between 1900 and 1913; those who came between 1914 and 1920 and became deans or department heads before 1931; others who came between 1914 and 1920 but did not serve in an executive capacity before 1931; those who came after 1921 and remained for long years of service at the college. Listed with these are some non-teaching staff members who came earlier. Emphasis is given to the earlier groups, for they made their chief contribution during the period[1] when the college was making its beginning.

The Early Faculty

CHARLES DUNCAN MCIVER, *1860-1906*. In 1893, a week after McIver had received the honorary degree of Doctor of Letters from the University of North Carolina, this tribute was paid him in the Greensboro *Record*: "By his broad scholarship, sound judgment, remarkable energy and perseverance, President McIver has achieved marked

1. The first four groups are arranged according to the year they came. Those who came in the same year will be in alphabetical order. The last group is alphabetized. The writer regrets that only a listing of the last group is possible. Many of these made her years at the college a rewarding experience, for which she is ever indebted.

success, and has done more for the cause of education—especially for the cause of public education, than any other man in the state.'"[2]

Not yet thirty-three, McIver had truly made a name for himself. After receiving his A.B. degree from the University of North Carolina in 1881, he taught at Buchanan's Academy in Durham, then served as teacher and principal of the high school and acting superintendent of the graded school in Durham.[3] In 1884 he took a position in the new graded school in Winston, where he met Lula Martin, whom he married in 1885. The following year he went to Raleigh as principal of the Literary Department of Peace Institute. In 1889 McIver and Edwin A. Alderman were selected by the State Board of Education to conduct county teachers' institutes throughout the state. Through these institutes both men inspired the teachers and aroused the interest of the people in education.

During this time McIver, Alderman, Finger, and others had been working to secure approval for a normal school. The bill to establish a normal school for girls was passed by the General Assembly on February 18, 1891. Four months later McIver was elected president, a post he held until his death in 1906.

In addition to his duties at the Normal, he held offices in many professional organizations: president of the North Carolina Teachers' Assembly; president of the Southern Education Association; president of the Normal School Department of the National Education Association; trustee and member of the Executive Committee of the Board of Trustees of the University of North Carolina; secretary and district director of the Southern Education Board. He was considered as a candidate for governor of North Carolina and for president of the university but refused to allow his name to be submitted, choosing to remain at the Normal.

Dr. McIver's death, in 1906, which occurred suddenly and unexpectedly, was a great tragedy, not only to the Normal but to the whole cause of education. On September 17, 1906, McIver went to Raleigh to join the special train of William Jennings Bryan, who was making a political tour of North Carolina. When the train reached Durham, McIver was not feeling well and did not attend Bryan's speech. Unable to purchase any medicine because the drug store was closed for the special visit, he returned to the train, where H. E. C. Bryant, a newspaperman, tried to render assistance. When the other

2. In 1904 the university awarded McIver an honorary LL.D.

3. Information not otherwise documented is from the Faculty File in the College Collection, Walter Clinton Jackson Library, University of North Carolina at Greensboro.

members of the party returned, McIver rallied for a time, but before the train reached Hillsborough, he suffered a severe pain in his chest and died. News of his death was met first with doubt, then with profound grief.

McIver was only forty-six when he died, but his ideals were already implanted. Once in a report to the Board of Directors, he had expressed the principles which he sought to develop in his college:

The Real Worth of a College

The worth of a strong college to a student is not as some suppose, the mere fact that it gives the opportunity to a student to perform systematic literary tasks assigned by teachers, or that it gives opportunity to work in laboratories and libraries. These are necessary and important, but the student's greatest advantage at college is the spiritual and mental atmosphere of the place. It is intangible, but you can feel it. It can not be measured, but its effect is everywhere manifest.

The love of truth for truth's sake; the belief in equality before the law; the belief in fair play and the willingness to applaud an honest victor in every contest, whether on the athletic field or in the classroom or in social life; the feeling of common responsibility; the habit of tolerance toward those with whom one does not entirely agree; the giving up of small rights for the sake of greater rights that are essential; the recognition of authority and the dignified voluntary submission to it even when the reason for the policy adopted by the authority is not apparent; the spirit of overlooking the blunders of others and of helping those who are weak; the contempt for idlers and shirkers; the love of one's fellow-workers even though they be one's rivals; patience in toil; self-reliance; faith in human progress; confidence in right; and belief in God—these are the characteristics of the atmosphere of a great and useful college. The young man or young woman who by association with faculty and fellow-students becomes imbued with these principles gains what never can be secured in the same degree in the best homes or small schools, or anywhere else except in a college.[4]

EDWIN A. ALDERMAN, *1861-1931.* Edwin A. Alderman was the first professor chosen for the State Normal, so active had been his support of the institution from the time the first resolutions were passed in the Teachers' Assembly.[5] As county institute conductor he eloquently pleaded the cause of higher education for women and with McIver

4. Charles Duncan McIver, ''Report of the President'' in *Report of the Board of Directors, 1892-1930,* Sept. 15, 1902, p. 21.

5. Alderman was president of the North Carolina Education Association in 1887 and in 1888.

and Finger wrote the training-school bill which was presented to the General Assembly in 1891.

Alderman was born in Wilmington and received his Bachelor of Philosophy degree from the University of North Carolina, where he first made the friends who were to be so important in the development of education in North Carolina: McIver, Charles B. Aycock, J. Y. Joyner, Walter Hines Page, and M. C. S. Noble.

After a year at the Normal, where he was recognized for his brilliant teaching, Alderman went to the University of North Carolina as professor of education and in 1896 was elected president. In 1900 he became president of Tulane University and in 1904 president of the University of Virginia.

Alderman's publications show his interest in education, history, and the South. He wrote a *Brief History of North Carolina*, biographies of William Hooper and J. L. M. Curry, *Southern Idealism, The Spirit of the South*, and several books and pamphlets on education.

A lifelong friend of President Woodrow Wilson, Dr. Alderman delivered the formal oration at the memorial ceremony for Wilson before the United States Congress in 1924. At that time Alderman was considered by some as a possible presidential candidate.

Many colleges and universities awarded him honorary degrees: the University of the South, Tulane, Johns Hopkins, Columbia, Yale, the University of North Carolina, Williams, Harvard, Dartmouth, the University of Pennsylvania, and the College of William and Mary.

LULA MARTIN MCIVER, *1864-1944*. Although Mrs. McIver was not an official member of the staff, she was nonetheless a valued member of the college community. By his marriage young McIver gained a lifetime partner in his educational interests and efforts. Miss Martin had attended Salem Academy and had experience as a teacher and as a business woman. An ardent advocate of women's education and women's rights, she influenced her husband to channel his energies and concentrate on the education of women.

Until his death, the two worked together for their common goal. Mrs. McIver taught with her husband at Peace Institute in Raleigh where he went in 1886 as principal of the Literary Department. There she read law with him, and later, while he was away conducting county teachers' institutes, she accepted a position as lady principal of the Presbyterian Female Institute in Charlotte. During that time she found time to study medicine with Dr. Annie Laurie Alexander, one of the first women to practice medicine in North Carolina.

Whenever her other duties would permit, Mrs. McIver assisted with the work in the institutes. Later, after the Normal School had been established by the General Assembly, she was invaluable to her husband in the planning, construction, and organization of the institution. When McIver was too busy to entertain visitors, he often sent them over to the President's House, where Mrs. McIver received them. Even after her husband's death, she remained on the campus and gained the love and respect of later generations of students. When she died in 1944, her funeral was held in the President's House, which had been her home for fifty-two years.

Dr. and Mrs. McIver had four children: Annie (Mrs. James R. Young); Lula Martin (Mrs. John Dickinson); Verlinda, who died as a child; and Charles, Jr. Only Mrs. Dickinson is still living.

VIOLA BODDIE, *1864-1940.* From 1892 until her retirement in 1935, Miss Boddie was head of the Department of Latin. Having won a highly competitive scholarship to the Nashville Normal School (now Peabody College), she made a brilliant record there. When she was graduated in 1891, her professor of Latin wrote, ''Her standing in the college, as a student and a woman, is of the highest . . . but it is not in Latin alone that her scholarship is of the best.''

One of the earliest students at the Normal remembered Miss Boddie as ''young, pretty, and wearing such fashionable clothes that the student's attention often wandered from the Latin which she had at her fingertips.''[6] She was also known for her love of flowers and for the arrangements which graced her classroom. Although she may not have been as close to the students as were some of her associates, she was by no means inhospitable. Once when some of the granddaughters of the college had come as students, she entertained them at a dinner party at the chrysanthemum show at West Market Street Methodist Church. ''This,'' the *State Normal Magazine* said, ''was characteristic of those pleasant parties which Miss Boddie so often gives the girls.''[7]

To those who knew Miss Boddie personally she represented intellectual integrity. She demanded thoroughness of her students and was not moved by the tears of those whom she found unprepared. There were many who felt she was too harsh, but there were others

6. Cordelia Camp (ed), *Some Pioneer Women Teachers of North Carolina* (Delta Kappa Gamma Society, North Carolina State Organization, 1955), p. 36.
7. *State Normal Magazine*, XXII (Dec., 1917), 98.

who expressed gratitude to her for instilling in them the desire to explore knowledge beyond the limits of the lesson and to find the satisfaction of a job well done.

DIXIE LEE BRYANT, *1862-1949*. Miss Bryant was born in Kentucky and grew up in Tennessee, where she received her preparatory education at Columbia Female Institute. She taught in the first public school in Columbia and at Hamilton College, a finishing school for girls in Kentucky.

After receiving a B.S. degree from Massachusetts Institute of Technology in 1891 (an unusual accomplishment for a woman at that time), Miss Bryant taught one year at the State Normal College in New Hampshire before coming to the State Normal School in North Carolina as a charter member of the faculty. The following year she persuaded her friend Dr. Anna M. Gove to come to Greensboro as college physician.

Miss Bryant taught science at the Normal until 1901, when she took a leave of absence to study in Germany. Three years later she received her Ph.D. in geology from the Bavarian University of Erlangen, where she was graduated *magna cum laude*. She was the first woman to receive this degree at Erlangen.

When Dr. Bryant returned for the year 1904-1905, she was the first with a Ph.D. to serve on the faculty. Dr. Eugene W. Gudger, who succeeded her in 1905, was the second.

Dr. Bryant taught in the public schools of Chicago from 1905 until 1931; she retired to Asheville where she died in 1941.

EDWARD JACOB FORNEY, *1860-1948*. When E. J. Forney died January 29, 1948, he was the last charter member of the college faculty. He had come in 1892 as secretary to McIver, head of the commercial department, and treasurer. He soon trained a student to take his place as secretary; the other positions he held until his retirement in 1940.

Growing up in the war-stricken South where educational opportunities were at a low ebb, Forney taught himself Latin and shorthand. McIver employed him because he was impressed with his proficiency in shorthand. Soon people were hiring his students because of their capabilities. Mrs. Fodie Buie Kenyon, the student whom he trained to work for McIver, said,

> He came at a time when the women of the state needed training of the type he gave. Up to then no lady went out alone; no

lady worked in an office; no lady went alone into a courtroom, or to a doctor's meeting. I shall never forget the day he sent me to the court in Greensboro—green, untried, right out of the classroom. I can still remember the stares and the wonderment of that group that a woman could write in shorthand what they had said—and read it back![8]

Forney thought that helping set up the state's budget accounting system was his major achievement, but he received the greatest commendation for his teaching. When he died in 1948, hundreds of tributes poured into the college.[9] Two members of the faculty, Cornelia Strong and Alonzo C. Hall, described him in this way:

> There was only one "E. J."; no campus, hardly a city could keep up with more than one like him. His very walk, the sparkle in his eyes, his lively sense of humor, his insatiable curiosity of mind, his indefatigable energy, enlivened those who responded to his enthusiasm, commanded the admiration (and despair) of his colleagues, and frightened, no doubt, many a student when she first met him in class. But in the end, if a student worked hard and dared to match skill with skill, and wit with wit, that student became a friend, and found a friend for whom she could always be grateful. . . . The man and the college were one; for the college, beyond the doors of his home, was his work and his life. He touched many of us personally; but he touched all of us through the character of the college; for the character of the Woman's College is largely the reflection of the personality of her teachers, teachers like Edward Jacob Forney. In honoring him, we honor, therefore, not only what is highest in a man but also what is highest in the institution he helped to shape.[10]

MELVILLE VINCENT FORT, *1868-1939*. A native of Mississippi, Miss Fort was graduated with honors from the Mississippi Industrial Institute and College. She was one of the charter members of the State Normal faculty and served as head of the Department of Art until 1919, when she resigned and moved to Raleigh. There she worked part-time in the office of the state architect and in the Revenue Department.

In the early days at the Normal, Miss Fort lived with Miss Mendenhall at the Green Cottage and increased its reputation for charm and hospitality by her own wit and friendliness. Although art did not become an important department for many years, students in her

8. Frances Gibson Satterfield, "E. J. Forney," *Alumnae News*, XXXVI (May, 1948), 7.

9. *Ibid.*

10. Cornelia Strong and Alonzo C. Hall, "In Memoriam," Faculty File in College Collection.

classes learned a respect for order, truthfulness of representation, and integrity which they did not forget.[11]

SUE MAY KIRKLAND, *1843-1914*. Miss Kirkland was eminently qualified to serve as "referee in matters social and domestic," for she was in every respect a true Southern lady, of a long line of distinguished ancestors. Born in Hillsborough, she was educated at Misses Nash and Kollock's Select School for Young Ladies in Hillsborough and taught at Peace Institute, a Presbyterian school for girls. The students at the Normal were impressed by her fine clothes and heirloom jewelry, her silver service which was used at her table in the dining hall, and by her personal maid who kept her apartment in Spencer Hall.

Students were required to have Miss Kirkland's permission to receive callers or to leave campus. Since brothers of students were more readily admitted, boys sometimes assumed the brotherly role in order to win their way past Miss Kirkland. She was not unaware of this subterfuge and on occasion challenged the identity of a real brother.[12] Some of her rules which appear ridiculous to a later generation were accepted as reasonable by her students.

One was a regulation that in all plays men's parts were to be played by girls and that the girls had to wear black skirts instead of trousers. Mary Cleveland Snuggs once borrowed Dr. McIver's coat to make her masculine costume. When asked about the rule years later she replied, "Of course we didn't wear trousers." She did think it a little unreasonable that Miss Kirkland required her to change from the jacket before she greeted her "caller" who had attended the play.[13]

Phoebe Pegram, one of the first students, had only five days of formal education before coming to the Normal. In 1937, she recalled Miss Kirkland's kindness to her:

> Many were the nights that she sent her maid to tell me to come down that she might help me with my lessons. She taught me how to read, how to talk, and many other things. Sunday mornings she would have me go by her room so that she could see that I was properly dressed. She never in any way criticized the homemade hat or dress. She told me instead such things as,

11. Personal interview with Mrs. Julius I. Foust, Aug. 25, 1964. Mrs. Foust was a student of Miss Fort's.

12. Personal interview with Professor J. Minor Gwynn, Dec. 17, 1963.

13. Personal interview with Mrs. F. N. Patterson, Sr. (Mary Snuggs), Dec. 28, 1963.

always to button my gloves, to walk straight, and to come right back after church.[14]

Miss Kirkland died on June 8, 1914, at her sister's home in Raleigh. President Foust paid this tribute to her:

> From the opening of the college twenty-two years ago Miss Kirkland has been one of the most important factors in its life. On account of her position she was brought into closer contact with the students than any other member of the Faculty, and for that reason it is impossible to estimate the influence that she exerted, not only upon the life of the institution, but also upon the life of the State through the young women who came under her care and supervision. Miss Kirkland possessed one of those strong, positive characters that made a deep impression upon all with whom she came in contact. . . . Her sympathy was strong and deep, and she met their problems with a fine spirit of co-operation which was always returned by the students.[15]

In recognition of her services, the Board of Directors named a dormitory for her in 1914.[16]

GERTRUDE WHITTIER MENDENHALL, *1861-1926*. Throughout the issues of the *State Normal Magazine* are references to Miss Mendenhall, to the Green Cottage in which she lived on Spring Garden Street, and to the many parties she gave. There were Easter egg hunts for the girls who sat at her table in the dining hall, picnics in the country for her mathematics students, and receptions for new faculty members. Although references are often made to her shy and gentle nature, she was obviously friendly and hospitable as well.

Miss Mendenhall grew up in the Quaker community of Guilford College and attended New Garden School there before going to Wellesley, where she received a Bachelor of Science degree. She taught at Peace Institute, and when New Garden School became Guilford College, she returned to her alma mater to teach. In 1892 she was persuaded to come to the Normal as head of the mathematics department and teacher of German. Her early students were hardly prepared for higher mathematics, since only a knowledge of arithmetic was required for admission, but she was noted for her patience and

14. Phoebe Pegram Baughan, ''Out of the Past,'' *Alumnae News*, XXV (April, 1937), 5.

15. Julius I. Foust, ''Report of the President,'' in *Report of the Board of Directors, 1892-1930*, Sept., 1914, p. 15.

16. This building was torn down in 1964. Its limited size by this time had made it obsolete, and it had been condemned.

perseverance in assisting those who were unprepared; the others she taught algebra, geometry, and trigonometry.

Miss Mendenhall's influence was not limited to the social and academic aspects of college life. A member of the Society of Friends, she made religion a pattern for living day by day. Even her love of mathematics was a part of her devotion to truth. One of the alumnae spoke of her gratitude to Miss Mendenhall: "For what am I most grateful to Miss Mendenhall? For not disappointing me. As a child I thought she was a rare, noble woman—as a woman, knowing more of human nature and life's pressures upon it, I *know* that it is lives like hers that give dignity to human existence."[17]

Miss Mendenhall established a scholarship fund to aid students who wished to study higher mathematics and allied sciences. In 1950 a residence hall was named for her.

PHILANDER PRIESTLY CLAXTON, *1862-1957*. P. P. Claxton's life followed the typical American success story. Born in a log cabin in Bedford County, Tennessee, he was forced to work his way through the University of Tennessee. Later he studied at Johns Hopkins University and in Germany.

Claxton joined the Department of Pedagogy at the Normal in 1893 and became its head in 1895. Under his supervision graduate work and correspondence courses were added to the curriculum and the training school was established. His efforts at developing the school were so successful that there were many who thought the building erected in 1902 should be named for him rather than for J .L. M. Curry.

In 1902 Claxton went to the University of Tennessee to establish a department of education and to serve as chief of the Bureau of Investigation and Publication of the Southern Education Board.

President Taft appointed Claxton United States commissioner of education in 1911. Of his service Julius I. Foust said, "The work of the Commissioner of Education before Claxton was chosen had been merely the assembling of statistics and statement of facts. Claxton put enthusiasm into his work and made the Bureau of Education a vital force in the United States. He traveled over the whole country creating interest for and confidence in the public schools."[18]

17. Camp, *Some Pioneer Teachers*, p. 130.
18. Julius I. Foust, ''The History of the Woman's College,'' MS, Chancellor's Office, The University of North Carolina at Greensboro.

The Faculty, 1892-1893

First row: Viola Boddie, Florence Stone
Second row: Edith McIntyre, Mary Petty, Dr. Anna M. Gove, Dr. McIver, Mrs. Lucy H. Robertson
Third row: E. J. Forney, Maude Broadaway, J. Y. Joyner, Melville Fort, P. P. Claxton
Fourth row: Sue May Kirkland, Dixie Lee Bryant, Gertrude Mendenhall (Clarence R. Brown not pictured)

First Graduating Class, 1893

First row: Minnie Hampton, Maude Broadaway, Zella McCulloch
Second row: Carrie Mullins, Annie Page, Mattie Bolton, Bertha Lee
Third row: Maggie McIver, Dr. Alderman, Lizzie Lee Williams, Dr. McIver, Maggie Burke

First Board of Editors, State Normal Magazine, *1897*

Frances Eskridge, Margaret McCaull, Cheves West, Mary Petty (advisor), Mary Faison DeVane, Sudie Hanes, Oeland Barnett (standing).

The 1898 seniors went with Dr. McIver and Dr. Gove on a trip to Washington, where they were entertained at the White House by Mrs. McKinley.

Later Claxton served as provost of the University of Alabama, superintendent of schools in Tulsa, Oklahoma, and president of Austin Peay College.

ANNA M. GOVE, *1867-1948*. A native of New Hampshire, a former student of Massachusetts Institute of Technology, and a graduate of the Woman's Medical College of New York Infirmary, Dr. Gove came to the college in 1893. Only two women doctors had been licensed in North Carolina before this time. When Dr. Gove took the state medical board in 1894, two other women took the examination, Dr. Clara E. Jones of Goldsboro and Dr. L. Hughes Brown[19] of Wilmington. A "female lady doctress" was such a rarity that a male physician was reported to have come from a nearby town to see what Dr. Gove looked like.[20]

The first infirmary was one room in Brick Dormitory. There Dr. Gove kept her books and collected money for all medicine dispensed, in addition to caring for the sick in office hours. On her rounds in the dormitory she made bedside visits and checked on the health habits of all the students. She taught classes in physiology and hygiene, was adviser in the physical education department, and instituted regular physical examinations when only Amherst and Vassar were requiring them.

Dr. Gove's large home on Highland Avenue (just behind the Green Cottage) was a center of hospitality, and she was a charming hostess. Her many leaves of absence enriched her life as well as her profession. In 1896 and again in 1913 she studied in Vienna; in 1901 she taught physiology at Vassar; from 1902-1904 she took the private practice of Dr. Miriam Bitting Kennedy in Yonkers, New York; in 1917 she studied at the Post-Graduate Hospital of New York and from 1918 to 1920 was a medical Red Cross worker with underprivileged children in France. In 1926 she took a year off for a world tour, and in 1936 she retired but continued to work part-time.

The regard which the students had for Dr. Gove is expressed in this yearbook dedication: "With admiration for one who has shown to us a beautiful character and a life made richer by the passing years, with true appreciation for her loyalty, her constancy, and her preparedness to meet each class, offering always her gift of Service, and

19. Dr. Brown was the first Negro woman doctor to be licensed in North Carolina.

20. Virginia Terrell Lathrop, *Educate a Woman* (Chapel Hill: The University of North Carolina Press, 1942), p. 14.

with sincere love for her who has become a part of all that we have loved, we dedicate this annual of the year 1931 to Dr. Gove.''[21]

The infirmary which was built in 1911 and the one which replaced it in 1953 were both named in honor of Dr. Gove. Another memorial to her is a collection of rare books in the Walter Clinton Jackson Library. The college received a bequest of $21,000 from a cousin, Maria C. Brace, who had been one of Dr. Gove's heirs. It was stipulated that the money be used for collecting rare books, one of Dr. Gove's particular interests.

Dr. Gove was an important member of that early group who launched the little school and fostered its development. ''Her life was a challenge to all who knew her well to perpetuate the beautiful example of high thinking, generous living, and unselfish service of which Dr. Gove was the gracious embodiment.''[22]

JAMES Y. JOYNER, *1862-1954.* James Y. Joyner, professor of English at the Normal from 1893 to 1902, was a North Carolinian who contributed selflessly to education in his native state. He was born in Davidson County and received his Bachelor of Philosophy degree from the University of North Carolina in 1881, the same year that McIver was graduated. After practicing law for a short time, he turned to education and was a teacher, principal, and superintendent.

In 1902 he was appointed state superintendent of public instruction, a post which made him an ex officio member of the Board of Directors of the state educational institutions.

During Joyner's administration, a compulsory attendance law was passed, a system of teacher certification established, and a vocational education program started. When Dr. McIver died, Joyner was offered the presidency of the Normal, but he declined that position to continue his work with the state education department.

In 1909 Joyner received two honors. His alma mater awarded him an honorary degree, and he was elected president of the National Education Association. In this election his campaign was managed by Julius I. Foust.

Declining health forced Dr. Joyner to resign in 1919, but he was not one to be idle. He turned to farming and was so successful that he was elected president of the North Carolina Tobacco Growers Association.

21. *Pine Needles*, 1931, p. 5.
22. Annie Beam Funderburk, chairman, ''Memorial,'' Faculty File in College Collection.

BERTHA MARVIN LEE, *1875-1954*. When Miss Lee was graduated from the Greensboro Female College in 1892, she gave the valedictory in Latin, as was the custom. That fall she entered the State Normal and was graduated in the first class. She remained, first as librarian and then as instructor in arithmetic and English.

In 1895 Miss Lee assisted Professor Claxton in German and in 1896 became head of the department. She later traveled and studied abroad. Active in the Alumnae Association and the YWCA, both of which she helped organize, she was a loyal member of the faculty until ill health forced her retirement in 1913. She was remembered by the students for her kindness and her deep devotion to religion.

Returning to her old home in Mocksville, she became active in church and civic affairs. She was the first woman to serve on the Mocksville Board of Education, and she initiated the study of the Bible in the public schools by volunteering her services in both the Negro and white schools.

MARY MACY PETTY, *1863-1958*. Miss Petty's life was in many respects similar to that of Miss Mendenhall. They grew up in Quaker communities (Miss Petty in Bush Hill, now Archdale), attended New Garden School, and received bachelor's degrees from Wellesley in 1885. They both taught at Guilford College and then came to the State Normal, Miss Mendenhall in 1892, Miss Petty in 1893. They were a part of that ''close-knit group of dedicated women, rich in culture and drawn from fields of widely varied interests, who gave tone and character as well as academic standards to the young institution.''[23]

From 1893 to 1934 Miss Petty was head of the Department of Chemistry.[24] She kept abreast of new developments in her field by doing advanced work at Harvard, Columbia, Cornell, and the University of California.

In addition to her work in chemistry, Miss Petty served on many important committees: the Faculty Cabinet, the Curriculum Committee, and later the Social Committee, of which she was chairman even after her retirement.

Active in club work, Miss Petty served as president of the Greensboro Woman's Club and the Friday Afternoon Club and as secretary of the State Federation of Women's Clubs. Miss Petty enjoyed

23. Elva Barrow, chairman, ''Memorial,'' Faculty File in College Collection, p. 4.

24. The Science Building was named in honor of Miss Petty in 1960.

travel and went to Europe several times. She also liked parties and frequently arranged dinners or house parties at her home in Archdale. Under her planning, an English classroom in McIver Building was fitted up as a faculty social center.

Miss Petty was very active in church work and was the first woman to serve on the Board of Trustees of Guilford College. One of her finest tributes came from Russell Branson, a young Quaker minister whom she had encouraged:

> In a remarkable way she was the fulfillment of one of the two types of Quakers. One type senses the moral wrong about him, and under divine compulsion sets about the task of making right and love prevail. The other type lives a life of pure goodness, almost oblivious of the evil and sordidness about him. His life is his testimony, his life is his witness, his life is his contribution. Miss Petty belonged to this latter type.[25]

MRS. LUCY H. OWEN ROBERTSON, *1850-1930.* Following Alderman's resignation in 1893, Mrs. Robertson became head of the Department of History at the Normal. Born in Warrenton, she had grown up in Hillsborough, where she attended Misses Nash and Kollock's School. She continued her education at Chowan Baptist Institute.

In 1870 she married Dr. David A. Robertson and moved to Greensboro. After her husband's death thirteen years later, she taught at Greensboro Female College. From 1893 to 1900 she was at the Normal, but she chose to return to the other college where she remained until her death.

For two years Mrs. Robertson served as principal, and in 1902 she was elected president, the only woman to serve Greensboro College in that capacity. During her administration occurred the episode which Dr. C. Alphonso Smith, well-known English professor at the University of North Carolina, the University of Virginia, and the United States Naval Academy, called "the romance of education in North Carolina." In 1882 "a syndicate of prominent laymen" had purchased the college because its very life was threatened by financial ruin. In 1903 these men decided that it was necessary for them to dissolve their company, and public notice was made of the sale of the institution. The Alumnae Association, under the direction of Miss Nannie Lee Smith and with the active support of Governor Aycock, secured enough money to purchase their alma mater.[26]

25. Barrow, ''Memorial.''
26. Samuel Bryant Turrentine, *A Romance of Education* (Greensboro, N.C.: Piedmont Press, 1946), pp. 120-36.

In 1913 Mrs. Robertson relinquished her office and returned to teaching, a position she was to hold until shortly before her death.

ANNIE PETTY, *1871-1962*. After graduation from Guilford College and a year of teaching at Red Springs, Miss Annie Petty, who was Miss Mary's sister, came to the State Normal in 1895 as librarian. The library was small, at that time only one room in the Administration Building, with six tables for reading and shelves around the side walls. There were few books other than textbooks, which the college provided in those days, but Miss Petty was kept busy receiving and sorting the mail, signing for express deliveries, and ringing the bells for classes every forty minutes.[27]

In 1898 Miss Petty was granted a leave of absence to study at the Drexel Library School of Drexel Institute. She returned to the college as the first trained librarian in North Carolina and in 1904 she organized the first library association in the state. Miss Petty left the college in 1921, going to Raleigh as assistant secretary of the State Library Commsision. There she was one of those responsible for the introduction of bookmobiles, and she took the first one in North Carolina to her native Randolph County.

LAURA HILL COIT, *1875-1944*. After receiving a diploma from Statesville Female College (now Mitchell College), Laura Hill Coit entered the Normal in 1894, became a student assistant in science, and was graduated in 1896. After teaching physical education, mathematics, and English until 1901, she became secretary of the college and administrative assistant. In this capacity she served faithfully for almost forty years, performing a multiplicity of tasks.

In addition to those tasks expected of a secretary, Miss Coit helped students and parents with problems, served as head of hall in Midway Dormitory, administered the student loan funds and scholarships, directed the self-help work of students, kept the minutes of the faculty meetings, and collected newspaper clippings of importance to the college for the scrapbook.

Miss Coit's most outstanding characteristic was her strong religious faith. Her early intention had been to become a foreign missionary, but the sudden death of President McIver convinced her that she was needed at the college. Her interest in missions continued and was evidenced by active participation in the YWCA and by the many Bible and Sunday school classes she taught on campus and in town.

27. Virginia Terrell Lathrop, ''The Petty Sisters,'' *Alumnae News*, XXXX (Feb., 1952), 11.

Another area in which she served was the Alumnae Association. First business manager of the *Alumnae News*, secretary-treasurer and twice president of the association, she was so important to the alumnae that they made her honorary president from 1922 until her death.

Chancellor W. C. Jackson said of her, "Miss Coit was the best loved person who ever served on our faculty. More certainly, perhaps, than anyone else she translated the reality of college into the lives of the students. She had a phenomenal memory for names and faces. Her devotion to the college was matched only by the devotion of the students to her."[28]

The devotion of the students to her is expressed in the 1933 *Pine Needles*, which was dedicated to her:

> Our loyal friend and wise counselor, whose abiding beauty and integrity of life have been to us an ideal of womanhood at its best, whose steadfast faith in us and genuine concern for our welfare have given us courage and renewed faith in our own abilities; to one who is abundantly dedicated to us, in token of our deep appreciation, we dedicate this the twenty-first edition of *Pine Needles*.

MINNIE LOU JAMISON, *1866-1948*. One of the first students at the State Normal, Miss Jamison was born on a farm in Rowan County. She devoted her life to her alma mater. After serving as a student assistant in domestic science, she became a member of the faculty in 1896. She taught many of the Normal girls to cook and to sew; still others in their letters to the *Alumnae News* expressed regret that they had not taken Miss Jamison's courses. As assistant to Miss Kirkland, she began what she referred to as her happiest work, her life with students in the dormitory.

Through the extension division of the college, her influence spread throughout the state. Her talks on menu-making and her demonstration of the fireless cooker entertained and instructed women's clubs and teachers' groups. An article that she prepared for the first college bulletin in 1916, "A Study in Foods and Household Equipment," was printed three times and was read throughout the United States and in several foreign countries. Her work as secretary of the College Volunteer Workers of North Carolina during World War I earned her a commendation from Herbert Hoover, then National Food Administrator.

After years of extension work and an illness of two years, she returned to the campus where she served as counselor in one of the

28. Camp, *Some Pioneer Teachers*, p. 52.

dormitories and as adviser to freshmen. In 1936 she became adviser in social affairs and director of the Students' Building. Although this constituted semi-retirement, she was still considered the campus hostess and was there ''to pour'' on all important occasions. Miss Jamison was well suited for such tasks because she was a beautiful woman of fine carriage. She was always impeccably dressed, and in later years her white hair was lovely. Her poise, graciousness, beauty, all made a great impression on the girls with whom she came in contact.

In the *Pine Needles* dedication of 1939, her last freshman class paid the most fitting tribute to her: ''Educator, Counselor, Believer in Youth, Miss Minnie Lou Jamison has served the college and the state since her graduation. Her work has been as distinctive for excellence as for length of service.''

MARY SETTLE SHARPE, *1863-1944*. The daughter of Judge Thomas Settle, Mrs. Sharpe was born in Rockingham County and educated at Salem Academy and St. Mary's School. In 1884 she married Benjamin Charles Sharpe of Edgecombe County, and in 1887 they moved to Greensboro.

Mrs. Sharpe joined the faculty of the Normal in 1896. Although for brief intervals she served as director of physical training and instructor of history, her special interest was in reading and elocution. As chairman of the faculty committee on entertainments, she brought grace and charm to social functions on the campus. As adviser to essayists, debaters, and thespians, she stimulated the students by her kindly criticism. Her most outstanding productions were the May Day Fetes held in 1912 and 1916, in which all the students of the college and the training school participated.

Mrs. Sharpe was also interested in politics. She served as the first chairman of the North Carolina Republican Executive Committee for Women and in 1920 was nominated for the office of state superintendent of public instruction. She was thus the first woman to be nominated by a political party for a public office in North Carolina.[29]

One of her colleagues, William C. Smith, said of her, ''Keen in intellect, yet kindly at heart, and democratic in sympathy, alert, resourceful, tactful, wise and always gracious, courteous, just and true—her college and community have looked to her constantly nor ever looked in vain.''[30]

29. *Carolinian*, March 13, 1920.
30. *Mary Settle Sharpe* (Philadelphia: Stackhouse, n.d.).

1900-1913

WILLIAM CUNNINGHAM SMITH, *1871-1943*. After receiving his Bachelor and Master of Arts degrees at the University of North Carolina, William C. Smith taught English and history there before coming to the Normal in 1900 as professor of history. In 1903 he became professor of English and in 1904 head of the Department of English. In 1938 he retired as head but continued to teach until within two weeks of his death in 1943. He had ample opportunity to display his remarkable administrative ability as dean of the college, 1905-1915; dean of the faculty, 1915-1922; dean of the College of Liberal Arts, 1922-1934. Editor of the *Catalogue* for many years, Smith was one of the leaders in the development of the curriculum of the college.

In an article in the Greensboro *Daily News*, January 23, 1944, E. J. Forney called Smith "our best scholar." He was a member of Phi Beta Kappa, Kappa Alpha, and Phi Gamma Mu as well as many other professional organizations. Although he wrote articles on a variety of subjects, his chief interest was in the Bible, an interest which drew hundreds of men to his Sunday school class at First Presbyterian Church. In English literature his area of specialization was Victorian literature. He edited the memorial volume *Charles Duncan McIver* and wrote *Studies in American Authors*, an extension bulletin. Once, when the copy for the *State Normal Magazine* was lost, he wrote enough material for the entire issue.

For his scholarship and his contribution to the college and the state, his alma mater, the University of North Carolina, honored him in 1920 with the degree of Doctor of Humane Letters. An editorial in the December 19, 1943, Greensboro *Daily News* said of him, "Quietly, unostentatiously and modestly Dr. Smith went about his business of living and of training through lecture and example, and influencing others in how to live. . . . These individuals who lose themselves in their work and earnestness of purpose in giving of themselves to their fellowmen constitute the salt of the earth."

T. GILBERT PEARSON, *1873-1943*. A Quaker from Illinois, T. Gilbert Pearson wrote to President Lewis Lyndon Hobbs of Guilford College offering his collection of bird eggs and specimens as an initial payment on a college education. He further suggested that he might pay his expenses by developing the first ornithologic museum at a North Carolina college. Dr. Hobbs accepted the young man's offer, and Pearson was graduated from Guilford College in 1897. In 1899 he earned a B.S. degree from the University of North Carolina, which awarded him an honorary degree in 1924.

Pearson taught first at Guilford and then at the State Normal. In the three years he spent at the Normal, he published his first book, *Stories of Bird Life*, made the study of biology more practical by field trips in Peabody Park, and organized the first Audubon Society in North Carolina, a project to which he was to devote the rest of his life.

From 1903 to 1910 Pearson was secretary of the North Carolina Audubon Society and state game commissioner. With other ornithologists he organized the National Association of Audubon Societies in 1905 and served as secretary and executive officer from 1910 to 1920 and as president from 1920 to 1935.

Pearson's autobiography, *Adventures in Bird Protection*, records his lifelong interest in ornithology. He was editor-in-chief of the three volume *Birds of America*, senior author of *Birds of North Carolina*, and co-editor of *Book of Birds*.

JULIUS ISAAC FOUST, *1865-1946*. When Dr. McIver died, the Board of Directors asked Julius I. Foust, dean of the college, to serve as acting president. The following May (1907) he was unanimously elected president.[31] At this time the Raleigh *News and Observer* said of him,

> He has scholarship, he has practical judgment, he has business ability, and he has the confidence and the esteem of the student body, the faculty, the trustees and the hosts of friends of the institution. He will continue it upon the high plane upon which it was established and under his presidency it will continue to grow in usefulness and power. The trustees made no mistake in the election of Mr. Foust to the presidency.[32]

A native of North Carolina, Foust had come to the Normal in 1902 to replace P. P. Claxton as head of the Department of Pedagogy and principal of the Practice School. He was well prepared for his work, having received his Bachelor of Philosophy degree from the University in 1890[33] and having served as teacher, principal, and superintendent of schools in Wilson and Goldsboro. After two years at the Normal he was named dean of the college.

31. When consolidation became effective in 1932, Foust became vice-president of the consolidated university and dean of administration of the Woman's College of the University of North Carolnia.

32. Raleigh *News and Observer*, May 30, 1907.

33. The university awarded him the honorary degree of Doctor of Laws in 1910.

As president, it was Foust's responsibility to solidify the gains made by McIver. Although his challenge may have lacked the glamor associated with the founding of the institution, it was certainly important. His genius for achieving material progress earned him the title "Builder."[34] When he became president in 1907, it was a normal school of some five hundred students and a few buildings. During his administration and under his leadership, the normal school became a college, a liberal arts college approved by the Southern Association of Colleges. Almost every year brought new buildings: eleven residence halls, three dining halls, a gymnasium, music building, auditorium, new demonstration school, home demonstration house, new infirmary, classroom building, and faculty houses. All of this expansion was made necessary by the growth in enrollment. The number of students increased from 461 in 1907 to 1,761 in 1931. In 1931 his was the third largest college for women in the country.[35]

This expansion would not have been possible except for Foust's remarkable ability to wrest funds from the state legislatures. At a reception that the students gave for him after a successful appearance before the legislature, W. C. Jackson said, "He presented with matchless skill and argument the cause which he represented, and I thanked God that we had a man with shoulders broad enough and strong enough to carry the burden." Turning to Foust, he added, "We wish you the greatest gift we can—our genuine affection."[36]

There were many evidences of the students' affection for their president. The yearbook of 1910 was dedicated to "the wise counselor, the just administrator, the skillful leader, the sympathetic friend, the courteous gentleman Julius Isaac Foust as an expression of sincere friendship." In 1916 a birthday dinner was given him in the dining hall with some of his favorite foods, oysters and mincemeat pie, and a large cake with fifty-one candles. The students presented skits based on scenes from his life.[37] In 1930 students and alumnae presented his portrait to the college.[38]

The way in which Foust managed the purchase of the Teague property (later the site of the new Curry Building, the laundry, and the heating plant) exemplifies the trust his students placed in him. The property was offered for sale at a time when the legislature was

34. Lathrop, *Educate a Woman*, p. 41.
35. "Vital Statistics," *Alumnae News*, XIX (April, 1931), 12. The enrollment of 1931 was smaller than that of the two previous years because of the Depression.
36. *Carolinian*, March 3, 1923.
37. *Alumnae News*, V (Feb., 1917), 5.
38. *Carolinian*, June 7, 1930.

not in session, and neither the board nor the president had the authority to make the $60,000 purchase. Foust asked the newly incorporated Alumnae Association to borrow the money and buy the land. This they did, confident that Foust would persuade the legislature to pay the debt. The fact that he was able to do so is another example of his influence with the legislature.

Foust retired in 1934 and was living in Florida when he died in 1946. At the Founder's Day program that year one of his former students described him as a man of courage, faith, and integrity. "He lit 15,000 candles in North Carolina and today their gleam illuminates the eager faces of children in schoolhouses in every corner of the state."[39]

MYRA ALDERMAN ALBRIGHT, *1867-1955*. When Mrs. Albright was a student at the Greensboro Female College, she received a gold medal for her accomplishments as a pianist. From 1903 to 1930, she taught piano at Normal and after her retirement gave private lessons. A charter member of the Euterpe Club, she was often accompanist for musical events in Greensboro.

MARY TAYLOR MOORE, *1884-1948*. Miss Moore spent most of her life in the service of the college. Coming as a member of the class of 1903, she was active in student organizations and served as president of her class. After graduation she taught Latin and in 1909 was appointed registrar, a position which she held until her death in 1948. At that time Chancellor Jackson said of her:

> In her capacity as Registrar, she virtually created the office, and brought it to a high state of efficient organization. She was recognized widely in educational circles as having perfected a remarkable organization of this especially difficult phase of educational work. Many other institutions of learning throughout the country learned much from her and used the methods and procedures she had established. The debt the Woman's College owes her is very great. We will not forget it.[40]

The debt was not forgotten, for in 1960 a residence hall was named in her honor.

39. Mildred Harrington (Mrs. Peter F. Lynch), quoted in "Founder's Day," *Alumnae News*, XXXV (Nov., 1946), 5.
40. W. C. Jackson, "Memorial," Faculty File in College Collection.

RUTH FITZGERALD, *1885-1966*. Born near Mocksville, Miss Fitzgerald received her diploma from the State Normal in 1905 and returned that fall to assist in the demonstration school. Except for a leave of absence during which she studied for her bachelor's and master's degrees at Teacher's College, Columbia University, Miss Fitzgerald taught at the college until her retirement in 1950.

Miss Fitzgerald's special field was elementary education. For nineteen years she was a supervisor at Curry Demonstration School; later she taught college classes for prospective teachers and for teachers and principals in service. To her, teaching was a noble calling, and one of the most important ideas her students learned was that teaching is a profession. She was a state founder and at one time state president of Delta Kappa Gamma.[41]

DR. EUGENE W. GUDGER, *1867-1956*. Dr. Gudger was educated at Emory and Henry, at the University of Nebraska where he received the Bachelor of Science and Master of Science degrees, and at Johns Hopkins where he earned the Doctor of Philosophy degree.

He acted as head of the biology and geology departments at the State Normal from 1905 to 1919. Although these years represent only a small part of a very successful career (he retired at the age of eighty-seven), they were important to the college. Prior to this time, science had not provided occupations for women, but Dr. Gudger soon began preparing a few students as laboratory technicians and directing a small number of his best students into the study of medicine. For the other students he wrote *Household Biology*. He left the college to go to the American Museum of Natural History in New York to edit the index volume of the *Bibliography of Fishes*, a monumental work containing 50,000 citations. He remained in New York until 1953 but did not lose interest in his former students. Several times he wrote to the *Alumnae News*, giving up-to-date information on their careers. Many of these young women, in writing to the *News* about trips to New York, said, "Of course, we went by to see Dr. Gudger." Dr. Gudger loved the mountains and kept his old home in Waynesville, where he went each summer to spend a vacation. On these trips he always visited the college.[42]

In 1942, when the college celebrated its fiftieth anniversary, Gudger presented to the library the *Bashford Dean Memorial*

41. Jane Summerell, "Miss Ruth Fitzgerald," *Alumnae News*, XXXX (Nov., 1951), 4.

42. *Alumnae News*, XIX (Nov., 1930), 22.

Volumes on Archaic Fishes, an eight-volume reprint collection of articles, which he had edited.

In a letter to Miss Barbara Parrish, alumnae secretary, Dr. Gudger said, "I have just read the excellent October issue of the *Alumnae News.* . . . I taught in the college 1905-1919 and in those years, I gave my students the best that was in me and they reciprocated." The letter[43] was dated October 30, 1955, less than four months before he died at the age of eighty-nine.

CORNELIA STRONG, *1877-1955.* A word often used by former students to describe Miss Strong was "brilliant." A native of South Carolina and the daughter of a Presbyterian minister, she received her early education at the Agnes Scott Institute. In 1903 she received her Bachelor of Arts degree from Cornell, where she was elected to membership in Sigma Xi. Professor John Henry Tanner was so impressed by her work that he later requested that she be given a leave of absence to return to Cornell to help him write a high school algebra book. Her quest for knowledge carried her to universities across the country, Cornell, Harvard, Michigan, California, Colorado, and Wisconsin, and in 1931 she received her Master of Arts degree from the University of Michigan. From 1905 to 1948 she was a member of the mathematics faculty at the Normal in Greensboro and one of the most valued members of the entire faculty. One of the achievements of which she was most proud was the introduction of astronomy to the curriculum in 1931.

From 1913 to 1937 Miss Strong was chairman of the Committee on Advanced Standing, a truly difficult task which concerned the many alumnae who returned to earn standard degrees after the college had been accredited. It was the task of her committee to evaluate the academic records of these students to determine how much work would be necessary to meet degree requirements. She also served on the Loan Committee, the Curriculum Committee, and the Consolidated University Administrative Council.

As a teacher, she was known for her "thoroughness, her insistence upon accuracy, her infinite patience. Her . . . students . . . came to understand and to apply logic in their reasoning . . . and (at least some of them) experienced . . . the rare moments in their lives when the wonder and the beauty of the mathematical universe flashed upon their sight."[44]

43. Faculty File in College Collection.
44. Jane Summerell, "Miss Cornelia Strong Retires after 43 Years," *Alumnae News*, XXXVII (Aug, 1948), 16. A residence hall was named for her in 1960.

ELIZABETH MCIVER WEATHERSPOON, *1870-1939*. Elizabeth McIver was one of the students who came in 1892 to the school that her brother had just established. Indeed, McIver's interest in educating women had been quickened by the fact that when his sister completed her studies at the local private school, the only educational opportunities open to her were both limited and expensive. From 1888 to 1890 she had attended Peace Institute, and after one year at the Normal she taught in the Greensboro city schools until her marriage in 1900 to James R. Weatherspoon of Sanford. When he died in 1906, she returned to Greensboro where she was a first grade supervisor at Curry School.

Mrs. Weatherspoon's abiding interest was in art. After a year of study with Professor Arthur Dow at Columbia, she taught art courses for elementary teachers at the Normal. She encouraged an interest in art for all students by sponsoring traveling exhibits, helped organize the Division of Art of the North Carolina Education Association, and was its first president.

Throughout the years she worked for the establishment of an art department at the college. When one was finally established in 1935, she was made an associate professor. Later, when an art gallery was provided at the college, it was named in her honor.[45]

MARTHA ELIZABETH WINFIELD, *1873-1936*. Miss Winfield, a native of Beaufort County, was graduated from the State Normal in 1906. Her performance as a student was so impressive that she was invited to return as a member of the English Department. Here she taught until 1936. Further study at Columbia brought her a Bachelor of Science degree in 1915 and a Master of Arts in 1923. In 1935 when the local chapter of Phi Beta Kappa was organized, she became the first alumna member.

For thirty years Miss Winfield shared with her students her vast knowledge and her great love of literature. The *Alumnae News* of April, 1937, said of her, ''In the teaching of Shakespeare her powers found their liveliest play. His language, his wit, and his wisdom she made her own; at her touch his robust qualities came spontaneously to life again, and the students whom she sent adventuring among the

45. The first gallery was in the old McIver Building, which was replaced in 1959. The new building contains excellent facilities for the gallery, which has a permanent collection of paintings, sculpture, textiles, and prints by contemporary American and European artists and designers and which brings to the campus a series of exhibits as a part of the instructional program of the Department of Art. The public is invited to attend the exhibitions.

creations of his mastermind gathered strength and understanding.''

In addition to her teaching responsibilities, Miss Winfield, through her work on many committees, played a vital part in administrative affairs. Her excellent lectures were in demand throughout the state. In the Phi Beta Kappa tribute to her, Winfield S. Barney said,

> We make no effort to define her contribution to the College, reaching back as it does over thirty of the forty-four years of the institution's life. . . . And we wish to inscribe permanently in the records of the Woman's College section of Phi Beta Kappa our deep consciousness that with her death a regal presence and cultural force have gone from us—a power memorable in moulding the destiny of this institution.[46]

Shortly after her death, friends donated to the library in her memory a copy of Sir Sidney Lee's facsimile of Shakespeare's First Folio. As further tribute, the Board of Trustees in 1939 named a residence hall for her. The Winfield scholarship was established by her to aid a junior or senior majoring in English.

ETTA RIDER SPIER, *1876-1938.* A graduate of the State Normal in 1895, Miss Spier taught first grade in Goldsboro for twelve years before returning as supervisor in the training school in 1907. She later earned her bachelor's and master's degrees from Teachers College, Columbia University.

After a few years at Curry, Miss Spier began teaching college courses, specializing in problems of rural education and in primary education. Her favorite courses were public education in North Carolina, kindergarten education, and children's literature. When the faculty was reorganized in 1921, she became a full professor.

Professional civic, and religious organizations benefited from Miss Spier's participation. An early member of the Progressive Education Association, she helped organize local chapters of the Association for Childhood Education and of Delta Kappa Gamma. She was given a leave of absence to visit alumnae groups across the state as field secretary for the McIver Loan Fund. The League of Women Voters and the American Association of University Women were other interests. She was a founder of Temple Emanuel in Greensboro and a member of its board of directors.

When Miss Spier died in 1938, Miss Ruth Fitzgerald said of her, ''Service is the ideal upon which this college was founded. *Service* is

46. Winfield S. Barney, ''Martha Elizabeth Winfield,'' *Alumnae News*, XXV (April, 1937), 6.

the motto of which we sing today. No finer example of the realization can be found than in the life of Miss Spier—service to the college, service to North Carolina, service to humanity.''[47]

WALTER CLINTON JACKSON, *1879-1959*. After receiving a Bachelor of Science degree from Mercer University in Macon, Dr. Jackson taught in the public schools of Georgia. In 1902 he came to Greensboro as teaching principal at Lindsay Street School. For six years he was at Greensboro High School, first as English teacher and then as principal. In 1909 he came to the Normal and except for an interval of two years remained until his retirement in 1950. He pursued his graduate studies at Columbia University and at the University of Chicago, attending several summer sessions. He was awarded two honorary degrees, the Doctor of Laws from Mercer in 1926 and the Doctor of Humane Letters from Bennett College in 1949.

Through the years Dr. Jackson held a variety of positions at the college, first, professor and head of the Department of History, and then in 1919, dean of the college. When the faculty was reorganized in 1921, he was named professor and chairman of the faculty of social science and vice-president of the college. During Foust's illness, Jackson was acting president. In 1932 he went to the University at Chapel Hill as dean of the School of Public Administration. When Foust retired in 1934, the board elected Jackson to succeed him. His title then was Dean of Administration of the Woman's College of the University of North Carolina and Vice-President of the University. In 1945 the title was changed to Chancellor of the Woman's College of the University of North Carolina.

Dr. Jackson once said to the seniors, ''great teaching is the most important fact connected with the building of a great college. If we have great teachers, all else will follow.'' Certainly in the person of Walter Clinton Jackson, the college had a great teacher. Under his dramatic touch, people and events in history came alive. He was such an imaginative lecturer that it was sometimes necessary to have extra chairs brought in for his classes, a practice reminiscent of the days when Alderman drew such crowds to his lectures. Respected by students and colleagues alike, Jackson was known as an ''artist-teacher.''[48]

47. Ruth Fitzgerald, ''Etta Rider Spier,'' *Alumnae News*, XXVII (Feb., 1939), 3.
48. Jane Summerell, chairman, ''Memorial,'' Faculty File in College Collection.

The Bailey Memorial Room in the Students Building was furnished in memory of Sarah and Evelyn Bailey, who died in the typhoid epidemic of 1899.

Minnie Jamison (left) presides over a luncheon prepared by a domestic science class.

Farmerettes, 1918

During World War I students operated the college farm.
First row: Nannie May Tilley, Martha Blakeney, Nell Robertson,
Marjorie Craig, Marguerite Brawley, Gladys Murrill, Mildred Ellis
Second row: Margaret Hayes, Mary Gordon, Mary York

WOOTTEN-MOULTON, GREENSBORO

The Cast of Craig's Wife, *Presented in 1927*

De Alva Stewart, A. T. West, Clara Gill, Elizabeth Howland, W. R.
Taylor, Phoebe Baughan, James Painter, Laura Orleans, Sally Connor,
H. R. Hulpien, A. C. Hall

Dr. Jackson took an active interest in civic and professional affairs. He served as president of the North Carolina Literary and Historical Association (1924), North Carolina Conference for Social Service (1925), Southern Commission on Interracial Co-operation (1928-1932), North Carolina Education Association (1937), North Carolina College Conference (1944), and the Greensboro Chapter of the National Conference of Christians and Jews (1950). He was vice-president of the Southern Political Science Association (1933) and of the North Carolina Council of Churches. He served for several years on the Editorial Board of the North Carolina Historical Review and on the Board of Trustees of Bennett College. Among his publications are *A Boy's Life of Booker T. Washington, Poetry by American Negroes,* with N. I. White, and *The Story of North Carolina,* with A. M. Arnett.

Frank Porter Graham said of Chancellor Jackson,

The sixteen years (1934-1950) during which Walter Clinton Jackson was administrative head of the Woman's College constitutes an historic epoch in the history of the College. The student body grew from 1,266 to 2,231, the faculty from 131 to 197, the number of buildings from 44 to 55. . . . This remarkable growth in buildings, equipment and size of the College was accomplished by no less notable developments in the strength and quality of the faculty, the richness of the curriculum, the self-government of the faculty and the student body, the growth and standards of the professional schools and the graduate school, and in the widening and deepening of the services of the College for all the people of the State. For several decades as teacher and administrator, he embodied the life, the meaning and spirit of the Woman's College for the students and people of North Carolina.[49]

In his farewell speech to the graduating class in 1950, Jackson said,

I have always believed, and after a long life I still believe, that the greatest thing in the world is love. . . . I am persuaded that mankind is good; that it is worthy of your affection and your loyalty. . . . That the rewards of trust and affection and loyalty will more than match the evil that you will meet. . . . It is with high hope that we send you forth secure in the faith that you will take your part in the great community that lies about you mindful that a measure of the destiny of many hundreds of us is in your keeping.[50]

49. Frank Porter Graham, "Walter Clinton Jackson," *Alumnae News,* XXXIX (Aug., 1950), 11.

50. MS, Faculty File in College Collection.

Students who heard these words knew that they came from the heart, for they had seen this philosophy in his life.

VIRGINIA RAGSDALE, *1870-1945*. Upon graduation from Guilford College, Miss Ragsdale won the first Bryn Mawr scholarship awarded at Guilford. Receiving her Bachelor of Arts degree from Bryn Mawr, she was then awarded a fellowship for graduate study at Bryn Mawr and at Göttingen, where she studied with Felix K. Klein and David H. Hilbert. Returning from Germany, she taught in the Bryn Mawr School in Baltimore until she was awarded another fellowship, which was used to complete her work for the Doctor of Philosophy degree in 1903. Miss Ragsdale was the third person with a Ph.D. degree to serve on the faculty. The others were Dixie Lee Bryant and Eugene Gudger.

Although Dr. Ragsdale taught at the college only seventeen years, she contributed greatly to the intellectual life, not only of her department but of the entire faculty. She came to the college in 1911 as professor of mathematics and in 1926 became head of the department. Her election to the important Faculty Cabinet as member-at-large was an indication of the confidence that her colleagues placed in her.

In 1928 Dr. Ragsdale resigned because of her mother's illness and returned to her family home in nearby Jamestown. She felt that there were others who could do her work at the college, but there was no one who could take her place at home. After her mother's death, she built a house on the campus of Guilford College, which was used as the Alumni House for many years and is now the president's residence.

In 1950 the Board of Trustees named a residence hall for her at the Woman's College of the University of North Carolina.

WADE R. BROWN, *1866-1950*. A native of Ohio, Brown was a graduate of Baker University, the North East Conservatory of Music, the Sternchen Conservatory in Berlin, and the Virgil Conservatory in New York. In 1921 he was awarded the honorary degree of Doctor of Music from Wake Forest College.

When Brown came to the Normal in 1912, the voice of opposition to state schools was heard once again. In criticizing Brown's being lured from Meredith College to the Normal by a one-third increase in pay, the editor of *Charity and Children*, a Baptist publication, declared that it was not the purpose of a state school to provide an excellent music program.[51] Obviously Brown did not share this conviction, for he soon made the Department of Music a vital force on the campus and in the state.

On October 5, 1912, Dr. Brown gave an organ recital at the First Baptist Church of Greensboro, the first in a series of recitals to be given by the faculty.[52] In the same month he organized a chorus of 125 voices and in a few years started a series of special choral programs. These became so popular and drew such crowds that sometimes it was necessary to limit admission, children under fifteen being excluded. The *Messiah* was the first oratorio he presented. There followed through the years performances of such works as Gounod's *Faust, The Creation, The Holy City, Elijah, Cavalleria Rusticana,* and Reginald De Koven's comic opera *Robin Hood.* He organized music festivals in Greensboro and in Asheville; in 1929 he arranged for the San Carlo Opera Company to present ten operas in Greensboro, and he originated the North Carolina Music Contest for High Schools. This contest, probably his best-known accomplishment, began in 1919 with fourteen piano contestants and grew to such proportions that even after district contests were organized, thousands of band, glee club, and orchestral contestants continued to come to the campus for the final contest.[53]

For years Dr. and Mrs. Brown took the music seniors to New York. They attended several operas, symphony concerts, recitals, and recording sessions. The tour included sightseeing in Washington, and on one trip they were greeted by President Coolidge when they visited the White House. Dr. Brown's enthusiasm touched all the students through the Friday chapel programs which were devoted to music: recitals, group singing, or appreciation programs for coming artists. The 1926 *Pine Needles* was dedicated to Wade R. Brown, "whose presence among us is like a melody that finds an echo in every heart."

In 1940, three years after his retirement, a series of faculty recitals was established in honor of Dr. Brown. The first recital was by George M. Thompson, organist and choirmaster of the college for many years. In 1960 the Music Building was officially named the Wade R. Brown Building.

51. *Charity and Children,* July 25, 1912.
52. *State Normal Magazine,* XVII (Oct., 1912), 33. The recital was held at the church because the college did not acquire a pipe organ until 1913. *State Normal Magazine,* XVII (May, 1913), 494.
53. In 1966 there were 3,250 students participating in the program.

Department Heads, 1913-1920

HARRIET WISEMAN ELLIOTT, *1884-1947*. The most apparent memorial to Miss Elliott is the student union building erected in 1953 and named for her. As the center for campus social activities, it is a symbol of the expansion of the program she fostered while dean of women. As the home of the Student Government Association, it is a symbol of the spirit of responsible freedom which she instilled in so many students.

Miss Elliott came to the State Normal from Carbondale, Illinois, in 1913, having received a Bachelor of Arts degree from Hanover College and a Master of Arts from Columbia. As a member of the Department of History and Political Science, she was vitally interested in current affairs, and she aroused this interest in her students. One of them said,

> As a teacher Miss Elliott awakened the students of this college to their responsibilities as participants in a democracy. She taught them to read newspapers, to cast their votes, to question again and again the why-fors of their local and national community. She forced open minds of her students, insisting that they think for themselves the difficult problems that beset young people of our complicated world.[54]

A prominent worker in the fight for woman's suffrage in this country, Miss Elliott maintained her legal residence in Illinois where she could vote. She brought such speakers as Dr. Anna Howard Shaw to the campus, encouraged the organization of suffrage groups, and went wherever she was called to plead the cause. When the Fifth Annual Convention of the National League of Women Voters selected America's twelve greatest women, a national magazine carried an article on twelve other women who, although they were not included in the first list, had nonetheless made important contributions to their country. Miss Elliott was selected because of her outstanding work in the woman's suffrage movement.[55]

Miss Elliott's greatest influence was felt in the years following consolidation in 1931. In 1935 she became dean of women, though she continued her teaching. She had the opportunity as dean of women to effect many of the changes she had envisioned for years—more freedom, she termed it "responsible freedom," for the students and the renovation and beautification of the dormitories. She devised a

54. Camp, *Some Pioneer Teachers*, p. 70.
55. Marjorie Shuler, "A Friendly Parallel," *Woman's Home Companion*, LI (Aug., 1924), 20.

counseling plan for the dormitories, with a trained counselor in each, that was studied and adopted by other women's colleges.

Miss Elliott was also active in state and national affairs. On the state level she was appointed by Governor J. C. B. Ehringhaus to serve on the State Emergency Relief Administration and by Governor Clyde R. Hoey as a member of the North Carolina State Committee of the Conference of Southern Governors, 1940. She also served as a member of several national committees. President Wilson appointed her to the Women's National Defense Council during World War I, and during World War II she was the only woman member on President Roosevelt's Advisory Commission to the Council of National Defense. She was Federal Consumer Commissioner, had a part in setting up the WAVES, and became director of the Women's Division of the War Bond Sales Campaign. In 1940 she was a member of former President Hoover's Conference on Child Health. In 1945 she went to the London Conference of the United Nations Educational, Scientific, and Cultural Organization.[56]

Miss Elliott's influence is perpetuated through the Harriet Elliott Lectures (formerly the Harriet Elliott Social Science Forum), which annually bring to an ever increasing group of students an awareness of the world in which they live and their responsibilities as citizens of that world.

JAMES ALBERT HIGHSMITH, *1886*——. In 1916 Dr. Highsmith was appointed principal of Curry School and associate professor of education. A North Carolinian, he had received his A.B. and M.A. degrees from the University of North Carolina. In 1923 he was awarded the degree of Doctor of Philosophy by George Peabody College for Teachers.

At that time, 1916, there was no separate department of psychology at the Normal, the psychology courses having been a part of the School of Education since the establishment of the college. In 1928 Dr. Highsmith became head of the newly established Department of Psychology, a position he held until his retirement in 1953. At his retirement, one of his associates wrote,

> As department head he has built a department founded upon the philosophy of freedom for the individual staff member—freedom to develop his teaching, his thinking, his research program in whatever way he might see fit.. This freedom and the sense of security he has provided, have led to a degree of self-expression and personal development on the part of staff mem-

56. Camp, *Some Pioneer Teachers*, p. 71.

bers which would not have been possible under less favorable conditions. For this, and for his generous and warm response to their problems, he has won the deep affection of all who have worked with him. And he has won also their respect for him as a scholar.[57]

Dr. Highsmith served in many positions of responsibility: chairman of the Admissions Committee, chairman of the Curriculum Committee for more than ten years, chairman of the Schedule Committee which prepared a permanent schedule of classes for the college, member of the Faculty Advisory Committee, member of the Administrative Council of the University, and chairman of the General Policies Committee. Dr. Highsmith also served as chairman of the committee appointed by the North Carolina College Conference to devise, administer, and score achievement tests for seniors in all the high schools of the state in 1926.

In concluding her tribute, Dr. Elizabeth Duffy said,

> Generous, tolerant, wise—such is the character of this man who has enriched Woman's College for these many years. The steadying power of his insistence upon an intellectual grasp of experience, his equanimity, good humor, and patience have been communicated to generations of students. "For he doth not only show the way, but giveth so sweet a prospect into the way, as will entice any man to enter it."

JOHN HARRISON COOK, *1880-1941.* John Harrison Cook came to the college in 1918 as head of the Department of Education and director of the Summer School. A native of Ohio, he had received a B.S. degree from Ohio Northern University in 1908, an A.B. from Miami University of Ohio in 1912, and an M.A. from Columbia University in 1917, and in 1925 he was awarded the Ph.D. from Columbia.

Director of the summer session for fourteen years, he arranged a program which attracted teachers in service, prospective teachers, and liberal arts students. The program was so good that at one time it enrolled a larger number of students than any other session in the state.[58]

In the *Carolinian,* February 1, 1941, Chancellor Jackson explained the debt which the teachers of North Carolina owed Cook. As president of the North Carolina Education Association and as a member of the committee on retirement allowance of the NCEA and of the

---

57. Elizabeth Duffy Bridgers, "Dr. Highsmith Retires as Psychology Department Head," *Alumnae News,* XLII (Spring-Summer, 1953), 6.

58. Ruth Gunter, chairman, "In Recognition—John Harrison Cook," Memorial, Faculty File in College Collection.

National Education Association, Dr. Cook had worked for many years to secure a retirement program for teachers. He was asked to help draw up the provisions for the system in North Carolina, but he did not live to see its enactment.

The faculty memorial concludes with the following tribute:

> His friendliness, his tolerant attitude, his tendency to see the good in people, his sincerely tactful consideration for others, his sense of humor, his fearlessness in standing for his own convictions, his wide range of human interests, his concern for the welfare of the common man, his zest for life, all are qualities which were unified in him in a way that endowed him as a personality with an influence that was consistently directed toward advancing the common good. We are enriched in that he lived among us and worked with us. Through his deeds his life continues to speak to us and to motivate us.[59]

CAROLINE P. B. SCHOCH, *1880-1961*. Miss Schoch joined the faculty of the State Normal and Industrial College as professor of German in 1918, a year in which that language was as unpopular as the nation from which it came. "Against this prejudice," said some of her colleagues, "Miss Schoch maintained a valiant and doughty beachhead."[60] So great was her enthusiasm for German culture that students sometimes had the impression that she was German by birth. She had studied in Germany, but it was her grandparents who had first come to America. After receiving a bachelor's degree from the University of Chicago and a master's from the University of Wisconsin, Miss Schoch studied for a year at the University of Marburg.

For three decades Miss Schoch shared her love of German art, literature, and music with her students. One should not infer that grammar was ever neglected; certainly Miss Schoch did not neglect it, and any student who did so found Miss Schoch's disdain very difficult to face. Grammar was basic, but even in first-year German, students saw it as the key to the richness of German literature. There were songs to sing, "Sah ein Knabe ein Roslein stehen," poems to learn, "Du bist wie eine Blume," and many etchings to admire. One of the rewards of studying German came at Christmas when Miss Schoch decorated her room on third floor McIver and served marzipan and other German candy and cookies while the students sang the German carols they had studied so hard.

59. *Ibid.*
60. Bernice Draper, chairman, "Memorial," Faculty File in College Collection.

BLANCHE E. SHAFFER, *1878——*. Blanche E. Shaffer, who received her B.S. and M.A. degrees from Columbia University, became dean of the School of Home Economics in 1918. The fifteen years she served were important ones, for it was during this period that the Home Economics Building and the Home Management House on McIver Stret were built and the master's degree in home economics was approved.

After her marriage to William Dickson in 1933, she lived in New York.

WINFIELD S. BARNEY, *1883-1955*. Dr. Barney was head of the Department of Romance Languages from 1919 to 1953. He had degrees from Dartmouth College (A.B., 1905), Hobart College (M.A., 1911), and Syracuse University (Ph.D., 1916), and he had studied at Grenoble. He helped to organize the division of modern language teachers of the North Carolina Teachers' Assembly and the South Atlantic Modern Language Association and served as first president of both organizations. He was a charter member of the local chapter of Phi Beta Kappa.

Among Dr. Barney's publications were *A Practical French Review Grammar* and *Corneille's Comedies as a Mirror of Polite Society in the First Half of the Seventeenth Century*. He edited Merimee's *Colomba*, Loti's *Pecheur d'Islande*, Daudet's *Le Petit Chose*, and *Premier Livre de Lecture*.

The faculty memorial to Barney reads, "He was open-minded and ever willing to accept suggestions. Never arbitrary, he allowed his colleagues to experiment and explore. A man of convictions and principles, he was tenacious of purpose. Although he was reserved and reticent, those who knew him found him to be exceedingly friendly and possessed of a delightful sense of humor."[61]

MARY CHANNING COLEMAN, *1883-1947*. A few hours before she died, Miss Coleman remarked to one of her classes, "History is being made every day in physical education."[62] Few women have contributed more to the making of that history than she. Having been prepared for college by private tutors, she was graduated from State Teachers' College (now Longwood College) in her native Virginia, took a special course at Wellesley, and received her Bachelor of Science degree from Columbia. She taught at Winthrop College from 1910

---

61. Unsigned memorial, Faculty File in College Collection.
62. *Carolinian*, Oct. 8, 1947.

to 1913, was assistant supervisor of physical education in Detroit from 1913 to 1916, worked as part-time assistant at Columbia from 1916 to 1917, and taught at Carnegie Institute of Technology from 1917 to 1920.

In 1920 the Department of Physical Education at the North Carolina College for Women offered gymnastics, outdoor sports, and folk and aesthetic dancing. For public school teachers there were one-hour courses in the theory of teaching these subjects. Miss Coleman so vitalized the work in this department that in 1923 the Faculty Council approved a course leading to the Bachelor of Science degree in Physical Education.[63] This advancement was typical of the pattern of progress she established for the department.

Miss Coleman's work was not limited to the campus. She went to neighboring towns such as Burlington and High Point and gave demonstrations in public school methods of physical training. She was one of the founders and first president of the North Carolina Physical Educators' Society and also served as president of the Southern District Association of the American Physical Education Association and of the American Association for Health, Physical Education, and Recreation. She was named Southern Regional Director of the American Folk Arts Association, an honor given in recognition of her service in the collection and publication for folk songs, games, and dances of the South. In 1935 she received the Honor Award Citation for meritorious service, the highest award of the American Association for Health, Physical Education, and Recreation. Miss Coleman wrote *Athletics for High School Girls* with Guy B. Phillips and wrote *Lessons in Physical Education for Elementary Grades.*

A tribute by Collins Bennett, one of the students, expresses very well the respect and admiration people felt for her:

> Miss Coleman was loved not only for her ability as a teacher but for her capacity for living, her beliefs, her dry wit, her love of a good story, her inimitable ways of effecting progress—"By hook or by crook, both ways are good ways"—for her untiring efforts to make and keep her department of Physical Education an institution in democratic living.
>
> She will best be remembered by her students as they pass on to others the rich philosophy gained in her classes, and by their feeling that their highest tribute is to be known as "one of Miss Coleman's girls."[64]

JOHN PAUL GIVLER, *1882-1957.* Following release from military service

63. Faculty Council, Minutes, III (Jan. 23, 1923), 71.
64. Collins Bennett, *Carolinian,* Oct. 3, 1947.

in 1920, John Paul Givler joined the faculty of the college as professor and head of the Department of Biology, a position he held for twenty-nine years. He had received his Ph.B. and M.A. degrees from Hamline University and had been working on his Ph.D. when the war broke out.

Givler served as vice-president and president of the North Carolina Academy of Science. He was also a fellow in the American Association for the Advancement of Science and a member of Sigma Xi.

In addition to articles for professional journals, Givler wrote a *Textbook of Biology* and collaborated on a *Laboratory Guide for General Biology.*

Givler had another interest quite apart from his successful career as a teacher. He was an accomplished cellist. Finding it difficult to have his cello repaired, he learned to do it himself and became so skillful that his services were much in demand.

Professors, 1913-1920

ALLEINE R. MINOR, *1892———.* In 1913 Wade R. Brown added to his staff Alleine R. Minor, who had been his pupil at Meredith, where she received a diploma in 1912. Later she earned a B.S. degree at Columbia and studied at the New England Conservatory of Music. She taught piano at the college until her retirement in 1956.

ELVA BARROW, *1889———.* Miss Barrow was a member of the Department of Chemistry from 1916 to 1954. She received an A.B. degree from Randolph-Macon Woman's College and an M.S. from the University of Chicago. Her area of specialization was physiological chemistry.

A. C. HALL, *1886———.* A. C. Hall joined the English Department in 1916, having earned an A.B. degree from Elon. Later he received his M.A. from Columbia. Hall aroused interest in courses in American literature and in creative writing. It was in one of his writing classes that efforts to establish the *Carolinian,* the college newspaper, began. Mr. Hall's hobby, collecting epitaphs, provided material for his book *Grave Humor.* After his retirement in 1956, he was chairman of the Greensboro Housing Authority for several years.

CLAIRE HENLEY ATKISSON, *1895———.* Claire Henley Atkisson received her B.M. degree from the State Normal in 1916 and joined the music department in 1917 as a teacher of piano methods. Later she studied at Columbia and was a pupil of Karl Bondam, Austin Conradi, and Lotta Hough. Although Mrs. Atkisson retired in 1962, she continued to teach part-time.

MAGNHILDE GULLANDER, *1890——*. Magnhilde Gullander joined the history faculty in 1918, two years after receiving her A.B. degree from the University of Wisconsin. In 1925 she earned an M.A. degree from the University of Pennsylvania. Miss Gullander, as a teacher of history, helped to organize and direct the International Relations Club. Her teaching was enriched by European travel and, until her retirement in 1956, she was known for her course in English history.

A. P. KEPHART, *1883——*. A. P. Kephart received his A.B. and M.A. degrees from Coe College and his Ph.D. from the University of Pennsylvania. He came to the college in 1918 and was professor of education and principal of the practice school until 1937. Dr. Kephart owned and operated a very popular summer camp at Blowing Rock, Camp Yonahlossee. He later published *A Mountain of Gold*, a collection of stories drawn from his travels over the world.

Newcomers, 1920-1931

Alice Abbott	Romance Languages	1927-1965
Mary Ruth Angle	Library	1923-1938
Alex Matthews Arnett	History	1923-1945
Helen Barton	Mathematics	1927-1960
Estelle Boyd	Supervisor of Dormitories	1913-1942
Clara Booth Byrd	Alumnae Secretary	1913-1947
Dorothy Lee Clement	Music	1929-1946
Oliver Perry Clutts	Education	1924-1953
Inez Coldwell	Biology	1922-1961
Ruth M. Collings	College Physician	1925-1962
Hope Coolidge	Dietitian	1917-1938
Agnes N. Coxe	Home Economics	1927-1958
Dorothy Davis	Physical Education	1930-
Marie B. Denneen	Education	1926-1956
Bernice E. Draper	History	1922-1960
James Arthur Dunn	English	1923-1953
Mary Lois Ferrell	Music	1922-1949
Mary Fitzgerald	Education	1924-1953
Edna A. Forney	Assistant Treasurer	1921-1950
Henry H. Fuchs	Music	1924-1937
Annie Beam Funderburk	Romance Languages	1921-1961
Mildred Gould	English	1921-1951
Earl H. Hall	Botany	1923-1947

René Hardré	Romance Languages	1925-1958
Mildred P. Harris	Health	1924-1956
Edith Harwood	Chief Clerk	1923-1956
Kathleen P. Hawkins	Student Aid Officer	1921-1967
Marjorie Hood	Library	1929-
Malcolm Hooke	Romance Languages	1922-1958
Leonard B. Hurley	English	1921-1961
Minnie M. Hussey	Library	1930-1957
Helen Ingraham	Biology	1923-1960
Clarence D. Johns	History	1923-1950
Glenn R. Johnson	Sociology	1923-1954
Albert S. Keister	Economics	1924-1956
Benjamin B. Kendrick	History	1923-1945
Herbert Kimmel	Education	1926-1951
Anna M. Kreimeier	Education	1927-1965
Jessie C. Laird	Romance Languages	1922-1947
Betty Aiken Land	Education	1923-1945
Vera Largent	History	1923-1961
Augustine LaRochelle	Romance Languages	1922-1958
Lila Belle Love	Biology	1926-1953
Miriam McFadyen	Education	1927-1945
William W. Martin	Psychology	1922-1944
Harriett Mehaffie	Education	1929-1962
Meta Helen Miller	Romance Languages	1922-1966
Grace Van Dyke More	Music	1925-1947
Victoria Carlsson Nielson	College Physician	1930-1948
Mildred P. Newton	Secretary to Registrar	1926-1959
James W. Painter	English	1926-1962
Kathleen S. Painter	English	1929-1962
Mollie Anne Peterson	Home Economics	1921-1943
Helen Lee Pickard	Secretary to Business Manager	1923-1953
Viva Playfoot	Home Economics	1925-1954
Abigail Rowley	English	1922-1954
Elizabeth Sampson	Library	1920-1961
Florence L. Schaeffer	Chemistry	1922-1964
Archie D. Shaftesbury	Zoology	1924-1959
Anne Shamburger	Health	1925-
James Moyer Sink	Superintendent of Grounds and Buildings	1911-1953
John Aaron Smith	Education	1927-1954
Patty Spruill	Commercial	1923-1954
Madeleine Street	Home Economics	1930-1965
Jane Summerell	English	1926-1956
Katherine Taylor	Romance Languages	1929-
William Raymond Taylor	English	1921-1960
Mary Alice Tennent	Assistant Registrar	1913-1956
George M. Thompson	Music	1923-1963
Nettie Sue Tillett	English	1924-1958

Virginia Trumper	Library	1922-1963
George A. Underwood	Romance Languages	1924-1944
Emily Holmes Watkins	Mathematics	1926-1958
Maude Williams	Biology	1927-1962
Sue Vernon Williams	Library	1926-1963
George P. Wilson	English	1927-1956

∾ *four* ∾

Buildings
and Grounds

A college is far more than bricks and mortar: it is people, students with dreams and teachers with vision. Together they form that vital spirit which is the very essence of a college. The campus itself is only the shell in which this being grows, but it is a visible, tangible symbol of that growth. Every student recalls a certain classroom in which she found inspiration or an office in which she found encouragement. In the dormitories friendships were born and in the soda shop opinions were shared. The campus holds memories for everyone, and the record of its development is one story of the college.

Early Development

The crowded conditions and limited resources of the first year proved to be chronic ailments of the struggling college. In his first report to the Board of Directors, McIver requested more dormitory space, more recitation rooms, a small building for a practice school, and additional equipment for the library and laboratories. In the second year there were 391 students.[1] When the third floor of Brick Dormitory was completed, there were twenty-two additional rooms, but 150 students had to board with private families. Three rooms in Midway Dormitory were used by the Commercial Department and the Practice School, and the library was placed in the rear of the assembly hall to provide another recitation room. Still the facilities were inadequate. Before the catalogues were issued in 1894, enough applications for the fall term had been received to fill all places.[2]

When the legislature of 1895 appropriated $10,000 for improvement of the physical plant, the Board of Directors voted to build an

1. Charles Duncan McIver, ''President's Report,'' in *Report of the Board of Directors, 1892-1930*, Dec. 20, 1892, p. 37.
2. Board of Directors, Proceedings, I (June 21, 1894), 109.

infirmary, to increase the dining room capacity, to provide better sanitary arrangements, to add porches to the dormitory and to do necessary painting and finishing inside, and to add two wings to Main Building as originally planned.[3]

One of Dr. McIver's primary concerns was the need for an infirmary. One room in Brick Dormitory had been set aside as an infirmary; not only was this inadequate, but it made isolation of patients impossible. During the second year there was more sickness because of the bad weather. Although there were no epidemics, there were several cases of grippe, and some students had to go home for rest and recuperation. Miss Sue R. Palmer of Warren County, who was living in town with her aunt, died, and though she was attended by her physician brother, by Dr. Gove, and by a consulting physician, Dr. McIver felt this pointed up the need for an infirmary outside the dormitories.[4]

When Dr. Gove went to Chicago for the summer, she left the floor plans for the new infirmary. On her return she was "horrified" that these had been disregarded and a dwelling house plan had been substituted, completely unsuited for its purpose. But it was, at least, a separate arrangement for the sick.[5] Built just north of Midway (Guilford Hall) on College Avenue, the infirmary had five small rooms and several baths and cost $2,100. Later, when a larger infirmary was built just to the west of it, it was known as Little Guilford and used for offices.[6]

The new dining hall adjoined Brick Dormitory. Built at a cost of $6,000, it seated 400. There were twenty sleeping rooms on the second floor.[7] The old dining room was then converted into rooms for students, increasing the dormitory capacity to 330. The cook was Uncle Henderson Feribault, who called his institution "The Enormous and Industrious School."[8]

During the first year all of the students took turns washing dishes, setting tables, and serving food. The second year a self-help program was instituted by which thirty girls earned expenses by helping in the dining room.[9] Meals had to be provided for no more than $8.00 a

3. *Ibid.*, I (May 23, 1895), 171.

4. *Ibid.*, I (June 21, 1894), 114.

5. Personal interview with Anne Shamburger, September 29, 1964.

6. In 1947 the building was torn down to make room for a soda shop, which was later converted to a faculty center.

7. Board of Directors, Proceedings, I (Nov. 20, 1896), 206.

8. Virginia Terrell Lathrop, *Educate a Woman* (Chapel Hill: The University of North Carolina Press, 1942), p. 39.

9. Fodie Buie Kenyon, "When We Came to College in '92," *Alumnae News,* XVI (Nov., 1926), 17.

month, and at the end of each year money left over was refunded to the students. The first year the meals cost $7.79 ⅝ a month. The remainder was given by the students to a scholarship fund. The second year the cost ran $7.93 ½; the remainder was given to the students.[10]

Two wings were added to Main Building in 1895, thus completing the original design. Work had been deferred because of lack of funds, and further delay seemed probable when the carpenters went on strike. Without notice they quit work one morning and sent for McIver, demanding an increase in wages from $1.25 to $1.50 per day.[11] Whether he met their demands is not known, but they did go back to work. The building was completed by fall and provided six more classrooms and laboratories. The cost of this work was $6,000.[12]

Another of McIver's favorite projects was a practice school. When the Executive Committee voted $700 for this purpose, McIver sought the help of R. S. Pullen and R. T. Gray for land and the city of Greensboro for assistance, hoping to make it part of the city school system. Pullen and Gray offered the land, but the city could not help. Therefore, McIver added a wing to Midway. This provided four recitation rooms on the first floor and space for twenty boarders on the second. The tuition gain of $800 from the additional students was to pay for the $1,572.67 addition.[13] These rooms were later moved and annexed to the infirmary.[14] When this addition was removed from the infirmary, the lumber was bought by Mrs. Nannie Johnson, who used it to build a house on McGee Street.

Modern conveniences were added gradually to life at the Normal. The buildings were heated by steam, and the heating contract required that the system be sufficient to heat the rooms to sixty-five degrees. During the second winter a committee found that ten rooms in the Brick Dormitory could not be brought up to the heating contract. Mr. Orlo Epps, the contractor, released the note due from the board at a discount of 30 per cent, and the board in turn released his bond for failure to carry out the contract.[15] The buildings had been designed to include bathrooms, but because of lack of sewerage, they were omitted. In the summer of 1895 the problem was solved and

10. McIver, ''President's Report,'' in the Board of Directors, Proceedings, I (Dec. 13-14, 1894), 146.

11. Greensboro *Record*, July 20, 1895.

12. Board of Directors, Proceedings, I (Nov. 20, 1896), 205.

13. *Ibid.*, I (Dec. 13-14, 1894), 131-32.

14. *Carolinian*, 1913, p. 72.

15. Board of Directors, Proceedings, I (June 21, 1894), 125.

bathrooms with hot and cold water were installed in all the buildings. Another improvement was the installation of gas lights to replace the kerosene lamps. With the addition of porches to Brick Dormitory and the liberal use of paint, the campus was far less forbidding. The connection of the school to the city telephone system was an event of note.[16]

Additions to College Property

One act which the President and board performed in 1895 was of particular significance to the development of the school. This was the purchase of 112 acres of land for $12,000.[17] The original ten-acre tract donated by Pullen and Gray was between Spring Garden Street, Walker Avenue, College Avenue, and a line which would be roughly equivalent to an extension of McIver Street. The land between College Avenue and Forest Street had been purchased from Pullen and Gray in 1892. When the large tract, bought from the same men, was added north of the college, the campus was almost complete. Later, the extension of West Market Street cut nine acres from the northern edge of the campus. These were sold for $6,000 and the money was used to purchase the land on the west side of McIver Street in 1907.[18] Foust thought it necessary to purchase the property between McIver Building and Tate Street to protect the campus and provide for future expansion. So that he might keep the price down, he bought the lots one at a time through A. M. Scales at a cost of $11,000.[19] There were several other tracts which Foust purchased for the college: two lots on Walker Avenue from Mrs. McIver for $1,500,[20] a house and lot on Lithia (now Tate) Street for $2,500,[21] the Coble lot on the corner of Tate and Spring Garden for $8,000,[22] the Teague property between Spring Garden and the railroad for $50,000,[23] the Currie lot west of the Coble property on Spring Garden for $12,000, and a farm

16. McIver, ''President's Report,'' in *Report of the Board of Directors, 1892-1930*, Sept. 30, 1896, p. 7.

17. Board of Directors, Proceedings, I (June 27, 1895), 178.

18. *Report of the Board of Directors, 1892-1930*, Sept. 15, 1908, p. 7.

19. Julius I. Foust, ''The History of the Woman's College'' (unpublished history, Chancellor's Office, The University of North Carolina at Greensboro), p. 131.

20. E. J. Forney, ''Report of the Treasurer,'' *Report of the Board of Directors, 1892-1930*, Sept. 15, 1914, p. 35.

21. *Ibid.*, p. 37.

22. Julius I. Foust, ''Report of the President,'' *Report of the Board of Directors, 1892-1930*, Sept. 15, 1916, p. 13.

23. Board of Directors, Proceedings, III (May 21, 1919), 145.

in Friendship township for $23,750.[24] With this last addition, the campus reached its maximum size for two decades.

In 1897 McIver decided to institute a Department of Horticulture and brought to the college Thomas L. Brown, who had been connected with the Vanderbilt Estate near Asheville. The department never materialized, but, as superintendent of grounds, Brown did much to beautify the campus. The land was drained, the driveway to Brick Dormitory was paved, and in front of Main Building a turn for carriages was built and a fountain was placed in the center.[25] While building the turn, the workmen discovered some granite, which was in pieces and appeared to have been "faced up." There was great speculation about the origin of the stones, Mr. Brown suggesting that they might be the remains of an old fortification 6,400 years old. Interest soon died down, however, and the stones were used to build the wall in front of the Main Building.[26]

Several practical additions were made at this time: a steam laundry (in the early days the laundry had been done by hand in large black washpots out-of-doors), a power house which made possible the extension of the heating system to all buildings, a new kitchen, a modern barn and dairy, and an iron bridge across the newly extended Walker Avenue. Despite these improvements, the list of needs was long: a practice and observation school, a gymnasium, additional library facilities, more classroom and dormitory space, society halls, a fence (the old wooden fence which had lined the eastern boundary of the campus had recently been torn down), and an auditorium.[27]

In 1899 the enrollment had grown from 409 to 490, necessitating more dormitory space. There were two dormitories on the campus, Midway and Brick, and the Teague House on Spring Garden Street (now the site of Curry Building) was rented. To provide for the increase, two other houses were rented, and the seniors gave up their rooms in the dormitories and moved into them. In anticipation of a

24. *Budget Request—Years 1925-1927*, North Carolina College for Women, p. 11.

25. When the fountain failed to work properly, it was filled in with dirt, and flowers, often cannas, were planted. As a gift to the school, the Class of 1928 had a new fountain built. *Alumnae News*, XVIII (Feb., 1930), 35. Although never an artistic achievement, the fountain was, in the summer, a refreshing sight, and on the coldest days of winter, a picture of icy beauty. In 1962 the fountain was torn down and parking places provided.

26. Greensboro *Record*, Jan. 31, 1898.

27. Charles D. McIver, "Report of the President," *Report of the Board of Directors, 1892-1930*, Sept. 30, 1900, p. 13.

new gymnasium, the old one in Main Building was converted into a library, and the library was used as a reception room for visitors and a meeting room for the faculty and Board of Directors. At this time the library had over three thousand volumes.[28] To provide for athletics, the Executive Committee ordered that an outdoor playing field be prepared, "surrounded by an evergreen hedge or some other construction to avoid observation from without."[29] Known as the Hockey Field, it was also used for outdoor gatherings, picture-taking for the yearbook, and bonfires. The space is now occupied by the Petty Science Building.

The Typhoid Epidemic

In November of 1899 a serious epidemic of typhoid necessitated the closing of the Normal.[30] Forty-eight students were too ill to travel, and seven weeks passed before the last patient was able to leave. During that time thirteen students and one staff member died. After extensive cleaning and disinfecting, the college was reopened on January 30.

Expenses incurred during the epidemic presented a serious problem. The $5,000 appropriation which the 1899 legislature had made for a gymnasium was used, but there was still a large deficit. Not only were there nursing and medical expenses, but there was also the cost of painting all the rooms and buying new furniture. The old double beds were burned and single beds substituted. A new filtering system was necessary, and new plumbing. All of this cost over $8,000. The loss of income from the laundry, the dairy, and the dormitory was $4,500.[31] It was 1908 before the college recovered financially from this tragedy.[32]

Peabody Park

In 1901 George Foster Peabody, a distant relative of George Peabody, gave $5,000 to develop an educational park in the wooded area north of the main campus. The original plan was to have markers honoring educational leaders of North Carolina. As the girls walked through the park during "walking period," they would learn the history of North Carolina education.[33]

28. Myrtie Scarboro, "Among Ourselves," *State Normal Magazine,* IV (March, 1900), 64.
29. Board of Directors, Proceedings, II (May 23, 1899), 49.
30. The epidemic is discussed in more detail in the chapter on student life.
31. Board of Directors, Proceedings, II (Dec. 20, 1900), 162-63.
32. Foust, "History of the Woman's College," p. 89.
33. Greensboro *Record,* June 24, 1901.

One of the former students, Kitty Dorcas Dees of Greensboro, obtained for the college the plans for the development of the park. While she was still a student at the Normal, the manager of one of the hotels in Pinehurst visited Mr. Forney's class, looking for a secretary. He so admired her "beautiful piece of work" that he hired her immediately. In Pinehurst she met Mr. Warren Henry Manning, a landscape architect of Boston, and went to work for him. When she asked him to lay out the grounds of her college, he agreed, and the college had to pay only the actual amount expended for clerical help, drafts, and traveling expenses. Dr. McIver was said to have considered Miss Dees' contribution the largest made to the college. Of this gift Mr. Forney said, "Let me project an earnest that at some future time, there will be another walk or lane or road or avenue laid off on the College grounds, more beautiful than anything now existing, and that its name will be 'Dees' lane, road, walk, avenue, and the mere fact of its existence will be a standing monument that a girl did a 'beautiful piece of work' in the classroom."[34]

Curry Building

February 17, 1902, marked the formal opening of the Curry Building, the training school for which McIver had worked so earnestly. The building was named for Dr. Jabez Lamar Monroe Curry, executive secretary of the Peabody Fund. In introducing Dr. Curry, McIver announced that the building had been so named because Curry had encouraged the legislature in 1891 when the founding of the institution was at stake and, as executive secretary of the Peabody Fund, had contributed to the School of Pedagogy through the years.[35] Other speakers that day were George Foster Peabody, Governor Aycock, President Charles G. Vardell of Flora Macdonald College, P. P. Claxton, and Julius I. Foust. An "elegant six o'clock dinner" was served in the dining hall by the students.[36]

Curry Building faced Walker Avenue, which then ran through the campus, and was on the east side of College Avenue.[37] On moving day

34. E. J. Forney, Fodie Buie, and Emily Semple Austin, *Leaves from The Stenographer's Notebook* (Greensboro: Harrison Printing Co., n.d.), p. 17.
35. "The Curry Building," *State Normal Magazine*, VI (April, 1902), 346. The treasurer's reports show that the contributions from the Peabody Fund through 1902 totaled $27,800. In the remaining years, $11,500 was donated.
36. *Ibid.*
37. The treasurer's reports do not give one cost for the building. The total of items listed in the reports for 1901 and 1902 is $15,009.36. The amount may have been more because there are bills for plumbing and roofing which are not explained.

Julius I. Foust, the new principal, led the parade of students and teachers as they marched, with banners flying, from their old quarters in Midway to the new school. This building served as the practice and observation school until it burned in 1926.

Students' Building

A cherished dream of the students began to materialize when the cornerstone for the Students' Building was laid in 1902. As sophomores, the students of the Class of 1899 had been inspired by a lecture by J. L. M. Curry to contribute something to their school. First they gave $40 for a North Carolina flag; then they set aside $400 for a building for the literary societies. This was to have been a two-room frame house, but when the students found that financial assistance would be available, they decided to wait for something better.

Major contributions came from George Foster Peabody and the members of the Southern Education Board. William Jennings Bryan and Dr. Claribel Cone[38] gave the receipts from their appearances on the campus. Performances by the University Glee Club and the First North Carolina Regimental Band also added to the fund. Students and faculty made personal contributions, and soon a handsome three-story building was underway. The Board of Directors decided to cooperate in the project and equip one floor for the domestic science department. To save money, McIver and the board did not let a contract, and the college supervised the work.[39]

The Students' Building stood at the southwest corner of Walker and College Avenues, facing College Avenue. The basement, which was open on three sides, housed the domestic science and manual training departments. In later years these rooms were used for the post office and book store. The main floor had two society halls, each seating about 300, and a reception or banquet hall. On the second floor were the auditorium seating 700, the meeting room for the Young Women's Christian Association, and the Bailey Memorial Room, which was dedicated to the memory of Sarah and Evelyn Bailey, who had died in the typhoid epidemic in 1899. In giving the money to furnish the room and establish the Bailey Scholarship Fund, Thomas Bailey said, "I establish this fund in memory of those who

38. Dr. Cone and her sister Miss Etta Cone were interested in modern art and for many years collected works by such outstanding artists as Matisse, Manet, Cezanne, Van Gogh, Degas, Picasso, Renoir, Gauguin, and Rouault. The major portion of their collection was bequeathed to the Baltimore Museum of Art, but the Weatherspoon gallery received over 175 works of art.

39. Charlotte *Observer*, Nov. 5, 1902.

were dearer than life, and in grateful appreciation of your kindness and of the many attentions and loving care rendered to my dear ones by the faculty.''[40] This room provided a place for quiet meditation for many students, and it was here that Lula Disosway, Class of 1918, committed her life to God as a medical missionary. After receiving her medical degree from Woman's Medical College in Philadelphia, she served in China.[41] The third floor had rooms for entertaining alumnae and former students during commencement, when they could rent a cot for fifty cents.[42] Completion of the building required several years, and it was not until 1906 that graduation could be held in the auditorium.[43]

Brick Dormitory Fire

On January 20, 1904, just after mid-term examinations, Eugene Osborne, the night watchman, discovered a fire in Brick Dormitory at 3:45 A.M. All of the 350 students were awakened in time to vacate the building, but 125 of them lost all their clothing. Years later Miss Emma McKinney recalled that night,

> One of the dormitory girls opened the door to my room and called out, ''Fire! Get out at once. Don't take time to get anything. Hurry.''
>
> I waked my roommate and we grabbed our robes and bedroom slippers and rushed to the stairway as quickly as we could. You would think on a winter night that we would have put on our shoes and a coat, but we didn't. Two of the teachers lent us some clothes to wear home.
>
> You can imagine how we felt as we watched the fire outside and thought of our cherished possessions being consumed in flames.
>
> I remember the nice breakfast the different hotels sent out to the College. You see the kitchen was burned and no food could be prepared out there.
>
> Dr. McIver had been to New York but returned to Greensboro early that morning. He had all of us assemble in the auditorium about 11 a.m., and I shall never forget his talk. He said his heart was filled with gratitude that not one girl or person had been burned or hurt. Then he said he was so sorry that many of us had had our clothes and others things destroyed, but material things can be replaced and human lives can't. His

40. ''Bailey Fund,'' *State Normal Magazine*, IV (March, 1900), 61.
41. *Alumnae News*, XVII (Nov., 1927), 14.
42. Charlotte *Observer*, Nov. 5, 1902.
43. *Carolinian*, 1913, p. 127.

talk was one never to be forgotten and I have thought of it many times. He was a wonderful person.[44]

At that meeting in the auditorium McIver walked out on the stage and asked that those students who had enough clothes to appear in should join in singing "Praise God from Whom All Blessings Flow."[45] Governor Aycock commented that he was glad to see them all "clothed and in their right minds."[46] Afterward McIver met with the Governor, members of the Council of State, and the Board of Directors to decide what to do.

The fire had destroyed the dormitory, the kitchen, the laundry, the newly erected cold storage plant, and the dining hall, to which two stories had recently been added. The total loss was $64,458.34 and the insurance was $32,678.09. School was suspended for three weeks to make temporary arrangements, and $80,000 was borrowed to build a new dormitory. The lower story of the Students' Building had been opened in the fall, and while the students were at home, it was fitted up as a dormitory with sheets serving as partitions between the small alcoves. This arrangement provided for about half the students; some found rooms in private homes, and others, about a hundred, remained at home.[47] A temporary building to be used for the dining room and kitchen was erected on the present site of Mary Foust Hall. These temporary arrangements cost $16,000, of which $6,390.70 was of little or no permanent value.[48]

Spencer Hall

As soon as possible, work was begun on a new dormitory, and the building was ready for occupancy when school opened on October 6, 1904. The Board of Directors named it in honor of Cornelia Phillips Spencer, who had been instrumental in having the University of North Carolina reopened after it had been closed during the Reconstruction period. Although not an advocate of co-education, she supported the first summer normal school at the university in 1877. A few months earlier Mrs. Spencer, her daughter June, and her niece Lucy Phillips had been permitted to attend lectures in botany on the condition that they sit in the back of the room and remain quiet. In

44. Personal interview, Nov. 8, 1964.

45. Forney, *et al.*, *Stenographer's Notebook*, p. 22.

46. Rose Howell Holder, *McIver of North Carolina* (Chapel Hill: The University of North Carolina Press, 1957), p. 233.

47. McIver, "Report of the President," in *Biennial Report of the Board of Directors*, Sept. 15, 1904, p. 21.

48. *Biennial Report of the Board of Directors*, Sept. 15, 1904, p. 6.

1895 she was awarded an honorary LL.D. by the university, the first woman to receive such recognition.[49]

Mindful of how disastrous the Brick Dormitory fire could have been, Dr. McIver was determined that the new building would be safer. This time only two stories were planned, with fire doors at intervals on the halls and many exits. Facing east on College Avenue, the building was 492 feet long from north to south, with a wing on the north end and a large dining room and kitchen running back from the center. The north wing seemed so far away the students often called it "Rockingham" for Rockingham County, which lies just north of Guilford.[50] When the south wing was added in 1907, the building was said to be the largest woman's dormitory in the nation.

Years later the building became outmoded and was considered a fire hazard. Until it was renovated, Dr. Jackson had policewomen patrol the halls each night to check for fire.

Carnegie Library

At commencement in 1904 Dr. McIver described the "donation of a library building by Mr. Andrew Carnegie in February of this year [as marking] a new epoch in the literary life of the college."[51] This gift was considered somewhat remarkable because Carnegie had just given a library to the city of Greensboro and because he did not usually give libraries to colleges.[52]

The nucleus of the library had been donated by McIver and other members of the faculty. Alderman set up a "what-not" in his classroom which he and his students filled with books for general distribution. The first year was half over before the college placed an order for books for the library. One of the largest contributions to the library came from the Dialectic and Philanthropic Literary societies of the University of North Carolina. When the two societies gave their libraries to the university in 1892, duplicates were given to the Normal and to the College of Agriculture and Mechanic Arts in Raleigh. Among these were valuable first editions of Irving and Cooper and first American editions of Sir Walter Scott and Bulwer-Lytton. The Cornelian and Adelphian societies at the Normal each

49. Phillips Russell, *The Woman Who Rang the Bell* (Chapel Hill: The University of North Carolina Press, 1949), p. 161.

50. Hazel Worsley and Vera Keech must have felt very isolated indeed when an owl flew into their room one night and killed a rat. *Carolinian*, Dec. 17, 1921.

51. *State Normal Magazine*, VIII (June, 1904), 246.

52. *News and Observer* (Raleigh, N.C.), Feb. 21, 1904.

contributed $150 a year to buy books for the library until the drive
to raise money for the Students' Building began.[53]

The Carnegie Library, which opened on October 2, 1905, was a
tremendous improvement over the classroom, the reception room, and
the gymnasium, which had served their turns as libraries. Miss Annie
Petty, who was the first trained librarian in North Carolina, described
her new library with some pride,

> Our new library, gift of Mr. Carnegie, has been completed
> and adds much to the attractiveness of the place, having, to
> quote one of the students, ''quite a literary look.''
> Entering the vestibule with its handsome tiled floor, you pass
> to the lobby. On the right is the general reading room where the
> newspapers, magazines and books of fiction are kept. Back of
> this room is the private office of the librarian which leads into a
> fireproof vault in which important papers are placed on file. To
> the left of the lobby is the history room and back of this a room
> for dictionaries and encyclopedias. Immediately behind the
> lobby is a fireproof stock [*sic*] room.
> On the second floor which is reached by two broad stairways,
> are the teachers' sitting and reading room which is just above
> the general reading room and one above the history room for
> government documents.
> The furniture and wood-work is all of natural oak. The
> building is heated by steam and lighted by electricity.[54]

The total cost of the library, $18,868, was paid by Andrew Carnegie.[55]

Improvements, 1906-1907

The President's report of 1906 announced the completion of the
laundry building and powerhouse, cold storage plant, the first floor
of the Students' Building, and fourteen music practice rooms around
the rostrum of the auditorium. At this time all the buildings were
connected to the central heating system, and Midway, the wooden
dormitory, was renovated.[56]

During the summer of 1907, the south wing of Spencer Hall was
extended to make room for seventy-five more students. This addition,
which included the enlargement of the kitchen and dining hall, cost

53. Elizabeth Jerome Holder, ''A History of the Library of the Woman's
College of the University of North Carolina,'' (Master's thesis, School of Library
Science, University of North Carolina, 1955), *passim.*

54. Annie F. Petty, ''Improvements at the College,'' *State Normal Magazine,*
IX (Nov., 1905), 17.

55. Foust, ''Report of the Acting President,'' in *Biennial Report of the Board
of Directors,* Sept. 15, 1906, p. 25.

56. *Ibid.*

$31,230.82.[57] Since there was still no gymnasium, the basement was fitted up as a large exercise room and shower baths were added. Facing Walker Avenue, the entrance with its tall white columns made this one of the most attractive buildings on the campus.[58]

The *Biennial Report of 1908* gave the final cost of the Students' Building, equipment included, as $49,813. Students, alumnae, and friends contributed about $18,000, and Mr. and Mrs. T. B. Bailey, about $2,000 for the Bailey Memorial Room.[59] The walls of the auditorium were hung with portraits of noteworthy people, most of which had been painted by W. G. Randall. Among them were McIver, Joyner, Curry, Finger, and Aycock, who had direct influence on the college, and Miss Frances E. Willard, Miss Dorothea Dix, John A. Mills, James C. Dobbins, Zebulon B. Vance, Calvin Wiley, and George Peabody.

McIver Memorial Building

In January, 1908, the board met to consider plans for the science building, which was to be named for McIver. Plans were drawn for a $125,000 building, but since that much money was not available, only the central section was built immediately. The cornerstone was laid at commencement, and the building was opened in the fall. Housed in the McIver Building were lecture rooms, laboratories, and offices for the departments of physics, domestic arts, and science. Erected at a cost of $54,451.35, the building had three stories and a basement.[60]

McIver Statue

After the death of McIver, a movement began throughout the state to raise money to erect a bronze statue in his honor. Even the school children brought pennies on North Carolina Day for this tribute. In January, 1910, J. Y. Joyner, chairman of the statue committee, announced that the contract had been awarded to Frederick W. Ruckstuhl, chief sculptor of the Louisiana Purchase Exposition, who was leaving for Paris immediately to begin work.[61] Working from pictures and a death mask, Ruckstuhl sculptured the statue, which was unveiled on the Capitol grounds in Raleigh on May 15, 1912. The death mask, which for years lay unmarked in the Southern Historical

57. Foust, ''Report of the President,'' in the *Biennial Report of the Board of Directors*, Sept. 15, 1908, p. 15.

58. *Biennial Report of the Board of Directors*, Sept. 15, 1908, p. 6.

59. *Ibid.*, p. 5.

60. *Ibid.*, p. 6.

61. *News and Observer* (Raleigh, N.C.), Jan. 8, 1910.

Collection, was later presented to the college and is in the College Collection in the Jackson Library.

At the suggestion of George T. Winston, a copy was made for the Normal, the two statues to cost $7,000.[62] The statue on the campus was unveiled on Founder's Day, October 5, 1912. After the invocation by the Reverend Mr. R. Murphy Williams of the Presbyterian Church of the Covenant, Greensboro, and the singing of "America," Foust introduced Miss Bertha Lee, one of the first graduates of the school and a member of the faculty. She, in turn, introduced P. P. Claxton, United States commissioner of education. After his address, the student body repeated McIver's favorite scripture, the thirteenth chapter of First Corinthians. Joyner then presented the statue, which was accepted by Foust. As McIver's eldest daughter Annie drew the veil, the students sang "The Old North State," one of McIver's favorite songs.

In 1959 when the McIver Building was torn down, the statue, which had stood in front, was moved to a more prominent position in front of the Walter Clinton Jackson Library on College Avenue. Here the daisy chain is spread out at commencement in the numerals of the graduation class.

Infirmary

The next major addition to the campus was a larger infirmary. The first one had never been completely satisfactory, and as the enrollment grew, it became even more inadequate.[63] The seventy-five bed capacity of the new building was designed to meet the requirements of the college for many years to come. Situated between Forest Street and the Students' Building, the infirmary had a basement, two stories, and an attic. One important feature was the quarantine ward, an important provision to the college, which had not forgotten the typhoid epidemic of 1899. In November, 1911, students, alumnae, and even daughters of alumnae gave a linen shower for the infirmary.[64] After another infirmary was built in 1953, this building had a varied career. Leased by the federal government for several years, it added mystery to the campus because its function was classified information.

62. *Ibid.*, Dec. 6, 1911. Dr. Winston had been president of the University of North Carolina, the University of Texas, and the College of Agriculture and Mechanic Arts. He was the only man to serve both of the North Carolina institutions in this capacity.

63. The enrollment reached 613 in 1909-1910.

64. Charlotte *Observer*, Nov. 6, 1911.

Later it served as a dormitory for graduate students and then as an office building for faculty. It was demolished in 1966.

Woman's Hall

In November of 1912 a new dormitory was opened, named Woman's for the women of the Confederacy. This building housed sixty students and cost $25,000.[65] Located on the edge of Peabody Park just west of Spencer Hall, this building soon became known as "Senior Hall" and was the recognized home of the campus leaders for many years. In 1931 it housed the president and vice-president of the Student Government Association and the two who had been elected to succeed them; the editors of the *Carolinian, Coraddi,* and the *Pine Needles*; the presidents of the three societies and of the senior class; four of the yearbook superlatives; and numerous legislators, judicial board members, marshals, minor officers and editors, and Playlikers.[66]

Pre-War Building

The first home management house was opened early in 1914. In rounding out the college property, Foust bought a small house on Lithia Street (Tate), which was remodeled under Miss Jamison's supervision. Seniors in domestic science lived there for a week, thus getting practical experience in housekeeping.[67]

When Woman's Hall was built, it was necessary to tear down the already dilapidated barn nearby and to build a new barn and dairy farther away.[68] Located on the site of the present golf course, the new facilities provided a picnic area for students.

At the same time, repairs were indicated in the Curry Building, where ceilings in some of the rooms were falling. The cost of repairs was $13,114.55.[69]

The year 1914 found another dormitory in progress. Later named Kirkland Hall in honor of the lady principal, this building was very similar to Woman's, beside which it was built.[70] Although these dormitories were considered models at that time, their limited capacity

65. Foust, "Report of the President," in the *Biennial Report*, Sept. 15, 1912, p. 23.

66. *Carolinian*, May 7, 1931.

67. *Twice-a-Week Dispatch* (Burlington, N.C.), Feb. 12, 1914.

68. *Biennial Report of the Board of Directors*, Sept. 15, 1914, p. 23.

69. *Ibid.*, p. 21.

70. *Ibid.*, p. 10.

made the cost of constant repair impractical, and they were torn down in 1964.

1914 Valuation

The insurance valuation list for July, 1914, gives a view of the size and value of the campus at that time.

Main Building	$ 60,000
Curry	27,000
Students'	60,000
Spencer	150,000
McIver	60,000
Mechanical	15,000
Guilford	10,000
President's House	3,500
Old Infirmary	3,000
New Infirmary	65,000
Woman's	30,000
Stewart	800
Library	15,000
Kirkland	35,000
Barn and Stable Building	8,000
Dairy	1,000
Janitor's Dwelling	700
1200 Walker Avenue	1,000
Ford House, 406 S. Lithia Street	3,000

All this plus furnishings and equipment totaled $712,000.[71]

For the next few years there was little change in the physical plant.[72] New insurance laws made it necessary to add fire escapes to many of the buildings, and Forest House, a small dormitory on the corner of Forest Street and Walker Avenue, burned. A house on Highland Avenue was rented to accommodate the thirty-two girls who had been left homeless.[73]

World War I Era

In the spring of 1917 the legislature voted to issue $3,000,000 in state bonds for the enlargement and improvement of the state's educational and charitable institutions. The college was to receive $500,000 of this amount and an annual appropriation of $125,000.[74] When

71. Executive Committee of the Board of Directors, Minutes, I (July, 1914), 23.

72. *Biennial Report of the Board of Directors*, Sept. 15, 1916, p. 12.

73. Greensboro *Daily News*, Feb. 11, 1917.

74. Foust, ''Report of the President,'' in the *Biennial Report of the Board of Directors*, Sept. 15, 1918, p. 8.

Foust returned from Raleigh, 700 students marched to his house to show their gratitude for his part in obtaining this generous appropriation. They burned "Hardtimes" in effigy, set off fireworks, and sang,

> This year we're crowded till we overflow
> Three in a room just two by four,
> We've got so many till we're short of dough;
> He's pulled the legislature for a whole lot more.
> Who? Dr. Foust!
> How much more? Five hundred thousand dollars.[75]

The appropriation from the bonds was delayed, however, because the federal government was selling bonds which paid a higher interest rate than the state. Only as bonds were sold could the appropriation be paid. The war brought increased prices, and, as a result, the seemingly generous annual allotment was insufficient. The college was faced with the necessity for strict economy and even debt.

The only building erected during this period was the YWCA Hut, which the students themselves helped to erect because of the shortage of labor and money.[76]

Anna Howard Shaw Hall

In 1919 a new dormitory, housing 125 students, was built on Walker Avenue, just west of Woman's Building, at a cost of $106,399. When Dr. Anna Howard Shaw spoke at commencement in 1919, the students and alumnae decided that they wanted the dormitory named for her because of her interest in the college and their interest in the suffrage movement.

Decade of the Twenties

The contract for the east wing of the McIver Memorial Building was let the same day war was declared on Germany, and resulting complications delayed the opening of the building until 1920. The History Department had offices and classrooms on the first floor; Mathematics on the second; and Domestic Science on the third. The Romance Language Department had the basement, which was above ground, and some of the classrooms on the first and second floors. The cost of this wing was $82,095.[77]

75. *State Normal Magazine*, XXI (April, 1917), 209.

76. The building of the Hut is described in the chapter on student life.

77. Foust, ''Report of the President,'' in the *Biennial Report of the Board of Directors*, Sept. 15, 1920, p. 8.

During the decade of the twenties, the college underwent a remarkable physical expansion. From 1915 to 1921 the enrollment was between 700 and 800. During the four years after that the number increased to a total of 1,636. The growth in enrollment was, of course, accompanied by a growth in buildings. In fact, more buildings were erected during this decade than had been built in the period from 1891 to 1920.

Spencer Dining Hall, which had been built for a student body of 500, was so inadequate that plans were made for a five-building complex, of which Spencer was to be the first part. The second, West Dining Hall, was erected in 1921. When completed, four dining halls and a kitchen extended from a central serving area like the spokes of a wheel. South was built in 1924, the kitchen in 1927, and North in 1939.

Additional dormitory space was always one of the more pressing needs of the college. Soon after the completion of Shaw, plans were made for a quadrangle of residence halls to be erected, with Shaw closing the southern end. The next one was built northeast of Shaw and was named for Robert T. Gray, one of the donors of the original land and for twelve years (1900-1912) member of the Board of Directors. This building was similar to Shaw, except that it lacked the tall white columns, and it served as a model for the other buildings in the group.[78] Each of these dormitories cost about $110,000 and housed 130 students. Three others were completed in 1922. At the request of the alumnae, one was named for Mrs. Sallie Southall Cotten, founder of the woman's club movement in North Carolina. The others were named Bailey and Hinshaw in honor of members of the board; Thomas B. Bailey had served on the board from 1902 to 1916, and Colonel G. W. Hinshaw had served from 1910 to 1918.

In 1923 two dormitories were added to the group. These were known as East and West until they were officially named for Minnie Lou Jamison and Laura Hill Coit, who had come to the college as students in 1892 and 1893, respectively, and had spent their lives in service to the college.

Since the shortage of faculty housing made securing personnel difficult, Foust sought to remedy the situation. In 1920 he purchased seven Alladin ready-cut houses. In a matter of a few weeks four were built on McIver Street and three on West Market Street. Three of those on McIver were for women faculty who boarded in the dining

78. *Ibid.*, p. 10.

hall; the others were for men with families.[79] The cost of the houses and of the construction was $51,189.27, which was to be paid from the income.[80]

In 1922 the west wing of the McIver Building was erected, thus completing the original plan. The first floor of this wing had six classrooms of varying size, a reference library, and five offices. The second floor was similar, but the third floor had a sewing laboratory, a cutting room, and an art room, all spacious and fitted with sky lights.[81] This addition cost $73,232.41.[82]

Another addition of 1922 was the Home Management House, then known as the Domestic Science Cottage, on McIver Street. This handsome brick building had on the first floor an entrance hall, living room, dining room, pantry, kitchen, bedroom, and sleeping porch. On the second floor there were four bedrooms. A large attic was designed for use with the groups of children participating in the child study program.[83] The cost of the house was $27,887.35.[84]

In 1923 annexation brought the dairy into the city, forcing the college to find a new location, for it was still considered practical to maintain a dairy to produce milk and cream for dining hall use. Since 1920 the only crops raised on the farm had been grain and feed for the cows and horses. At a cost of $23,753.54 the college bought a 250-acre farm in Friendship township, eight miles from Greensboro.[85]

A drive was started in 1924 to raise $250,000 for a "non-academic activities building." The plan was to raise $25,000 on campus, $75,000 in Guilford County, and $150,000 in the state. The building, "constructed along the lines of the finest of the Old Southern architecture," was to contain reception rooms, dining room, banquet hall, smaller parlors, kitchenette, combined reading and music room, offices for student organizations, a lounge and kitchenette for day students, club rooms for faculty, guest rooms for visitors and alumnae, and a little theater.[86] Despite the initial enthusiasm which brought pledges

79. *Carolinian*, Sept. 25, 1920. The houses on West Market Street are now used for home management houses. One of the houses on McIver is the residence of the director of student services. The others have been removed.

80. Foust, "Report of the President," in the *Biennial Report of the Board of Directors*, Sept. 15, 1920, p. 12.

81. *Carolinian*, Oct. 29, 1921.

82. Foust, "Report of the President," in the *Biennial Report of the Board of Directors*, Sept. 15, 1922, p. 10.

83. *Carolinian*, March 10, 1923.

84. Forney, "Report of the Treasurer," in *Biennial Report of the Board of Directors*, Sept. 15, 1922, p. 52.

85. Greensboro *Daily News*, Dec. 19, 1923.

86. *Carolinian*, Feb. 9, 1924.

of $150,000 and a snake dance of a thousand students, singing and cheering through downtown Greensboro, the college had to wait thirty years for the student union building that fulfilled most of the dream.

Alumnae Tea Room

In 1922 the Alumnae Association started construction of its own building on the site occupied by the Teague House on Spring Garden Street. Originally the plan called for twenty-eight bedrooms, a large club room, swimming pool, nursery, dining room, and kitchen.[87] In 1920, Mr. Julius Cone, Mr. Bernard Cone, and Mrs. Ceasar Cone donated $2,500.[88] A bazaar was held in the YWCA Hut in December, 1920, at which novelties, toys, lingerie, and refreshments donated by alumnae were sold to raise money for the building.[89] During the summer of 1921 a tea room was opened in the Old Infirmary to raise money during summer school.[90] In 1922 the Teague House was moved south to a site nearer the railroad, and work was begun on the Alumnae Building.

The first section, the Alumnae Tea Room, was completed in October. The basement held the laundry, heating plant, store room, and servants' quarters. The first floor had a large dining room, kitchen, lavatories, and enclosed porch. The dining room was decorated with ornamental plaster and handblocked draperies. These draperies were designed by students in Miss Beatrice D. Craig's art class and depicted such campus scenes as Zeke[91] ringing the college bell and students walking across the iron bridge over Walker Avenue. Miss Harriett Hylton supervised the Tea House, which offered three meals a day, a la carte service, and afternoon tea. There was also a showcase displaying handiwork sent by the alumnae to be sold for the fund.[92]

Unfortunately the Tea House was not successful. Since the Alumnae Association had originally purchased the property to hold it for the college, Miss Byrd, alumnae secretary, asked Dr. Foust to buy the Tea House and land in 1925 and to permit the association to erect another building at some time in the future.

87. *Ibid.*, Jan 27, 1923.
88. *Ibid.*, Oct. 16, 1920. The Cone family have, throughout the years, been benefactors of the college. The ballroom in Elliott Hall was named for them.
89. *Ibid.*, Dec. 11, 1920.
90. *Alumnae News*, X (June, 1921), 7.
91. Zeke, Ezekial Robinson, served the college for over fifty years as ''general factotum extraordinary, as janitorial lighter of fires and polisher of lamps, as driver of the college surrey, as mail carrier, as presidential coachman and porter and valet.'' Holder, *McIver of North Carolina*, p. 125.
92. *Pine Needles*, 1923, p. 22.

Outdoor Gymnasium

The Department of Physical Education also found a home of its own in 1922, an outdoor gymnasium. When the college was first opened, a classroom in the Administration Building was used, but that became the library when money was appropriated for a gymnasium. This money had to be used for the typhoid epidemic, and for a few years there was no space available for athletics. The chapel of the Curry Building and later the basement of Spencer Building were used by the department. The outdoor gymnasium was 90 by 50 feet. Around three sides there was a wall six feet high with a screen above, stretching to the roof. Canvas drops were provided for rainy weather. This structure, which cost $9,871.83, was west of Shaw Building.[93]

President's Residence

When McIver died in 1906, the legislature invited his widow to remain in the President's House. Not until 1923 was a residence provided for his successor. In that year a lovely tapestry brick house, costing $22,408.37, was built on the northeast corner of Spring Garden and Forest Streets. This was occupied by Foust when he returned from Asheville, where he had been recuperating from a stroke he had suffered in April.[94]

Expansion of Library

In 1922 renovation of the Carnegie Library was begun. While the work was being done, eight rooms in the basement of the east wing of McIver were used as a temporary library. In March, 1923, the library reopened with three times as much space as the old building. There were rooms for periodicals, documents, fiction, American authors, and reference works. The periodical and reference rooms had long tables divided into compartments which afforded some privacy. There were two floors of stacks with room for more to be added. The total cost of expansion was $100,000.[95] The number of books was increasing as well. In June, 1920, the number of volumes in the library was 13,721; in 1922, 16,817; and in 1924, 25,167.[96]

93. Marion O'Neill, ''A History of the Physical Education Department at the Woman's College of the University of North Carolina'' (Master's thesis, Department of Physical Education, Woman's College of the University of North Carolina, 1955), pp. 92-96.

94. *Alumnae News*, XII (Oct., 1923), 7.

95. *Carolinian*, March 3, 1923.

96. Holder, *McIver*, p. 45.

Rosenthal Building

Under the leadership of Mary Channing Coleman, the Department of Physical Education was making such strides that new facilities became necessary. In March, 1925, a modern, well-equipped building was opened with a gymnasium 78 by 98 feet with a spectators' gallery, a corrective room and auxiliary gymnasium, a swimming pool 25 by 75 feet with thirty-six marble showers, and an administrative section with offices and a lobby.[97] Before the plans were made Miss Coleman was asked whether she preferred a gymnasium or a swimming pool. After she chose the pool, the board realized that the gymnasium was needed too, and so she got both.[98] In 1928 the Alumnae Association asked that the building be named for Joe Rosenthal, whom a yearbook dedication called, "a faithful friend whose genuine interest in our college was demonstrated during seventeen years of unstinting service as a trustee, whose progressive policies were influential in expanding our school, whose unostentatious generosity and personal interest in our faculty and students won our love."[99]

Music Building

In 1925 the School of Music moved into its new $200,000 home on the corner of Walker Avenue and Tate Street. The organ,[100] which had been in the Students' Building, was remodeled and placed in the auditorium, which was also equipped with two Mason and Hamlin grand pianos. The auditorium had a seating capacity of 250 and was designed for small recitals. There were sixteen classrooms, nine offices, and fifty practice rooms. Although not perfect, the soundproofing was very good. The equipment used daily included seven grand pianos, thirty-six uprights, one Duo-art instrument, two pipe organs, one pedal reed organ, and one practice pedal piano.[101] The building was named for Dr. Wade R. Brown in 1960.

New Curry Building

The college had its third fire when the Curry Building was destroyed in March of 1926. The old structure with its wooden floors

97. *Carolinian*, Jan. 17, 1925.

98. O'Neill, "History of the Physical Education Department," p. 96.

99. *Pine Needles*, 1928, p. 6.

100. This organ had been installed in the Students' Building in 1913. It had 1,114 pipes, 30 speaking stops, and 21 accessories. Roanoke-Chowan *Times*, Nov. 27, 1913.

101. Wade R. Brown, "Report of the Dean of the School of Music," in *Report of the Board of Directors for the Years 1924-1926*, p. 53.

burned rapidly and only the records of the principal, Dr. A. P. Kephart, were saved. John H. Cook, dean of the School of Education, lost his records, which included the summer school applications and the superintendents' requests for teachers. Fortunately, classes in the training school had been dismissed before the fire was discovered by students playing ball on the hockey field.

Because the old Curry had proved inadequate, a new building was already under construction. The insurance money and $47,000 from the emergency fund made it possible to complete more of the building than the board had expected.[102] The new building was erected on Teague field, incorporating the Alumnae Tea Room in the central portion. Two wings extended southward from this section; at the eastern end was the elementary school wing, and in the center, the auditorium. In 1927 the west wing was added for high school classrooms, and a gymnasium was built behind the auditorium.[103]

Aycock Auditorium

Since the seating capacity of the auditorium in the Students' Building was only 700, the student body had outgrown it by the early twenties. It was necessary to divide the students into two groups and have them alternate in chapel attendance. When it was important to have all the students together, assemblies were held in the Spring Garden Street Methodist Church (now College Place Methodist). When the new auditorium was being built, the Alumnae Board requested the Board of Directors to name the building for Dr. Foust. When he heard of this, he wrote the Board of Directors and asked that the request be refused, for he did not think the best interests of the college would be served in that way.[104] Then the alumnae asked that it be named for Charles B. Aycock, "the great apostle of public education in North Carolina," who had always been a friend of the college, particularly at the time of the fire. Because Aycock had been such a great public speaker, it seemed fitting that an auditorium be named for him.[105]

102. Foust, "Report of the President," in *Report of the Board of Directors for the Years 1924-1926*, p. 15. The cost of the original part was $340,930.02. Forney, "Report of the Treasurer," Dec. 1, 1928, p. 79.

103. *Carolinian*, Sept. 22, 1927. The state, of course, paid for the building, but the General Education Board gave $100,000 to maintain the high school. The cost of this wing was $89,238.48. Forney, "Report of the Treasurer," Dec. 1, 1928, p. 79.

104. Letter from Julius I. Foust to the Board of Directors, May 14, 1926, College Collection.

105. Board of Directors, Proceedings, IV (June 19, 1928), 136.

The auditorium was dedicated at the commencement of 1927. This was the year of the great homecoming, when all former students were asked to return regardless of their class colors or year. Between 1,200 and 1,500 returned for the excellent program which included the auditorium dedication by Dr. Stephen A. Wise of the Free Synagogue of New York, a performance of *Alice Sit by the Fire* by the Play-likers and of *Elijah* by the orchestra and chorus, Park Night,[106] a bac-calaureate sermon by Dr. William P. Merrill of New York City, and the graduation address by Judge N. A. Townsend of Dunn on ''The Building of a Greater North Carolina.''[107]

At the dedication of the auditorium Foust made a statement which expresses his devotion to the college and his vision of its purpose:

> We enter upon this new era in college life, not boastfully, but very humbly, and at the same time with the confident hope and expectation that this college may be able to serve the people of North Carolina better than it has served them in the past. . . . I know I speak the sentiments of both faculty and students when I say that we all commit ourselves and dedicate our lives to those high ideals which must dominate a people who hope to make a college that will be a vital force in this state and in the world where so much clear thinking and unselfish idealism is needed.[108]

Additional Residence Halls

The legislature of 1927 appropriated $820,000 for permanent im-provements. Because this could not provide for all the needs of the college, it was necessary to select those which seemed most im-portant.[109]

Two dormitories, with a combined capacity of three hundred, were built on College Avenue at the northern end. More attention was given to making these buildings attractive and comfortable than formerly was given to beauty on the campus. The alumnae asked that one be named Guilford because the first Guilford would someday be removed and they wished to preserve ''a name that is already dear to the hearts of so many alumnae and that acknowledges our indebted-ness to the county in which our college is founded.''[110] For years after the first Guilford was torn down, its namesake was known as

106. See below, p. 132.

107. *Alumnae News*, XVII (July, 1927), 5-15.

108. *Ibid.*, p. 10.

109. Foust, ''Report of the President,'' in *Report of the Board of Directors for the Years 1926-1928*, p. 7.

110. Board of Directors, Proceedings, IV (June 19, 1928), 136.

New Guilford. The other dormitory was named for Dr. Foust's daughter, Mary Foust Armstrong, who was graduated from the college in 1920 and died in 1925. The recommendation from the alumnae committee said, ''In her short life she typified the fine ideals that characterized the best in North Carolina womanhood.'' Each of these buildings cost $167,704.00.[111]

Home Economics Building

In October, 1928, the Home Economics Building was opened.[112] The first floor had offices, lecture rooms, and an art room. Since there was no art department, the only art instruction outside the School of Education was that offered in home economics—costume design, house planning and furnishing, and art appreciation. On the second floor were the sewing rooms and food laboratories. In the basement was the nursery school. One important addition was the cafeteria, with adjoining kitchen, which was frequented by faculty members and sometimes visited by students who wished a change from dining hall fare.[113]

Improvements

From the beginning, muddy streets and walks had been a problem to the pedestrian society. The plank walks had gradually been replaced by concrete, but paving the roads took longer. The treasurer's report of 1918 lists $517.60 for street paving. This may have been College Avenue. McIver Street was paved in 1924; Forest Street in 1925; and Walker and West Market in 1926.[114] In 1928 the iron bridge over Walker was replaced by a concrete one. In 1929 the other roads through the campus were hard-surfaced.[115]

In 1929-1930 the Administration Building was completely renovated. This was the last improvement before the Depression years, which were to decrease the enrollment by a third, reduce faculty salaries, and delay further physical expansion for several years.[116]

111. E. J. Forney, ''Reports of the Treasurer to the President,'' Dec. 1, 1930, in *Report of the Board of Directors, 1928-1930*, p. 30.

112. This building was erected on the northwest corner of Walker Avenue and McIver Street at a cost of $136,103.49. *Ibid.* It is now only a wing of the Stone Home Economics Building.

113. *Carolinian*, Oct. 26, 1928.

114. Letter from Julius I. Foust to Henry Burke, Aug. 13, 1928, College Collection.

115. *Carolinian*, Sept. 27, 1929.

116. In 1967 the University of North Carolina at Greensboro comprised 135 acres and was valued at $31,000,000.

∾ five ∾

The Development
of the Curriculum

In many respects the curriculum of 1892 at the Normal was the equivalent of a high school program. The purpose of the institution was always to serve the needs of the young women of the state, and at that early date the girls needed something more akin to a high school than a college. As interest in education grew and more high schools were built, the students were prepared for a more advanced program; therefore the curriculum was up-graded. Since improvements at the Normal were dependent on conditions in the state, changes were made gradually and developments were not often outstanding.

The first period was that during which diplomas were awarded for work which was distinctly below college level (1892-1902). The next period was that of the first degrees (1903-1908), although still not college level, the work was being improved. The third period was marked by the expansion of services through extension and summer schools and by the introduction of new courses to develop a program worthy of accreditation (1909-1920). In 1921 the Association of Secondary Schools and Colleges of the Southern States gave its stamp of approval to the college, and the fourth period began, that of physical and academic expansion.

The First Course of Study and Diplomas

The curriculum was designed to comply with Section 5 of the legislative act establishing the institution as a normal and industrial school. The three courses of study were in pedagogy, domestic science, and business, but there was little difference in the requirements. Everyone studied English, science, history, mathematics, a foreign language, drawing, vocal music, physical culture, elocution, and pedagogy. Students in the course designed for prospective teachers were required to take more mathematics. Domestic science students took sewing, cooking, and household economics; and the commercial students studied bookkeeping, shorthand, and typewriting.[1] These three courses formed the basis of the curriculum for the first few years. In 1897 a fourth was added, providing for concentration in the study of foreign languages.

Until 1901 graduates received licenses to teach in North Carolina without further examination. In that year the legislature ruled that those graduating from the Normal College should take the examinations required for other teachers of the state in order to secure certificates.[2]

Because of the scarcity of high schools in North Carolina, entrance requirements could not be raised immediately. The required subjects were still arithmetic, English grammar, geography, United States history, and North Carolina history. Classification examinations were given to all students entering the college to determine advanced standing, as well as to check on entrance requirements. For a time, physiology and hygiene were added to the requirements, but they, with North Carolina history, were soon dropped. Otherwise, entrance requirements remained the same until 1905 when the four-year degree program was established.

During the first ten years, 1892 to 1902, only diplomas were awarded by the college. On the surface the course of study was limited and rigid, but in actuality it provided for a variety of needs. Some girls, graduates of other institutions, were able to earn the diploma in a year or two, as did the earliest graduates. Others, who came with meager preparation, sometimes studied five or six years without receiving the diploma. One such student came to the college with less than five full days of formal education. Although she never received a diploma, she studied diligently for six years and was awarded the Curry medal for the "most deserving student."[3] Every effort was made to meet the needs of the students, but the vision of a college "good enough for anybody" was never forgotten.

Changes in the Curriculum

In the early years, there were few changes in the curriculum. Some time was to pass before the results of Governor Aycock's expan-

1. Information on the curriculum was obtained from the catalogues unless otherwise noted.

2. Julius I. Foust, "The History of the Woman's College" (unpublished history, Chancellor's Office, The University of North Carolina at Greensboro), p. 64.

3. Phoebe Pegram Baughan, "Out of the Past," *Alumnae News*, XXV (April, 1937), 5.

sion of public education would bring many graduates of accredited high schools to the college. Meanwhile, the program had to be suited to the needs and abilities of the applicants. Nevertheless, President McIver and his carefully selected faculty were determined that they would, as quickly as possible, make theirs a real college.

Since the preparation of teachers was the main function of the institution, it was natural that more attention would be paid to the development of the Department of Pedagogy. P. P. Claxton, who joined the department in 1893 and became its head in 1895, was responsible for many advances.

The first important change was the addition of the practice school for teachers in 1893. Dr. McIver often used the expression, "A normal school without a practice school is like a swimming school without water." As soon as it was possible, he established one. Located in Midway Dormitory, it had ten pupils, aged five to eight, none of whom had ever attended school before. Among them were two of McIver's children, Charlie and Annie. Seniors were required to do three hours of work in the school each week and were allowed to observe at any time. Mrs. Fannie Cox Bell was the teacher, and Claxton, the director.

In 1894 McIver ran an advertisement in the Greensboro *Record*:

PRACTICE
AND
OBSERVATION SCHOOL
The capacity of the model pri-
mary school, connected with
The State Normal and Industrial School
having been enlarged, children
will be admitted this year whose
ages are from six to nine years.
There Will Probably Be Three Grades.
This School will begin its
work on
Monday, October 8th.
Tuition Will Be $12.00 a Year.
Application for admission should
be made at once so that the proper
preparations may be made for in-
creased attendance. For further
information apply to
Charles D. McIver, Pres.

Since there were so few pupils in the beginning, Professor Claxton had difficulty dividing them among the seniors. In the third year there were seven classes and ninety-seven pupils. Enrollment increased steadily, and by 1898, when it became part of the Greensboro school system, the school had 200 pupils. Classes were crowded into Midway until the spring of 1902, when Curry School was opened.

To widen the area of service Claxton added a graduate program and correspondence courses in pedagogy in 1897. Of the first 118 graduates (1892-1898), 20 had returned for graduate work by 1899. From 1897 to 1901, 46 non-residents were enrolled in correspondence courses.

Another development in the Department of Pedagogy was the establishment of short courses for teachers. The first such course was held in 1902 and was popularly known as the May school. The teachers who attended were dubbed "May pops" by the regular students and were subjects of derision when, already tired from a year of teaching, they sometimes fainted from exhaustion at the college pace.[4]

After a few years a short course was offered for teachers who wished to come for a year of study. This was similar in outline to the May school, but was more advanced. The May school continued until it was replaced by the regular summer school in 1912. The one-year course was offered until the college was accredited in 1921.

In a few of the other departments significant changes were made. With the advent of the Spanish-American War came an interest in the Spanish language. A three-year course was introduced at the Normal in 1898, but when interest declined after the war, the subject was temporarily dropped in 1905.

Physical culture changed little until 1900, when the gymnasium was converted into a library in anticipation of a new building. The appropriation for the gymnasium, however, was needed more urgently to defray part of the expenses incurred during the typhoid epidemic of 1899, and other measures were adopted for physical exercise. For more than twenty years "walking period" was an institution at the college. Each catalogue carried the statement: "Owing to present lack of adequate provision for a gymnasium, a systematic course of physical culture is not available, but each student is required to spend some time each day, if weather be suitable, in out-door exercise, walking or games."[5] Each afternoon when the bell rang, the girls opened the windows in their rooms, propped open the doors, and went for a forty-five minute walk while their rooms were aired.

Because the college had been established as a normal and industrial

4. Personal interview with Miss Jane Summerell, Aug. 21, 1964.
5. *Ninth Annual Catalogue*, p. 36.

institution, the development of the music department was difficult. The vocal music which was offered in the beginning was justified as a preparation for public school music, but students who wanted instrumental music were forced to seek private lessons. In 1899 the Board of Directors passed a resolution to extend the music department to include instrumental music. Charles J. Brockman and his sister Laura gave lessons in piano and stringed instruments. The charge for lessons was $40 a year, the same as for tuition.

In 1901 a new course of study was established making it possible for students who were concentrating in music to receive diplomas. Similar to the other programs, this included two years' work in harmony, one year in the history of music, and one or more in ensemble playing. Diplomas were given only for voice, violin, or piano majors. The first two graduates in music were Jeanette Trotter of Mt. Airy and Sudie L. Harding of Greenville. Assisted by Mr. Clarence Brown and Mr. Charles J. Brockman, they gave their senior piano recital on April 23, 1903.

In other departments, few course changes were made, but the general quality of scholarship was improved. Recognizing this, the General Assembly voted in 1897 to amend the act establishing the institution, changing its name to State Normal and Industrial College.[6]

The First Degrees

In 1901 the General Assembly authorized the college to grant the usual degrees conferred by other colleges upon the completion of such courses of study as the authorities of the institution prescribed.[7] Because Dr. McIver still did not think the regular program of the college warranted a degree, he set up a degree program which required a year of graduate study and invited seven former students to return: Lewis Dull of Forsyth County (1899), Margaret Perry of Wilkes (1895), Mary C. Wiley of Forsyth (1894), and Frances Winston of Franklin (1901), all of whom earned the Bachelor of Arts degree; and Virginia Brown of Guilford (1902), Lyda Humber of Moore (1897), and Emma Lewis Speight of Edgecombe (1900), who earned the Bachelor of Science degree. The only difference in requirements for the two degrees was that the A.B. included Latin instead of science. A granite marker engraved "Bachelors of 1903" was erected in Peabody Park to commemorate the granting of the first degrees. Only a few degrees were awarded from 1904 to 1908.

6. *Public Laws and Resolutions of the State of North Carolina Passed by the General Assembly at its Session of 1897,* c. 230.
7. Board of Directors, Proceedings, II (June 6, 1901), 191.

In 1904 the University of North Carolina admitted to its senior class students from the Normal who had completed the diploma programs with concentrations in education or foreign languages, making it possible for them to earn the bachelor's degree with one year of additional study.

At this time the General Education Board gave to the college a grant of $2,500 a year for three years to establish a Department of Manual Arts to prepare teachers in this field.

Four-Year Degree Programs

When Dr. McIver and his faculty were convinced that they could offer a four-year program of merit, they changed the degree requirements, and in 1905 three degrees were offered: Bachelor of Pedagogy, Bachelor of Arts, and Bachelor of Science. All new students were enrolled in a degree program except those who sought special work in music, domestic science, and commercial subjects, which were still only one-year courses.[8]

The new program provided greater flexibility than the old courses of study. Even in the freshman year some selection of courses was offered. The three degrees had similar requirements. In addition to the general courses the Bachelor of Arts required only an additional language, Bachelor of Pedagogy required only education courses, and the Bachelor of Science required more mathematics and science courses.

Admission requirements were raised when the four-year degree programs were established. Prospective students had to pass examinations in arithmetic, elementary algebra, United States history, English history or ancient history, English, physics, physical geography, and Latin, German, or French. Those who wished to enter the Bachelor of Arts program were required to present two years of Latin. The subject matter to be included in the high school courses was outlined in the catalogue.[9]

Exempt from the examinations were graduates of the ten-year program of public schools in cities where the course of study was approved by a committee from the college. Cities on the approved list in 1905 were Greensboro, Rocky Mount, Winston, Wilmington, Salisbury, Smithfield, Reidsville, and Durham. Others had entrance conditions

8. The one-year courses in music and domestic science were discontinued when the college became accredited, but the Commercial Certificate was offered even after the college became a university.

9. *Thirteenth Annual Catalogue*, p. 39.

in science: Tarboro, Oxford, Asheville, Goldsboro, Monroe, Shelby, Burlington, Scotland Neck, Wilson, Gastonia, Graham, Kinston, and New Bern.[10]

In 1909 the first students were graduated from the four-year degree program. They were Jean Booth, Oxford; Bessie Cauble, Salisbury; Okla Dees, Grantsboro; Nettie Dixon, Greensboro; Edna Duke, Hamlet; Evelyn H. Gudger, Marshall; Cora Hart, Weldon; Pauline Hassell, Edenton; Katherine Jeffreys, Goldsboro; Flieda Johnson, Greensboro; Florence Pugh Landis, Oxford; Lola Lasley, Burlington; Mary B. Mitchell, Wilmington; Hal Morrison, Statesville; Velna Pope, Jackson; Linda Shuford, Newton; Clara Sloan, Belmont; Jessie Smoak, Wilkesboro; and Claude Umstead, Rougemont.

Bachelor of Music Degree

The degree of Bachelor of Music was first offered in 1907. In addition to a list of courses, requirements stipulated "a certain degree of talent." The first degree was awarded in 1911 to Huldah Slaughter of Goldsboro. When she gave her graduation recital consisting of works by Beethoven, Chopin, and Grieg, she was assisted by two vocalists, Frances Broadfoot of Black Mountain and Agnes Wills of Brinkleyville.

Preparatory Department

Since rural schools were frequently inadequate to prepare girls for the degree program of the college, a preparatory department of two years was established at this time by the college. Students might take any courses they needed. This department was, for many years, larger than any other class. In 1911 there were 91 First "Prep" and 71 Second "Prep" in a student body of 568. In 1913, First "Prep" was abolished, but there were still 148 preparatory students that fall. The number had dropped to 23 in 1916, the last year there was such a classification.

Bachelor of Science in Home Economics

The next degree to be established was the Bachelor of Science in Home Economics, which was offered in 1911. Unlike the other programs, this allowed no electives. Special courses were given in sewing, house architecture and sanitation, cooking, laundry, textiles, food and dietetics, home nursing, and household management. All students

10. Faculty Council Minutes, II (Sept. 16, 1905), 7.

were required to take pedagogy courses. The first to earn this degree was Mazie Dell Kirkpatrick of Haywood County, who graduated in 1915.

Interest in Rural Education

In 1912 agriculture was accepted as an elective for entrance, and elementary agriculture was added to the home economics program. A two-hour course in school gardening was required of students in pedagogy. The reason for this interest was well explained in a discussion of the objectives of rural economics, the name by which these courses came to be known:

> More and more the public is demanding that the school shall be a source of uplift for a community in its economic, social, and religious relations—that it shall assist in educating the whole people. . . . A teacher who appreciates her real mission will do something to improve the health of the community; awaken civic pride; relieve the physical drudgery, and intellectual and social barrenness which is the lot of so many farmers' wives and daughters, and give to the farm community some of the enthusiasms of life. She will hold community meetings, educational rally days; be interested in co-operative societies for buying and selling; take a part in the organization of women's clubs and betterment associations; organize a school and community library; and take an interest in farm sports and athletics.[11]

It is interesting to compare this with a report sent the *Alumnae News* in 1917. Because of her health, Mamie Griffin of Goldsboro had been ordered by her doctor to go to the country where she was to get twelve hours sleep each night. She went to a school four miles from Kinston, where she taught fifteen pupils. She organized box suppers and pie parties to raise money to paint the school inside and out, remodel and refurnish the building, and improve the grounds. She also "had a Betterment Association, Sunday school class, Debating Society, Music Club, *etc.*" She added that she was healthier, happier, and had a larger bank account.

Changes in Admission Requirements

In 1914, 12½ units were stipulated for admission: English 3, history 2, science 1, foreign language 3, algebra 1½, plane geometry 1, and 1 elective (science, history, or foreign language). In 1916 the

11. *Twenty-second Annual Catalogue*, p. 83.

number of units was increased to 14, and the list from which electives could be selected was broadened to include sixteen courses: Latin, French, German, history, chemistry, physics, general science, biology, agriculture, physical geography, botany, civics, physiology, zoology, domestic science, and music. This standard was not changed significantly in the fifty years that followed.[12]

Summer School

The first summer school was really just a special course in Latin which Miss Viola Boddie sometimes taught. It was first offered in 1898 and was repeated, but not with regularity. One student remembered that seniors liked to take the course in the summer so that their last year would not be ruined by the fear of Miss Boddie's failing them.[13] Although the May school was a summer program for teachers, it met during the regular session. Faculty members taught teachers' institutes during the summer without further compensation, but the first regular summer session on the campus was held in 1912.

No money was appropriated for the first summer classes, but members of the faculty gave their services, so strongly did they feel the necessity for offering work to those who were unable to attend the regular sessions. During the first year 416 students were enrolled in the eight-week program. Of these, 100 were pupils in the practice school, which was open to provide an opportunity for practice teaching and observation. Although the emphasis was on pedagogy, courses were offered in household economics, manual arts, agriculture, and music. Special features were a teachers' institute and a homemakers' conference. Visiting lecturers were J. Y. Joyner, state superintendent of public instruction; Miss Jessie Field, superintendent of public instruction in Page County, Iowa; Charles DeGarmo, professor of science and art of education at Cornell; P. P. Claxton, United States commissioner of education; and D. J. Crosby, of the United States Department of Agriculture.

So successful was this first venture that the General Assembly appropriated money for its continuation. During the first years much of the work was elementary, for many of the students were not high school graduates. John H. Cook, director of the Summer Session, estimated that one-half or more of the summer school students in 1919

12. In 1967 the requirement at the university in Greensboro was 15 units: English 4, foreign language 2, mathematics 2½, social science 2, science 1, electives 4½. The list of courses from which electives might be chosen included some which appeared to be easier than those that were accepted in 1916.

13. Personal interview with Miss Emma McKinney, Nov. 17, 1964.

and 1920 had less academic training than that of high school graduates. In 1921 a state certification regulation stipulated that only those with the equivalent of a high school education should be permitted to attend summer school at a college or university. Others were to go to county summer schools.

Despite this change, the enrollment increased. In 1921 there were 741 students, 64 of whom were college graduates, making this the second largest summer school in the state. Two sessions were arranged for 1923, and men were admitted for the first time. They lived in private homes and took their meals at the Alumnae Tea Room. Peak enrollment, at least until after the Depression, came in 1926, when almost 2,000 students were enrolled for the two sessions. At that time it was still possible for high school graduates to earn an Elementary B Teacher's Certificate with two units of summer credit. Such a certificate would not have been adequate for use in the city schools or in the schools of the more progressive counties. In 1928 the enrollment had dropped to 1626, but there were more graduate students than before. Most of the courses carried college credit, and it was possible to earn a Master's degree in four summers.

Summer school followed much the same pattern as the regular session in extracurricular activities. The Student Government Association was active and many of the same rules applied. There were concerts, plays, excursions, stunt nights, and lawn parties.

Through the years many important lecturers were brought to the campus: H. H. Horne of New York University, William Lyon Phelps of Yale, Charles A. Beard of Columbia, Frank P. Graves of the University of the State of New York, W. H. Kilpatrick of Columbia, Frederick L. Paxson of the University of Wisconsin, N. L. Englehart of Columbia, Hazel Gertrude Kinscella of the University of Nebraska, Charles A. McMurray of Peabody, and C. Alphonso Smith of the United States Naval Academy (formerly of the University of North Carolina).

Growth of Extension Work

Since the college had long recognized its duty "to that great body of people who will not enter this or any other school or college," extension work was a logical means by which to discharge this duty. In 1899, P. P. Claxton gave the first impetus to correspondence work, teachers' institutes, and the May school.

The next development in this program was the publication of the *Bulletin*. Some issues contained the catalogues and the biennial re-

Mathematics Faculty

In the back are Gertrude Mendenhall, Virginia Ragsdale, and
Cornelia Strong, for whom residence halls have been named. In
front is Nettie Leele Parker.

Commencement, 1931

(from right to left) Marshal Anne Griffin, Dr. Jackson (partially
visible), Dr. Foust, Deets Pickett, Dr. Gove, the Reverend Albea
Godbold, E. J. Forney, Dr. Wade Brown, Blanche E. Shaffer,
J. P. Givler

The first McIver Building stood for fifty years as a memorial to the first president. It has since been replaced by a modern classroom building, also named for McIver.

College Avenue, About 1914, Looking South

On the left: Hockey Field, Old Curry Building, Carnegie Library
(now Forney Building)
On the right: Spencer Building, Students Building, Guilford Hall,
President's House

ports of the Board of Directors. The others provided information relative to the departments of the college.

The first bulletin, issued in November, 1910, was the "Domestic Science Number" written by Miss Jamison. There followed "Rural School Number," 1911; "Studies in American Authors," 1913; "The Teaching of Mathematics," 1913; "The Teaching of History in North Carolina High Schools," 1914; "The Teaching of Algebra," 1915; "Arbor Day," 1916; "A Primer of Household Biology," 1917; "Methods of Saving Wheat, Meat, Sugar, and Fat," 1917; "The Teaching of Modern Languages in High School," 1918; and "Community Projects and School Credits for Home Projects," 1919.

Faculty members contributed other publications. In the training school Anna Meade Michaux, Mary Owen Graham, and J. A. Matheson collaborated on *Phonic Drills* to help the teacher of reading.[14] E. J. Forney wrote *Inductive Lessons Adapted to Isaac Pittman Phonography*, and W. C. Jackson edited *Ante Bellum Builders of North Carolina* and *Revolutionary Leaders of North Carolina*, both collections of lectures given at the college by R. D. W. Connor. In the English department, A. C. Hall wrote *Topical Outline of American Literature* and collaborated with Leonard B. Hurley on *Topical Outlines of English Literature*. The Department of Economics was represented by Albert Keister's *Our Financial System*, and the Department of Sociology by E. C. Lindeman's periodical *North Carolina Community Progress*. Winfield S. Barney edited several French works and wrote a French grammar. A *Textbook of Biology* and a *Laboratory Guide for General Biology* were written by John P. Givler. Although not complete, this listing shows the range of fields represented in faculty publications.

The first extension lectures were given under the auspices of the Federation of Women's Clubs of North Carolina in Goldsboro, Asheboro, and Morganton by E. W. Gudger, Mary Petty, Minnie Jamison, E. E. Balcomb, and W. C. A. Hammel. Miss Jamison was chairman of extension work until 1921. Most of the lectures offered during this time were for the homemaker, but some literary lectures were offered by the English Department.

In 1921 Charles B. Shaw was appointed director of the Extension Department in addition to his duties as librarian. Among the courses

14. Miss Graham was a sister of Edward Kidder Graham, president of the University of North Carolina. She later became president of Peace Institute at Raleigh and was the first woman to be president of the North Carolina Education Association (1915). Mr. Matheson was president of the organization in 1907 and 1908.

which were taught in Greensboro and Winston-Salem were history of English literature, contemporary American history, introductory psychology, introductory sociology, citizenship, educational tests and measurements, public school music, primary methods, and grammar grade methods. The charge for each course was five dollars.

In 1923 W. H. Livers became director of the Extension Division and business manager of the college. Courses were given in other parts of the state, with the territory divided between the North Carolina College for Women and the University of North Carolina. Since Mr. Livers was able to devote more time to extension work, more services were offered: Bureau of Parent-Teacher Service, Bureau of Pre-school and Parental Training, Bureau of Library Service, Club-Study Service, Bureau of Tests and Surveys, Bureau of Judging, Bureau of Community Service, and the Lecture Bureau, which served the largest number of people (Livers estimated that it reached 10,000 in 1925-1926).[15]

Period of Transition

In 1914 the course of study was revised by the Curriculum Committee. Recitation periods were increased from forty-five minutes to an hour, and more latitude in electives after the freshman year was permitted. New courses included astronomy, comparative anatomy, poultry raising and gardening, and counterpoint.

Although the curriculum was designed for concentration in areas, departmental majors except for music, home economics, science, and education had not developed. In English and in history, for example, the maximum number of hours a student could take was twelve, including basic courses.

Course offerings had increased so that a student who elected a particular subject often had some choice of course within that department. A freshman electing history would have no choice, for there was only one freshman course offered. A senior, however, could choose from five elective history courses: introduction to economics, American history from 1783-1865, American history from 1865-1917, North Carolina history, and American citizenship.

The program at this time illustrates the transition from limited offerings of the early years to the departmental majors which were to follow in a few years.

15. W. H. Livers, ''Report of the Director of Extension,'' in *Report of the Board of Directors for the Years 1924-1926*, p. 59.

Expansion of Curry School

With the establishment of high schools over the state, the demand for high school teachers increased greatly and the college was faced with the responsibility of helping to meet this demand. Until 1913 the practice school had only seven grades, but in that year the eighth grade was added, with Miss Jane Summerell as teacher. (Miss Summerell had been graduated from the Normal in 1910, and after graduate study and teaching at Winthrop, she returned to the college to teach in the English department from 1926 until 1958. In 1963 she received the Alumnae Service Award.)

In 1914 and in 1915 the ninth and tenth grades were added, and there were eighty-five pupils in the three high school grades. The eleventh grade was then added and the first class was graduated in 1917. The high school offered both general and college preparatory courses. When the high school was temporarily dropped in 1917, arrangements were made for prospective high school teachers to observe and to do student teaching in the Greensboro, Pomona, and Bessemer high schools.

To prepare teachers and supervisors for rural school work, the college operated a rural school at Rocky Knoll, about six miles south of Greensboro. Miss Etta Spier was in charge of the school, which was under the supervision of the college for four years.

Course for Home Demonstration Agents

A twelve-week course for home demonstration agents was offered in 1915-1916. Fourteen students were enrolled in the course, which included biology, chemistry, domestic science, domestic art, and other subjects connected with homemaking. This program grew out of the Smith-Lever Bill, which appropriated funds to employ demonstration agents. Although the college received no funds from this source, it sought to supply agents for the state. The first venture was such a success that the course was continued.

Bachelor of Science in Nursing

In 1911 a special course for nurses had been instituted, but not until 1918 was a degree program approved. The earlier course, which included household biology, household chemistry, dietetics, English, hygiene, laundry and textiles, physiology, and physical training, was designed only as a preparation for professional study.

The degree program called for three years of work at the college to be followed by two years in an accredited hospital. Students completing the course were awarded the Bachelor of Science degree.

Revisions of the Degree Programs

From 1916 to 1918 the faculty worked on the courses of instruction, revising them so that they would conform to the standards of other colleges. A group system was established for the freshman and sophomore years, and an elective system for the junior and senior years.

The group system was based on previous preparation and the degree program to be followed. Differences between groups involved requirements in foreign languages and science. During the junior and senior years students took twenty-four to thirty-six semester hours[16] of work in a major subject. Electives were chosen to complete sixty hours.

In 1916 the Faculty Council voted down a proposal to change the Bachelor of Pedagogy degree to Bachelor of Arts in Education. For two years it was called Bachelor of Education. When the program was revised at this time, it was made a Bachelor of Arts.

These changes in curriculum made it easier for graduates to gain admission to the graduate departments of leading colleges and universities, but the name State Normal and Industrial College was considered by many to be a drawback. In 1916 the Alumnae Association had petitioned the Board of Directors to rename the college. They suggested North Carolina State College for Women or preferably McIver College. When the board considered the name change in 1919, four names were submitted: McIver College, which received one vote; North Carolina Woman's College, one; McIver College, the North Carolina College for Women, two votes; North Carolina College for Women, five. On a motion by Edward E. Britton, the name North Carolina College for Women was adopted by unanimous vote.[17] This name was then approved by the General Assembly in 1919.

Department of Economics and Sociology

The first courses in sociology and in economics had been offered by the Department of History in 1913 and 1914. Their popularity was such that a separate department was organized in 1918. Years later

16. Semester hours are used here although the college was still using year hours at this time.

17. Board of Directors, Proceedings, III (Feb. 25, 1919), 142.

the Department of Sociology and Economics was divided into two separate departments.

New Areas and Degrees

Although the college maintained a strong teacher-training department, efforts were made to give preparation in other areas as new fields were opened to women. In addition to the program for nurses, the faculty began planning a course of study for welfare workers. In 1919 the Board of Directors changed the regulation concerning free tuition, which had previously been given to students who agreed to teach in North Carolina, to include students who wished to go into public welfare work.

Also in 1919, the State Board for Vocational Education chose North Carolina College for Women to prepare vocational home economics teachers. Under the Smith-Hughes Act, the college received an annual appropriation for this work. In 1919-1920 the amount was $10,800; in other years it ranged from $4,000 to $10,000.

In 1920 a degree for home demonstration agents was introduced. Called the Bachelor of Science in Home Economics, it was similar to the B.S. in Home Economics offered in the teacher-training program.

The first graduate degree was approved in 1920. Requiring thirty-two semester hours of work, the degree, Master of Arts, could be completed in one full college year or four summer terms. Courses were selected from one major subject and one or two minor subjects. All courses had to be of at least senior rank. The first M.A. was awarded to May Meador of High Point in 1922. Twelve more students earned the degree before 1931. Of these, two were from other states.

The United States Interdepartmental Social Hygiene Board made an appropriation of $10,800 to organize a department of health at the college in 1920. The object of the program was to teach the students, especially the prospective teachers, the fundamental laws of "health and right living." Known as the Department of Health, it was to be staffed by two physicians, an executive secretary, a biology teacher, two nurses, and at least three teachers of physical education.[18] As a result of this, the lectures in hygiene were replaced by an organized course in health, which was required of all freshmen.

Intelligence tests were first administered in 1920.[19] Until that time only achievement tests had been given. James A. Highsmith, who

18. Foust, "Report of the President," in the *Biennial Report of Board of Directors,* Sept. 15, 1920, p. 18.
19. Faculty Council Minutes, III (May 24, 1920), 146.

supervised the testing, was later chairman of the committee to establish a battery of tests for the North Carolina College Conference.

Accreditation by the Southern Association

In December of 1921 the college finally achieved recognition as a standard college. It was approved by the Association of Secondary Schools and Colleges of the Southern States. Meredith and Wake Forest were also admitted in 1921. Only three colleges and universities in North Carolina—Trinity (Duke), the University of North Carolina, and Davidson—had been admitted earlier. This recognition was a source of pride to teachers and students alike. At last the state could be sure that its institution, so reluctantly established for the higher education of women, was "good enough for any of its citizens."[20]

After the admission of the college to the Southern Association there was a reorganization of the faculty. W. C. Jackson was named vice president, a new office. Members of the faculty were classified as professor, associate professor, assistant professor, and instructor. All department heads and chief executive officers were professors. Minimum requirements for full professorships were: (1) Doctor of Philosophy degree or (2) Bachelor's or Master's degree and ten years' acceptable service in the college or (3) Master's degree and demonstrated ability in serving the college in the capacity of department head or director.

The following were elected to the rank of full professor:

Gertrude W. Mendenhall, B.S.
Viola Boddie
Mary M. Petty, B.S.
Anna M. Gove, M.D.
E. J. Forney
William C. Smith, Ph.B., L.H.D.
Walter C. Jackson, B.S.
Wade R. Brown, Mus. D.
John H. Cook, M.A.
Winfield S. Barney, Ph.D.
Carolina Schoch, M.A.
William T. Wright, M.S.
Blanche E. Shaffer, M.A.
John Paul Givler, M.A.
Cornelia Strong, A.B.
Martha Winfield, B.S.

Virginia Ragsdale, Ph.D.
James A. Highsmith, M.A.
A. P. Kephart, Ph.D.
Harriet W. Elliott, M.A.
Alonzo C. Hall, M.A.
Etta R. Spier, M.A.
G. Scott-Hunter
Richard H. Thornton, M.A.
Charles B. Shaw, M.A.
Alice E. Bivins, B.S.
W. R. Taylor, M.A.
Mary C. Coleman, B.S.
John D. Hicks, Ph.D.
Laura H. Coit, Secretary
Mary Taylor Moore, Registrar
Nell Farrar, M.A., Adviser
      of Women

20. *First Annual Catalogue,* p. 16.

Associate professors were:

Mary F. Seymour, M.A.
Leonard B. Hurley, M.A.
Frances V. Womble, M.A.
L. E. Yocum, M.S.
Elizabeth McI. Weatherspoon
Ruth Fitzgerald
Elva Barrow, A.B.
C. A. Williams, M.A.

Bessie Noyes, Ph.D.
Mollie A. Peterson, M.A.
Leo Rogin, B.S.
Mary J. Hogue, Ph.D.
M. K. Hooke, A.B.
Louise Irby, M.A.
W. W. Martin, M.A.
John T. Miller, M.A.
Eva M. Locke, M.D.

Those named assistant professors were:

Magnhilde Gullander, A.B.
Alleine R. Minor
Ellen K. Wright, M.A.
Ailsie M. Stevenson, M.A.

Inez Coldwell, A.B.
Meta Miller, Ph.D.
Benjamin Bates

In addition to the new classification of faculty, there was a new organization of departments:

1. College of Liberal Arts and Science, W. C. Smith, Dean
    a. Languages and Literature, W. S. Barney, Chairman
    b. Social Science Division, W. C. Jackson, Chairman
    c. Division of Mathematics and Pure Science, John P. Givler, Chairman
2. School of Education, John H. Cook, Dean
3. School of Home Economics, Blanche E. Shaffer, Dean
4. Summer Session Division, John H. Cook, Director
5. Extension Division, Charles B. Shaw, Director

The Faculty Council was the general legislative body, composed of professors and associate professors. The Faculty Cabinet was an administrative body which advised with the board and the president and acted in an executive capacity. Serving on the cabinet were the president, vice-president, deans and chairmen of divisions, and two members elected from the council. The first members so chosen were Miss Mendenhall and Dr. Ragsdale.

Many of the students who had graduated from the college before accreditation returned to earn a standard degree after the accreditation. Miss Strong, chairman of the Committee on Advanced Standing, evaluated the students' records to determine just how much further work would be required for the degree. During the first seven years, sixty students returned to take the degree.[21]

At the end of the first three decades, enrollment had passed the 1,200 mark and the faculty numbered almost 120. Most of the grad-

21. *Alumnae News*, XVII (April, 1928), 7.

uates still became teachers; 93 per cent of the graduates from 1919 to 1922 had taught by the fall of 1922. The college was the first in the South to offer a four-year course for music supervisors, and although almost all the graduates of the music department went into teaching, the supply met only half the demand.[22]

Bachelor of Science in Physical Education

The next major development in the curriculum was the approval of the Bachelor of Science degree in Physical Education in 1923. There were so many requirements in science, health, physical education, and education that few electives were permitted.

Master of Science in Home Economics

A Master of Science in Home Economics degree was approved in 1924 but was not immediately implemented. In 1928, when it was first included in the catalogue, the requirements were the same as for the Master of Arts: thirty semester hours of work and a thesis. At least six hours of the work was to be in a minor.

Department of Psychology

The Department of Psychology was established in 1924. For many years general, educational, and child psychology had been taught by one person in the Department of Education. Increased demand for courses for the general student as well as for prospective teachers made it necessary to start a separate department. In 1927 a major in psychology was offered.

Development of Curry High School

For many years majors in secondary education had done student teaching at Pomona, Bessemer, South Buffalo, and Greensboro high schools because there was no high school at Curry. When the new building was erected in 1926, a grant from the General Education Board made possible the re-establishment of a high school. The first two grades were added in 1926, the third and fourth in 1927. Teachers employed for the high school often taught methods courses which had previously been taught in each department.

22. In 1923 the Bachelor of Music degree was changed to Bachelor of Science in Music. This degree could be in piano, organ, violin, voice, or public school music.

Provisions for Differences in Ability

Although the college had achieved accreditation, there was still concern about the quality of the work. In 1926 the faculty heard a report from a committee studying the problem. Dr. Virginia Ragsdale, one of the members, spoke in favor of honors courses to provide for the very able student. Another member, Dr. Albert Keister, considered the first two years of work still of high school level. He asked whether the college should set the pace without regard for the slow student or whether students should be grouped by ability.[23]

One of the first efforts to meet this problem was the grouping of students in freshman English in 1928. During Freshman Week the students were given tests sponsored by the North Carolina College Conference. According to their achievement scores on the English test, the students were placed in four advanced sections, fourteen intermediate groups, and four sections for those of low ability. This last group received less credit and were required to take an extra English course. Later, this was changed to a non-credit course which was followed by the regular freshman course.

Library Science

The first course in library instruction had been offered in 1922. Six years later two courses of study were instituted in library science, one for those who wished to major in library science and one for those who were majoring in another subject but wished to be part-time librarians.

In 1931 the Department of Library Science was fully accredited as a junior undergraduate school by the board of education for librarianship of the American Library Association.[24]

Degrees Conferred

A summary of the degrees conferred during the years before consolidation illustrates the development of the degree programs.[25]

	1926	1927	1928	1929	1930	1931
Bachelor of Arts	199	232	248	268	232	215
Bachelor of Science in Home Economics	33	32	16	15	22	38

23. Faculty Council Minutes, IV (May 17, 1926), 140.

24. The Department of Library Science was abolished with consolidation because of the School of Library Science in Chapel Hill.

25. Mary Taylor Moore, ''Report of the Registrar,'' in the *President's Report to the Board of Directors, 1928-1930*, pp. 23-24. Figures for 1931 were taken from the commencement program.

Bachelor of Science in Music	18	20	15	19	23	17
Bachelor of Science in Physical Education	9	8	8	11	12	11
Bachelor of Science in Nursing		1				
Master of Arts	1		1	3	4	

This was the development of the curriculum as it had grown from 1892 when the students received diplomas for work that was generally considered the equivalent of high school studies. At that time the course of study, which was designed to meet the needs of the young women of North Carolina, was divided into only three areas.

In 1931, when the North Carolina College for Women was changing into the Woman's College of the University of North Carolina, students were majoring in home economics, physical education, music, and thirteen departments in the college of liberal arts. More students received degrees in 1931 than were enrolled in the first year. Such progress was predicted by a newspaper editor in 1894 when he said that it would be "just as easy to stop the flow of the Mississippi River to the ocean as to keep this school from being a success."[26]

26. *Patron and Gleaner* (Lasker, N.C.), May 31, 1894.

∾ six ∾

Student Life

When the college was established, the campus lay outside the city limits. The only means of transportation was the Tallyho, the four-seated carriage of "unlimited capacity," in which the students could ride to town on Friday or Saturday afternoons. Drawn by two large black bays, the Tallyho made trips every thirty minutes to the heart of the city at a charge of ten cents for each passenger,[1] but even so, Greensboro, with its unpaved streets, offered little attraction, particularly for the many students who lived on limited budgets. The first motion pictures came to town in 1907,[2] but for years the Normal girls were not allowed to attend. It was an event of some interest when a local furniture store, Huntley-Stockton-Hill, gave a demonstration of the Edison phonograph, and the students contributed ten cents each to buy one for the students' sitting room.[3]

Although there were visiting lecturers and performers, the students lived a somewhat cloistered existence and were forced to rely on themselves for entertainment. Their diversions took many forms. There were parties and trips, banquets and entertainments. Almost any important day served as an excuse for a celebration of some kind, Halloween, North Carolina Day, Valentine's Day, Arbor Day, May Day. Students entertained faculty, faculty entertained students, and almost everyone entertained the seniors. Many of these observances developed into traditions which lasted for years, but with the coming of motion pictures, television, and frequent week ends off campus, some have been abandoned. However, no picture of college life would be complete without a description of them. These activities have been divided into two groups: one, customs and traditions, and the other, student organizations.

1. *State Normal Magazine*, III (Dec., 1898), 361.
2. Ethel Stephens Arnett, *Greensboro, North Carolina* (Chapel Hill: The University of North Carolina Press, 1955), p. 301.
3. *Alumnae News*, VI (April, 1917), 5.

Customs and Traditions

COMMENCEMENT. Although the faculty is primarily responsible for commencement, it is one of the most important events of the year, and many interesting student customs have grown up around it. One of the most outstanding commencements of all was that in 1894. The whole city joined in the celebration by decorating in the school colors, yellow and white. The depot, residences, stores, street cars, hacks, and drivers were bedecked in ribbon and bunting, and the daisy was the popular boutonniere. Although the town did take pride in the college, the main reason for the decorations was a visit by William Jennings Bryan and John B. Gordon, Confederate general who had led the last charge at Appomattox.

Bryan's address at the Normal on Wednesday morning drew a record audience. Speaking for almost two hours without notes, Bryan discussed money, an unusual topic for a commencement address. The auditorium had been decorated with the great seal of North Carolina over the center of the platform. On one side was the seal of Nebraska in honor of Bryan, and on the other the seal of Georgia, in honor of Gordon.[4]

On Wednesday afternoon the students presented a physical culture exhibition for the ladies, which lasted two hours. The hall was so crowded that some stood on chairs, looking through the transom. The evening program was Class Night. After an address by Class President Susan Ellen Israel, three class essays were read by Mary C. Wiley,[5] Mary Lewis Harris, and Mary Katherine Applewhite. Virginia Taylor read the Class History; Annie Lee Rose, the Class Poem; and Gertrude M. Bagby, the Class Prophecy. Rachel C. Brown was the eighth member of the graduating class. Sixteen students received certificates in teaching, and six received certificates in the commercial department.

On Thursday the commencement sermon was delivered by the Rt. Rev. Edward Rondthaler, Moravian bishop, before the diplomas,

4. Greensboro *Record*, May 24, 1894.

5. Miss Wiley, the daughter of Calvin Wiley, taught in Winston-Salem for almost fifty years. She was awarded an honorary degree of Doctor of Education from the Woman's College of the University of North Carolina in 1946. These class essays continued to play an important part in the commencement program until 1912. All of the seniors wrote essays, and a committee selected ten to be read before the faculty, who picked the ones to be presented. When Ceasar Cone heard Pearl Wyche deliver her essay in 1903, he hired her as head of the Cone Welfare Department, a position she held for forty-eight years. *The Textorian* (Greensboro, N.C.), June 22, 1951.

Bibles, and copies of the constitutions of the United States and of North Carolina were presented.

On Thursday evening General Gordon spoke on ''The Last Days of the Confederacy'' for an hour and a half. One hundred veterans sat on the stage with Gordon, and the auditorium was overflowing with guests. One thousand were said to have been turned away. In his moving address, he made a plea for ''continued fraternal relations between the different sections of the country—for one flag, one country.''[6]

In 1895 the Honorable Carroll D. Wright, first United States commissioner of labor, and Dr. Nicholas Murray Butler, president of the National Education Association and later president of Columbia University, gave the principal addresses. The remainder of the exercises were the same as they had been in 1894 except that an alumnae meeting was added. In 1896 copies of the constitutions were presented by Colonel R. M. Douglas, son of Stephen A. Douglas, who repeated his father's dying words, ''Tell them to obey the laws of the United States.''[7]

In 1897 the commencement began on Saturday night with an alumnae meeting and reception by the faculty. On Sunday there was the commencement sermon, on Monday an address by the Honorable J. L. M. Curry, on Tuesday morning another speech, and on Tuesday night the class essays. Wednesday morning memorial exercises were held for Major Sidney M. Finger, who, from the beginning, had been a staunch supporter of the Normal. A member of the committee appointed in 1886 by the North Carolina Teachers' Assembly to petition the legislature to establish a normal school, he later served as president of the first Board of Directors responsible for the establishment of the Normal. The major address was by a North Carolinian, Walter Hines Page, editor of the *Atlantic Monthly* and later ambassador to Great Britain. On Wednesday night the societies presented a play by William Dean Howells. A portrait of McIver by William G. Randall was unveiled at this commencement.

The citizenry may have been surprised three years before at Bryan's choice of topic, money, but they were shocked by Page's speech, ''The Forgotten Man.'' The graduates, dressed in their frilly white frocks, who sat waiting for the usual words of praise and inspiration, were stunned by the picture he drew of poverty and illiteracy in North Carolina. The speech, which was later published,

6. Greensboro *Record,* May 25, 1894.
7. *The Messenger* (Wilmington, N.C.), May 22, 1896.

stirred up comment over the state. The editor of one newspaper said, "His long speech put into plain English was this: 'You complain of being made poor by the gold standard! but I will condescend to tell that you are poor only because you are too lazy to work and too stingy to educate your children.' "[8] Another was more sympathetic in his reaction: "Yes, 'Mr. Page's address is about the only one delivered in North Carolina this year that has outlived the moment of its delivery.' And why? 'Because he said something.' He told us the Truth about ourselves, and it hurt. Yes, Lord, it hurt.' "[9]

Commencement changed little in the years that followed. Class Day was moved to Peabody Park and then to the front lawn. The daisy chain became one of the most important traditions of the event.

In 1914 there was an eccentric speaker, the Reverend William Wilkinson of Trinity Parish, New York City. Before the program started, he was passing out religious literature in the audience, and it took President Foust several moments to get him on the stage. Foust had prevailed upon him not to preach in the streets of Greensboro before the service, but he had attracted attention by passing out red neckties,[10] a practice that he had followed in other cities.

The first woman commencement speaker was Mrs. Walter McNab Miller, first vice-president of the National American Woman Suffrage Movement and chairman of the National Thrift Committee, who spoke in 1917. The next was Anna Howard Shaw, who spoke in 1919, the first year that the students were permitted to wear caps and gowns.

The commencement of 1927 was another grand occasion because of the dedication of the new auditorium and the reunion of all classes. On Saturday there were the dedication program, a buffet luncheon, a general assembly of alumnae, class reunions, and in the evening a play. On Sunday the usual sermon was followed in the afternoon by a performance of *Elijah*, and in the evening by vesper services. On Monday morning the seniors presented the Senior Unmusical and the societies gave teas. Class Day and Park Night were both in the afternoon, and graduation was Monday night.

CHAPEL. In the early years chapel attendance was required of both students and faculty. The daily programs were generally religious in nature. When Dr. McIver presided he read a bit of Scripture, made announcements, and commented, if necessary, on any problems of

8. *Webster's Weekly* (Reidsville, N.C.), July 17, 1897.
9. Charlotte *Observer*, June 24, 1897.
10. *Ibid.*, May 25, 1914.

college life. On some days other faculty members would present a devotional program, or a guest speaker would appear. Almost every day in the spring the students got out the blue books to sing "Come and Search for Violets."[11]

Chapel changed little through the years. Sometimes it was held after breakfast, and sometimes just before lunch. A special music program was given on Fridays, and before concerts or recitals members of the music faculty gave "appreciation programs."

In 1922 there were so many students that they were divided into two groups. One group attended on Monday and Wednesday, the other on Tuesday and Thursday. Attendance was optional on Friday.

Dissatisfaction with chapel grew through the years, until complaints reached a peak in 1923-1924. The "Community Opinion" column in the *Carolinian* carried objections to compulsory attendance, to the time of the exercises, and to the lack of student participation. In February it was decided that the students were to have full charge of chapel on Monday and Tuesday. These programs were so well received that when a plan to abolish chapel was considered, the students objected.[12]

In 1926 voluntary attendance was tried, but when it proved unsatisfactory, required attendance was reinstated.[13]

LECTURES AND ENTERTAINMENT. One important phase of student life has always been the lectures, concerts, and plays which have come to the campus or the community. From the earliest years, an effort was made to secure speakers who could broaden the outlook of the students and performers who could provide entertainment while serving as a model to aspiring young actresses, dancers, and musicians. The names of many of those who came have long since been forgotten, but there were others whose names have been established for all time.

By later standards, the early years seem somewhat barren, but newspaper accounts indicate that the students enjoyed the programs. In 1893-1894 a minister from Hickory delivered a lecture on Marshal Ney, a traveling actor gave readings from Shakespeare, Dr. Kemp P. Battle (University of North Carolina history professor and former president) spoke on Sherman's entry into Raleigh, and Dr. D. C. Potter gave a lecture on Rome "with the finest stereopticon illustrations." This was so popular that on the next night he had a program

11. For years the walks around the campus were bordered with violets.
12. Personal interview, Miss Elizabeth Hathaway, Nov. 17, 1964.
13. After Aycock Auditorium became too small to accommodate all the students, seniors were not required to attend.

on the World's Fair exhibits at Chicago. One of the big events of the year was an excursion to Pilot Mountain, Mount Airy, and the granite quarry. Seven hundred Normal students and citizens of Greensboro joined Dr. Holmes of the University and his geology class.[14]

The next year music was added to the entertainment. The students heard the Schubert Symphony, the Lady Quartette Club, Miss Kellogg's recitations, and Master Tommy Purcello, a five-year old prodigy who presented humorous recitations and songs. One well-publicized event was the appearance of George R. Wendling, nationally known lawyer and lecturer, who lectured on Stonewall Jackson and on Saul of Tarsus.

In 1895 the Greensboro Female College and the Greensboro Young Men's Christian Association joined with the State Normal in sponsoring a Combination Entertainment Course. Eight entertainments were offered for one dollar general admission, two dollars for reserved seats. The program consisted of lectures and recitals.[15] More important than any entertainment in the course was the visit of the Liberty Bell to Greensboro. Businesses were closed, floral offerings were laid on the flat car, and special exercises were held at Guilford Battleground.[16]

The following year the Combination Course was not repeated because the Ladies' Aid Society of the West Market Street Methodist Church planned a course of entertainment to be given at the Academy of Music.[17] Two women were among the speakers at the Normal that year, Miss Helen Morris Lewis, president of the North Carolina Equal Rights Association, and Miss Dora Duty Jones, former lady principal of Greensboro Female College, whose father had been president of that institution.[18]

In 1897 the Entertainment Course was offered again at the Normal. A two-dollar season ticket "entitled the bearer to attend five lectures and three concerts." This pattern was followed more or less faithfully through the years. In 1913 the fee was still two dollars. The girls from Greensboro College had a block of seats. In 1926 the Civic Music Association was formed by the college and the city of Greensboro. All students were automatically members of the associa-

14. Information on the lectures during the second year was found in clippings in the Woman's College Scrapbooks, II (collected by Dr. Spainhour).

15. Greensboro *Record*, Oct. 9, 1895.

16. *Ibid.*, Jan. 31, 1896.

17. *Ibid.*, Sept. 26, 1896.

18. *Ibid.*, March 22, 1897.

Music Education Students, 1926-1927

In the background is Myra Alderman Albright, who
taught at the college for almost thirty years.

*Laura Coit, secretary of the college
and administrative assistant, came to
Normal in 1894 as a student. For
almost fifty years she was a beloved
member of the college community.*

*Harriet Elliott, teacher of political
science and dean of women, inspired her students to "responsible
freedom."*

The Y.W.C.A. Hut, built by the Carpenterettes in 1918, stood at the northern end of College Avenue. For thirty years it was a recreation center for students and faculty.

Junior Basketball Team, 1913

Effie Baynes, Eleanor Morgan, Margaret Smith, Mary Green, Louise Bell, Winifred Turlington, Willie Mae Stratford, Fannie Robertson, Nina Garner

tion, and one dollar of the student fee was set aside for lectures. In 1927 the fee for both concerts and lectures had gone up to five dollars.

Some of the better-known speakers who appeared through the years were Susan Blow of the Hearst Kindergarten Training School; Vice-President James S. Sherman; Alfred Tennyson Dickens, whose subject was "My Father and His Works"; John Spargo, socialist and author; Maud Ballington Booth, daughter-in-law of General William Booth, whose theme was prison reform; Dr. Harvey Wiley, the scientist who was instrumental in securing passage of the Food and Drugs Act by Congress; Ida Tarbell, who spoke during the war on the need for efficiency; Billy Sunday, who discussed education; William Lyon Phelps, whose lecture was the climax to Better Speech Week; Count Ilya Tolstoy, the son of the Russian novelist; Jane Addams, who spoke at West Market Street Methodist Church[19] on "America's Contribution to International Problems"; Judge Florence E. Allen,[20] the first woman in the United States to be a state supreme court judge; Dr. Henry Seidel Canby, editor of the *Saturday Review*; Nellie Tayloe Ross, first woman governor of a state (Wyoming); Clarence Darrow, who spoke on crime prevention; Anna Louise Strong, American author, who had lived in Russia as a newspaper correspondent; Maude Royden, English social worker and evangelist; Dr. William E. Dodd, native of North Carolina who became professor of history at the University of Chicago and ambassador to Germany; Vilhjalmur Stefansson, the Arctic explorer; Dr. George Washington Carver, who filled the auditorium even during examination week; Dr. Alexander Goldenweiser, anthropologist and sociologist; Lorado Taft, noted American sculptor; and Bertrand Russell, the English mathematician and philosopher.

Some of the authors who read or talked about their works were Hugh Walpole, Carl Sandburg, John Cowper Powys, Richard Halliburton, Louis Bromfield, Edna St. Vincent Millay, Will Durant, Frank R. Kent, Robert Frost, Sherwood Anderson, James Boyd, Cornelia Otis Skinner, Du Bose Heyward, Hamlin Garland, Vachel Lindsay, Carl Van Doren, and Lew Sarett.

Among the well-known musicians were Marcella Sembrich, Galli-Curci, Ethel Leginska, Geraldine Farrar, Florence Macbeth, Efrem

19. For several years before Aycock Auditorium was built, the most popular attractions did not come to the college auditorium, which was not adequate to seat even the students.

20. In 1939 Judge Allen received the first honorary degree awarded by the college.

Zimbalist, Frieda Hempel, John McCormack,[21] Josef Hofmann, Fritz Kreisler, Jascha Heifetz, Bronislaw Hubermann, Vladimir de Pachmann,[22] Paul Whiteman, John Charles Thomas, Percy Grainger, Gladys Swarthout, Alexander Brailowsky, Ernestine Schumann-Heink, and Helen Traubel.

Only a few musical groups appeared: the Boston Women's Symphony, the Pennsylvania Opera Company, the Russian Symphonic Choir, the Little Symphony Orchestra of Chicago, and the Minneapolis Symphony. One of the biggest musical events was Opera Week in 1929. During that time the San Carlo Grand Opera Company presented *Aida, Tales of Hoffman, Tosca, Faust, Cavalleria Rusticana, Pagliacci, Madame Butterfly, Rigoletto, Hansel and Gretel,* and *Carmen.*

Two famous dance groups came to the college, the Duncan Dancers, who had been organized by Isadora Duncan, and the Denishawn Players, with Ruth St. Denis and Ted Shawn. The most famous dancer was Anna Pavlova, who appeared with the Ballet-Russe Symphony Orchestra at the National Theater in 1922.

Many of the students were privileged to see another of the theater's greatest talents when Sarah Bernhardt played at the Municipal Theater in 1917. At the college they saw Charles Coburn and the Coburn Players in *The Yellow Jacket* and the *Imaginary Sick Man.* When the Shakespeare Playhouse Company of New York presented *Beyond the Horizon,* the audience was so noisy that a meeting of the Student Government Association was held the next day to discuss the conduct.[23] Madame Borgny Hammer's Norwegian Company presented *The Master Builder* and *Ghosts,* and the Theatre Guild gave *The Silver Cord,* starring Florence Eldridge and George Gaul (Frederic March was in the supporting cast).

INTER-CAMPUS ENTERTAINMENT. Although the rules were strict, there were opportunities for the Normal girls to meet students from the University of North Carolina. One of the first occasions was a reception in 1893. Students from Chapel Hill were invited to "a splendid sociable in the school building on Thanksgiving night. Flowers [were] engaged for the occasion and the grounds [were] brilliantly lighted by electricity."[24]

When the glee club made its annual visit to the campus, a reception

21. McCormack appeared at the National Theater.
22. De Pachmann played at the Grand Theater.
23. *Carolinian,* Nov. 26, 1921.
24. *News and Observer* (Raleigh, N.C.), October 20, 1893.

was always held. Susan Israel Wolfe, writing in the *Alumnae News* in 1926, recalled the decorations of 1894. The students brought their own furnishings to grace the reception room and, to carry out the blue and white scheme, they used a pair of blue and a pair of white stockings on the table legs.

In 1903 the glee club was joined by the orchestra, the Quartette, the Guitar Club, and the Mandolin Club. The reporter for the *Magazine* liked the orchestra and the Quartette but added that the glee club sang too loudly to be artistic. ''The boys closed with a genuine 'Yackety Yack,' and the crowd went mad. Some had heard *of* a college yell but few before had been so fortunate as to hear one.''[25]

Ten years later the University Dramatic Club presented *What Happened to Jones* under the auspices of the freshman class.[26]

The boys from the Agricultural and Mechanical College in Raleigh made an appearance in 1906 when the glee club and orchestra conducted their first annual concert tour.[27] By 1923 the choirs from Davidson and Trinity had also performed at the college.[28]

TREE DAY. Because the front campus had so few trees, the Class of 1895 instituted the custom of planting a tree on Arbor Day. To make it a festive occasion, they arranged a special program, and all the members dressed in white and gold. The Class of 1896 chose suits of white crash with jackets trimmed in buttons and brown braid. They later erected a marble slab for their tree, which had died. The next class met twelve times before deciding on their costumes.[29]

The tradition was established to plant the class tree in the freshman year and in the following years to hold a celebration to commemorate the occasion. In the senior year the class records were burned and buried around the tree.[30]

The Class of 1905 decided they would be different. Dressed in Grecian robes and singing ''Planting Tonight,'' they planted ivy around the stone wall in front of the Administration Building. Since only one piece of ivy survived, the class held memorial services on the first anniversary. They wore black arm bands, sang ''Weeping Tonight,'' gave sad addresses, and laid flowers at the foot of the wall.

25. *State Normal Magazine*, VII (April, 1903), 236.
26. *Ibid.*, XVII (April, 1913), 407.
27. *Telegram* (Greensboro, N.C.), Feb. 11, 1906.
28. *Carolinian*, Feb. 24, 1923.
29. *Decennial*, p. 38.
30. *Ibid.*, p. 49.

Other classes chose to plant the more traditional tree until 1910, when the Class of 1913 "adopted" a tree instead of planting one because there seemed to be no appropriate place. The practice of either planting or adopting a tree was continued for many years, and some of the stateliest trees on the campus bear the markers of the classes.[31]

CLASS COLORS. The Class of 1898, the first to choose class colors, picked green and white. The three classes that followed chose red and white, lavendar and white, and blue and white. These became the official colors, and they have rotated through the years. The first classes wore hats in their class colors, but later groups substituted coat sweaters. In 1927 the sophomores chose blue flannel blazers with white piping around the cuffs and down the front. On the pocket was "N.C.C.— '29." Wearing their new jackets, they made the usual parade through the dining hall, joined by Miss Jamison, whose class (1893) was considered a blue and white class. This practice has been continued, although the lavendar and white classes have often made such substitutions as black, charcoal, or beige.[32]

Class colors were used in naming the traditional sister class entertainments. Juniors welcomed the freshmen with a Green and White–Lavendar and White Service or with a Blue and White–Red and White Wedding. At one time both groups had a Sister Song, but it was the Blue and White–Red and White song which became traditional.

> May God build for you a harmony
> That will be both great and strong,
> Making all your life a melody
> And every day a song.
> It is here in our hearts, O Sisters dear,
> And we sing it now to you,
> We love you, yes, we love you,
> We love college and that means you.

31. Although the practice of tree planting is no longer followed, the Class of 1960 planted crabapple trees along College Avenue to replace the Japanese cherry trees that were dying. The cherry trees were planted in 1940. Before that time the street was lined with cedars.

32. When the Class of 1934 ordered their jackets, they knew that the name of the college was to be changed, and, therefore, they had the new name put on their emblems. When the jackets arrived, the administration was very displeased, but by the next year, the new name was adopted. Personal interview, Margaret Winder (Mrs. A. B. Dusenbury), Nov. 17, 1964.

SENIOR CLASS ENTERTAINMENT. The seniors have always constituted an important group, but in the early years so few girls were graduated that the senior class was very honored, and many entertainments were given for them. There were receptions, dinners, drives around town, picnics at Guilford Battleground, and trips to Raleigh given by the faculty, as individuals and as a group. The twenty-six seniors in 1898 went to Washington with Dr. McIver and Dr. Gove. While there they were entertained by Mrs. Marion Butler and Mrs. Zebulon B. Vance, wives of the North Carolina senators. They met President McKinley at a private reception given at the White House by Mrs. McKinley.[33]

The most traditional entertainment has been that given by the juniors. In 1899 they gave a supper, in 1900 a hayride, and in 1904 a theater party. In time, however, a banquet became the customary event. In 1915 Dr. Foust gave permission to invite boys for the first time, and the juniors promised to have one for every girl. The really big affair came in 1930 when a dance was permitted. Two dining halls were used; South, decorated with palms, Spanish moss, and magnolia blossoms, was the dancing room, and West was the lounge. It was also decorated with palms and had a fountain in the center with colored lights.[34]

THE TYPHOID EPIDEMIC. During the summer of 1899 there had been a marked increase in the extent and seriousness of contagious diseases in the state. Health authorities had warned of malaria epidemics in several counties including Guilford, but when school opened in the fall, there seemed to be no serious health problems. The first girls who contracted malaria recovered within a few days. Rapidly, however, the number of cases grew, and some of them did not respond to treatment. On November 15, Linda Toms, of Shelby, died of malaria and heart complications, and four other girls were seriously ill. Three days later Dr. Gove diagnosed the illnesses as typhoid fever. Immediately the students were summoned by the large bell behind the Main Building and were told that typhoid had been discovered and that school would be closed until the epidemic was over. That night Abbie S. Deans, of Wilson, died, and on the following day Mr. and Mrs. John Caldwell, of Davidson, sat by the side of their only child Daisy, as she passed away.[35]

Most of the students went home, but forty-eight were too ill to

33. *Decennial*, p. 49.
34. *Carolinian*, May 1, 1930.
35. Greensboro *Record*, Nov. 21, 1899.

travel. These were gathered into one dormitory where they were attended by Dr. Gove, Dr. W. P. Beall,[36] faculty members, and Greensboro ladies. Nurses were recruited from as far away as Richmond, Virginia. Some of the girls had their own physicians, and frequently relatives came to nurse the sick.[37] The next death was that of Susie Ivie, who died at home in Leaksville on November 25. On Thanksgiving Day the grief-stricken families of Sarah Bailey, of Mocksville, and Flora McGoogan, of Lumber Bridge, took their daughters home for burial.

The first days of December brought four deaths, Katie Hailey, of Fairly in Scotland County; Pattie Babbitt, of New Bern; Sadie Colson, who died at home in Norwood; and Ada Ader of Reedy Fork in Davidson County. By December 16 only ten patients were left at the college. One of these was Evelyn Bailey, who died three weeks after the death of her only sister. Another was Ina Davis, of Grissom in Granville County. She recovered from typhoid, but when gangrene set in, her leg had to be amputated above the knee. Because of her weakened condition, she never recovered from the shock. Her death was followed by that of Mary Lou Cromartie, of Clarkton, who died at home on January 6. The last patient, Frances Wright, of Macon County, left Greensboro on January 4.

Another victim of the epidemic was Miss Fannie W. Turner. A former student of the college, Miss Turner became assistant matron in 1896 and matron in 1898 when Mrs. Carraway's health failed. She helped nurse the students until she, too, became ill and died. Dr. McIver, in whose house she had lived as a student, paid tribute to her honesty, industry, and sense of humor. He credited her with handling the self-help program in such a way that the students were not ashamed. He wrote in the *State Normal Magazine* of December, 1899, "She was grateful to the college for the opportunity it gave her and others, and she by her faithful work for the college and its students had discharged any obligation of that kind long before she gave her life in its service. The Institution would do well to keep her character and example before future students." Later in 1921 the Alumnae Association recommended that the new dining halls be named for Miss

36. Dr. Beall, a prominent Greensboro physician, served the college as resident physician during several of Dr. Gove's leaves of absence. At another time her place was taken by one of her classmates, Dr. Edith Blackwell, who was a niece of Dr. Elizabeth Blackwell, pioneer woman physician and founder of the New York Infirmary where Dr. Gove studied.

37. *The Morning Post* (Raleigh, N.C.), Nov. 23, 1899.

Turner and Mrs. Carraway. Unfortunately, the recommendation was not followed.

Although the epidemic attracted much attention, there were only a few outspoken critics of the college. A Stoneville physician, Dr. G. M. Ivie, whose sister had died, wrote a letter to the Raleigh *News and Observer* in which he criticized the college.[38] The *Biblical Recorder* carried an indictment: "The epidemic was not necessary. Some one has blundered badly."[39] Most people waited for the report of the medical examiners. When the information was published, the college authorities were cleared. The trouble had come from a defective sewer which had contaminated the main well. When school reopened on January 30, almost three-fourths of the students returned.[40] Some stayed away because of illness; others, because they had gone to another school during the epidemic.[41] It was obvious from the number who returned that the students had not lost faith in the college authorities.

SPECIAL HOLIDAYS. In addition to the usual holidays, students at the college observed County Fair Day and George Washington's birthday. Attending the fair was an exciting event, and when the holiday was abolished in 1920, the editor of the *Carolinian* expressed the students' regret at missing the rides, the exhibits, and especially Esmeralda the Spider Girl and the wild man from Borneo.

George Washington's birthday continued to be a holiday a few years longer. The main event of that day was the reception which the seniors gave for the faculty. Since the theme was usually colonial, the students dressed in appropriate costumes. In 1923 the seniors deviated from the custom and served a Southern breakfast.

U.N.C.–VIRGINIA GAMES. For many years Carolina's major rival in athletics was the University of Virginia, and since the baseball game was often played in Greensboro, it became a grand occasion for everyone in town. In 1908 the seniors rode to the game at Cone Park[42] in a trolley car decorated in blue and white, and many of the citizens of

38. Dec. 17, 1899.
39. Dec. 20, 1899.
40. Greensboro *Record*, Feb. 1, 1900.
41. One such student was Katherine Smith, of Mount Airy, who went to Salem. Although she never returned to the Normal, the Katherine Smith Reynolds Scholarships were established there in her memory by the Zachary Smith Reynolds Foundation. In 1963 a six-story dormitory on the south edge of Peabody Park was named for her.
42. Now the site of the Oaks Motel on Summit Avenue.

Greensboro draped their carriages and automobiles in the Carolina colors.

In 1913 the *Carolinian* listed the following items in a Calendar of Events:

February 8...... U. N. C. Glee Club entertained
February 10..... Loads of mail from Chapel Hill
April 12......... Virginia-Carolina game. Rah! rah! Carolina.
April 14......... Bad lessons today—couldn't study
                  Saturday night. Refer to the 12th
                  instant of this calendar for further
                  information.

A College Week End was scheduled in 1917, which included a reception at the Country Club for the students, a concert by the College Chorus and Glee Club from Chapel Hill, and the Virginia-Carolina game. The games were not always part of such a big week end, but they continued to be important for many years. Elizabeth Hathaway, who was graduated in 1925, remembered riding the open street cars to the game, cheering all the way.[43]

Football gained in popularity and in 1919 the students received a telegram: "The real men of U.N.C. want the real girls of N.C.C. to be their real guests at that real game on Thanksgiving Day."[44] The seniors, who were given permission to attend, went on a special train and carried a laundry basket of lunch. Some days later the newspaper received a letter:

Won't you please tell me which of you girls who came to the game will fit the following description: She wore a coat suit, a large fur piece, a hat with a plume on it, had brown eyes, was pretty, and sat in front of me on the grandstand. I will never see another moment's peace without her, because I fell desperately in love with her. Please identify the girl and wire me at once.[45]

Unfortunately the paper failed to report the outcome of this query.

Later, the underclassmen were allowed to attend the game, and another popular custom was established.[46]

FOUNDER'S DAY. Until 1909, North Carolina Day was celebrated at the college by a program which included papers written and read by the students, recitations, addresses, and music. In that year, North

43. Personal interview, Nov. 17, 1964.
44. *Carolinian*, Nov. 22, 1919.
45. *Ibid.*, Dec. 6, 1919.
46. In recent years the students have attended the annual Carolina-N.C. State game, which is usually followed by a dance.

Carolina Day, October 12, was dedicated to the memory of Dr. McIver. Alumnae met in groups over the state, and students at the college placed wreaths on his grave in Green Hill Cemetery. In 1910 the same date was observed in his honor, and wreaths were presented by the societies, the classes, the faculty, and the YWCA. In 1911 Founder's Day was changed to October 5 and was a holiday for years. Since that time the annual observance has included an address and the placing of wreaths on McIver's grave and at his statue on the campus.

MAY DAY. The first May Festival was a musical program in 1904 featuring the Boston Festival Orchestra and vocal soloists from Boston, New York, and Chicago. They were joined by a chorus of seventy Greensboro people and the college Glee Club. This was such an important event that the railroad offered special rates.

The most outstanding May Day celebrations were in 1912 and 1916. All of the students in the college and in the training school participated. In 1912 the day began with a parade down College Avenue and the crowning of the May Queen at Curry School. Three plays were presented at different spots on the campus and were repeated twice so that the 3,000 spectators could see five hours of continuous entertainment by going from one play to the other. The theme for both programs was that of an old English May Day.

Less ambitious May Days were presented in the intervening years. In 1915 the program began at 6:45 A.M., with singing from the high balcony of the Administration Building, followed by traditional dances.

The war interrupted May Day programs and they were not resumed until 1926. That year Nellie Irvin was crowned May Queen on the South Spencer lawn, with dances by the classes and songs by the Phoenix Club, an organization of public school music majors. Never was there to be another program, however, to equal the Old English Fetes of 1912 and 1916.

THE COLLEGE SONG. In 1908 the Alumnae Association offered a prize of ten dollars in gold to the person who would write a song which would represent the spirit of the college. There was no response to this announcement, but in 1910 Laura Weill of Wilmington wrote the college song, which was first sung at her graduation.

> We raise our voices; let them swell
>   In a chorus loud and strong;
> The rolling hills send back the sound
>   Of our triumphant song.

For in one great unbroken band
 With loyal hearts and true,
Your daughters stand, and hand in hand
 Sing, college dear, to you.

Our college days run swiftly by
 And all too soon we part;
But in the years that are to come
 Deep-graven on each heart
Our motto, ''Service,'' will remain,
 And service we will do,
And as we serve, our hearts will turn
 O college dear, to you.

Dear Alma Mater, strong and great,
 We never shall forget
The gratitude we owe to you—
 A never-ending debt;
All honor to your name we give,
 And love we pledge anew,
Unfailing loyalty we bring,
 O college dear, to you.

COLLEGE NIGHT. After 1913 the first party of the year was College Night. It began with a program which introduced the new students to college life through a series of skits illustrating the organizations and customs. Frequently there was a theme, such as ''College As It Ain't'' in 1916 or the visit of Sir Overseas and Marquis d'Altitude in 1927. After the program, there was a reception in the society halls with refreshments and songs.[47]

COLLEGE PARTY. About 1916 the students originated an annual party to celebrate the end of midterm examinations. It was usually a costume affair, and students took the opportunity to poke good-natured fun at the faculty. In 1927, it was called the Senior Un-musical Recital, and the lecture-entertainment programs as well as the faculty were satirized. Eventually this custom was changed to an annual chapel program, but the habit of faculty satire was firmly entrenched.[48]

47. College night was also called Festival Night and Stunt Night.
48. In recent years the Senior Unmusical has become the Junior Show, a much more elaborate performance in the style of a musical comedy. The faculty and campus life still serve as the source of humor.

THE SUFFRAGE MOVEMENT. One of the first recorded references to woman's suffrage at the college was an editorial on reading newspapers, which appeared in the *State Normal Magazine* in 1914: "At least, we had better get accustomed to doing this sort of thing, because we will *have* to do it some day, you know—that is, when we vote." In February, 1915, approximately 250 students held a suffrage parade during walking period. Led by a band composed of members of the orchestra with drum and cornets and of amateurs with combs and tissue paper, they marched to the main entrance of Spencer Building where they heard speeches by student leaders: Carey Wilson (Asheville), Mary Worth (Wilmington), Carrie Goforth (Lenoir), Edith Avery (Winston-Salem), and Annie Beam (Shelby).[49] At commencement that year they refused to applaud Governor Locke Craig, who spoke against suffrage, until he said that if the women really desired the franchise, he would give it to them. He added that when women took over government, men would have to rock the cradle and wash the dishes and the cradle would not be well rocked.[50]

Dr. Anna Howard Shaw first spoke on the campus in 1917 and so inspired the students that they wrote a letter of appreciation which they all signed. In acknowledging their letter, Dr. Shaw wrote,

> There is nothing which gives me greater comfort in life than to know that I have been able to be of service to the young womanhood of the country, and to stir in them not only a desire to do things but the recognition of their own value as human beings. Too long the world has taught young women that their personal work in life was to inspire and build up the work of men, failing to realize that each girl was a distinct individual in herself, and that it was as great a service to build up her own character and make it worthy as to assist in the building up of another, and that the greatest service a woman could render was to become herself a strong and noble and self-respecting human being.[51]

They were further inspired by a visit from Miss Jeanette Rankin of Montana, first woman to serve in the Congress of the United States. In 1918 the students held a mass meeting at which 575 of them signed a petition urging Senators Overman and Simmons of North Carolina to vote for the proposed Nineteenth Amendment. "We hope that this is the last time that such an opportunity will present itself."[52]

49. *State Normal Magazine*, XIX (March, 1915), 219. Annie Beam, later Mrs. Kemp Funderburk, was a member of the French Department from 1921 to 1961.
50. High Point *Enterprise*, May 26, 1915.
51. Letter from Anna Howard Shaw, May 17, 1917, College Collection.
52. *State Normal Magazine*, XXII (March, 1918), 211.

When Dr. Shaw returned to the Normal in 1918, the students, dressed in white, lined the walk from Students' Building to Spencer Dining Hall to pay tribute to her as she and Lucile Reams, student body president, walked to the luncheon being given in her honor.[53] When she died, she left money for scholarships to leading women's colleges to be selected by a committee. The only college she specified was the North Carolina College for Women. In honor of her, the building which had been known as New Dormitory was named the Anna Howard Shaw Building in 1921.[54]

THE WAR YEARS. The girls at the Normal were eager to make their contribution to the war effort. Herbert Hoover and the National Food Administration had made the students conscious that knitting and sewing for the soldiers were not enough. They needed to conserve food; so they observed meatless days and wheatless days and saved a barrel of sugar a week.[55] One group stayed in Greensboro during the summer of 1918 and worked on the farm which the college had rented. These Farmerettes—Nannie May Tilley (Bahama), Mary Gordon (Monroe), Martha Blakeney (Monroe), Nell Robertson (Rowland), Mildred Ellis (Wilson), Gladys Murrill (Kinston), Margaret Hayes (Burlington), Marguerite Brawley (Mooresville), Marjorie Craig (Reidsville), and Mary York (High Point)—did all of the farm work, not only the manual labor but the operation of machinery. They raised and canned 3,000 gallons of beans and tomatoes and 2,000 bushels of corn.[56] In 1919 students operated the farm again.

Another group was known as the Carpenterettes: Camille Campbell (Salisbury), Louise Davis (Mt. Olive), Josephine Hopkins (Brown Summit), Elizabeth Jones (Charlotte), Mary D. Murray (Greensboro), Lula Martin McIver, youngest daughter of Dr. McIver (Greensboro), and Evelyn Hodges (Greenville). These girls came to the campus in August, 1918, to build the YWCA Hut. They cleared

53. *Alumnae News*, VII (June, 1918), 5.
54. *Carolinian*, April 23, 1921. The name change of the college came in 1919, the year Dr. Shaw died. The present Anna Howard Shaw Scholarship Fund was established by Miss Lucy B. Anthony to keep alive the memory of Dr. Shaw. A scholarship is awarded annually to an outstanding student in the field in social science.
55. "We're with you, Mr. Hoover," *State Normal Magazine*, XXII (Dec., 1917), 63.
56. Personal Interview, Mary York, Feb. 2, 1965. Martha Blakeney married Luther Hodges, who later was governor of North Carolina and United States Secretary of Commerce. Marguerite Brawley's tragic death by drowning during the summer of 1919 gave impetus to the movement to provide physical education facilities and to a subsequent requirement that all students learn to swim.

the land at the north end of College Avenue, cutting up the trees for firewood to be used in the large fireplaces. After they learned to lay brick, they laid the foundation while the workmen built the chimneys, and then all worked together on the framework. The story is told of one girl who would have fallen off the roof if she had not had the presence of mind to pour a bucket of tar in front of her to stop her slide. When college opened, the girls had to leave the inside work for the men.

A rustic, brown building with four large fireplaces, deep window seats, and comfortable chairs, the Hut was used as a recreation building for thirty years. Mrs. Janet Weil Bluethenthal and Miss Gertrude Weil of Goldsboro gave $1,000 for furnishings, and Thomas A. Edison gave a phonograph.[57] Meetings and receptions were held there regularly; small groups sometimes cooked meals in the kitchenette; and individuals went there just to sit before the fireplace and to read books from the library given by the faculty and students. During the influenza epidemic of 1918, when the students were quarantined for about two months, the YWCA arranged to have "Main Street" moved to the Hut so that the girls could do some Christmas shopping. Some of the stores that set up booths were Meyer's Department Store, Odell Hardware Company, S. H. Kress and Company, R. C. Bernau Jeweler, and Wills Book and Stationery Company.[58]

By doing all the mowing and raking on the grounds, other students played their part. *Educate a Woman* has pictures of the Campus Squad in neat white middy suits, of the Carpenterettes in overalls, and the Farmerettes in uniforms. There was also a Normal regiment, which drilled on the Curry athletic field. Led by Colonel Mary Fay Davenport on horseback, the girls joined in the Third Liberty Loan drive parade, which marched to the Normal hockey field (now the site of the Petty Science Building), where Charles Lapworth, former editor of the London *Daily Times*, and Charlie Chaplin spoke.[59] In all the war efforts, the students gave their time, their money, and their energy. When they were awakened by sirens and bells announcing the Armistice, they built a bonfire on the hockey field and sang the "Star Spangled Banner," "Keep the Homes Fires Burning," and the "Battle Hymn of the Republic." The next day, dressed in white and carrying flags, they marched in a parade down-

57. *Students' Handbook: 1921-1922*, pp. 28-29. Mrs. Bluethenthal attended the Normal from 1910 to 1912.
58. *State Normal Magazine*, XXIII (Feb., 1919), 139.
59. *Ibid.*, XXII (May, 1918), 291.

town. Later one of the students wrote, ''The cheering and flag waving, however, still go on in our hearts and minds; and registered there in black letters, two inches high is the glorious headline, 'War Is Over.' ''[60]

PARK NIGHT. Park Night was instituted in 1920 as a means of honoring those students who exemplified the ideals of the college. A Grecian pageant was presented in the amphitheater in Peabody Park, usually at commencement time. By secret ballot, the girl who had best served the college and who best represented its ideal and motto was elected as Service. Her attendants were Mind, Body, and Spirit. The students who were elected Service from 1920 to 1931 were Lena Kernodle of Washington, D.C., Gladys Wells of Clinton, Mabel Stamper of Leaksville, Virginia Terrell of Raleigh, Loula Woody of Richmond, Virginia, Rosalynd Nix of Shelby, Georgia Kirkpatrick of Efland, Josephine Hege of Rosemary, Ernestine Welton of Portsmouth, Virginia, Ruth Clinard of High Point, Betty Sloan of Franklin, and Mary Jane Wharton of Greensboro. Miss Hege, who was president of the Student Government Association in 1927, received the Weil Fellowship for graduate study. In 1934 she returned to the college to join the Department of History.

JUNIOR WEEK END. When there was still a sharp distinction between the privileges of the seniors and the restrictions on the other students, the juniors were granted one week end in the spring when they could visit other students during study hour and ignore the lights-out regulation. During the 1920's, this was a big event, but as class differences were eliminated, the custom died.

SOPHOMORE CHRISTMAS PROGRAM. In December, 1925, the sophomores were given permission to present a Christmas program in the auditorium, to be followed by carols sung around an outdoor tree. This observance was so well received that it became a custom.

LANTERN FESTIVAL. The Young Women's Christian Association instituted the Lantern Festival. On this beautiful and solemn occasion, the students marched with lanterns and candles from Shaw Hall to Spencer to Peabody Park. Each dormitory was assigned a folk song and these were sung in the park. Then all the girls marched back to

60. *Ibid.*, XXIII (Dec., 1918), 106.

the Administration Building where they sang the college song and dispersed, singing "New Lamps for Old."

Student Organizations

From the beginning of the college the students joined together to form organizations which give them an opportunity for fellowship, for the development of their talents and interests, and for service to their school and their fellow students.

LITERARY SOCIETIES. The literary societies, which were organized in the first year, remained the most important organizations on campus for more than a quarter of a century. In May, 1894, the Adelphian and Cornelian societies were "authorized and empowered . . . to select marshals and such other assistants as may be necessary to keep order during the commencement."[61] In 1896 the Board of Directors went on record as opposing Greek-letter fraternities and all secret societies except the two literary societies. Considering the others harmful, the board directed the president and faculty to prevent them.[62]

The identity of the society officers was always kept secret until 1918, but membership in the organizations was open to everyone. The first year's practice of compiling matching lists with the names of all the new girls was followed, and Aunt Amanda Rhoads[63] usually drew the lists. Many girls came to the college hoping to be admitted to a particular society, but they could only hope. One year the list-makers had a difficult problem. One of the new students had four older sisters who had all been Adelphians; another had four sisters who had been Cornelians. Both names were put on one list, presumably to insure the happiness of one rather than to risk the unhappiness of both. The list with the two names was drawn for the Adelphians, and one of the disappointed girl's sisters came to the college to help her accept the decision.[64]

61. Board of Directors, Proceedings, I (May 23, 1894), 104.

62. *Ibid.*, I (May 20, 1896), 209. Virginia Terrell Lathrop, *Educate a Woman* (Chapel Hill: The University of North Carolina Press, 1942), has a picture of five girls who organized a secret society with a Greek letter name. When McIver heard of it, he forced them to disband. In the picture, the Greek letters have been covered over with a heart.

63. Aunt Amanda was one of the most faithful servants the college ever had. She remained to nurse the patients during the typhoid epidemic, she attended athletic contests, and she baked cakes for the seniors. A poem she wrote to accompany the cakes for the Class of 1917 was published in the yearbook with her picture. She also wrote a poem in honor of Dr. McIver after his death.

64. Personal interview, Miss Jane Summerell, Sept. 21, 1964.

In the early years the societies served as an important force in discipline at the college. When Dr. McIver disapproved of some behavior on campus, he often called the leaders of the societies to his office to discuss it with them. They carried the problem to the regular Saturday night meetings, and frequently no other action was needed.[65]

The social life of the college was also directed by the societies. When there were programs or parties, the students brought their own lamps, rugs, sofa pillows, and rocking chairs to decorate the classrooms, where the meetings were held before the Students' Building was available. The popular refreshments in those days were chicken salad, oysters, beaten biscuits, pickles, olives, ice cream, and cake. The literary programs were frequently papers read by students or speeches by faculty members or guests.

The important social function of the year was the initiation banquet. Souvenirs, such as jewelry boxes, letter openers, and jeweled hat pins, were given. The toasts provided entertainment in themselves. At the Greek banquet given by the Adelphians in 1911, there were toasts to the new members, to the faculty, to Dr. Foust, to the Cornelian Literary Society, to the honorary members of the Adelphian Society, to the Adelphian Society, and to the future. There were responses to all except the last. In 1920 permission was granted to invite boys to the banquet, but boys and girls were not permitted to dance together until 1930.

Many organizations had their beginning in the societies. The first plays were given by these groups, each taking turns yearly in presenting a public performance. The literary value of the plays varied. In 1903 the Cornelians gave *Under the Southern Cross*, a play written by a Southern lady in which Southern ladies were heroic and lovely, Southern gentlemen brave and chivalrous, and Yankees absolutely detestable. In 1908 the same society presented *A Midsummer's Night's Dream*. These groups also sponsored professional entertainment.

In 1897 the societies started the *State Normal and Industrial Magazine*, the first student publication.[66]

Another important event of the year was the annual debate between the societies. The first public debate was held on November 25, 1910, when Minnie Littmann and Lucy Landon, Adelphians, met Nora Carpenter and Lelia White, Cornelians, to debate the topic: "Resolved, That our immigration laws should be further restricted by

65. *Ibid.*
66. The *Magazine* is discussed as a separate organization.

an education test.'' On that day the Cornelians won, and a serious competition was born.

Traditionally the debate was held on Thanksgiving Day. Early in the morning the seniors serenaded the faculty who lived near the campus before going to the dining hall where they sang to the underclassmen. At 9:30 a visiting minister conducted a worship service, and at 1:30 a festive turkey dinner was served. In the afternoon there was sometimes a mock field day, but the main event of the day was the annual debate in the evening. The topics reflected the interests of the time: military draft, prohibition, capital punishment, women's suffrage, and the League of Nations.

It is probably difficult for a later generation of students to understand the importance and excitement connected with the debates. Winning the cup donated by R. C. Bernau was perhaps the most coveted honor at the college, and the debaters worked long and hard. For years townspeople and former students attended the popular debates. In 1921, however, their importance was questioned by a *Carolinian* editorial entitled ''Down with Debates.'' The editor thought there was too much work and strain on the debaters. In 1922 the societies voted to discontinue the debates because so much importance was attached to winning that other values were lost. Tradition, however, was not so easily broken, and they continued for several years.

The societies also had service projects. For several years each donated $150 a year to buy books for the library. When the Greensboro Public Library was opened, they gave books on American history and a bust of William Shakespeare. Later they sponsored a short-story contest for high school girls in North Carolina and awarded the O. Henry Loving Cup for the best entry.

Despite these and other activities, the societies declined in influence and importance. New societies were organized, the Dikean in 1918 and the Aletheian in 1923, in an effort to improve the organizations by reducing their unwieldy size. The societies continued to hold initiation each fall, threatening the new girls with the Cornelian goat, the greasy pole of the Adelphians, the Dikean skeleton, and Lady Maud, the donkey of the Aletheians; however, their decline in influence was apparent when the 1919 Red Cross Drive was conducted through the classes because ''class spirit was strongest.'' The societies continued to initiate new students and give a dance each year until they were abolished in 1953.[67]

67. *Alumnae News*, XLI (Winter, 1953), 9.

YOUNG WOMEN'S CHRISTIAN ASSOCIATION. Another early organization was the Young Women's Christian Association. Growing out of Miss Gertrude Mendenhall's Bible class and several circles of King's Daughters, this group was formally organized in December, 1892. It conducted a Sabbath service, a mid-week prayer meeting, and a well-organized Sunday school. In 1895 Susie Dalton of Rockingham County was sent as a delegate to the first Southern Summer Conference, in Rogersville, Tennessee, thus strengthening the organization by association with other college groups. In 1902 Miss Coit was sent to a conference in Toronto. The local group began work with the World Student Christian Federation and the Student Volunteer Movement, and in 1906 it became a charter member of the Young Women's Christian Association of the United States.

One important function of the YWCA was the publication of the *Students' Handbook.* The copy for 1897-1898 announced that new students would be welcomed by members of the YWCA, who would be wearing the heliotrope and lavendar badge of the association. It advised that "the College discouraged extravagant dressing on the part of students and teachers" and suggested that school dresses should be made with pockets. A list of dues showed that membership in the literary societies cost $1.00, the YWCA 25c, the WCTU[68] 35c, and the lawn tennis club charged a nominal fee.

Until 1926 the YWCA was solely responsible for the *Handbook.* For ten years the Student Government Association assisted with the publication and in 1936 assumed complete responsibility. The *Handbook* included the constitutions of one or both organizations, rules and regulations, helpful information, and descriptions of other clubs.

On campus the YWCA used the Students' Building for religious meetings and the Hut for recreation. Since the Blue Ridge Conference near Black Mountain, North Carolina, was one of the exciting events of the year, they had a cottage there. Their activities were not limited to meetings, however, for they gave support to missionaries, sent boxes of clothing and gifts to orphanages, and helped finance a

68. This organization was originally a standing committee of the YWCA; however, so many members were "not interested in temperance in regard to spiritous liquors," it was decided that a separate group would be more effective. One of the main speakers was Miss Frances Willard, founder of the WCTU, and Professor Claxton recruited members for the "White Ribbon Army." *Decennial,* p. 109. This lack of interest in temperance is reflected in an anecdote related by a former student. Because she was underweight, she received a pint of cream each day from the infirmary. Her roommate's father had given her the ingredients for a scalp tonic, one of which was rum. The two girls used these, with eggs, to mix eggnogs.

student from Brazil, who came to the college in 1904. Money for these projects was raised by dues, a Christmas bazaar, and a small shop known as the Retreat. On occasion they sponsored some outside entertainment such as the Ibsen players in 1922.

Like the societies, the YWCA gave rise to several activities and organizations. One was the Student Volunteer Band, whose members signed a declaration card, "It is my purpose, if God permit, to become a foreign missionary." The group was active for several years, with Miss Coit as its adviser. Several of the members went to the foreign field, and some went into religious or social work in this country.

Denominational groups developed through the years, and some of them had their own buildings. One of the first was St. Mary's House, the Episcopal student center on Walker Avenue. Bishop Edwin Anderson Penick conducted the first service of Holy Communion there, and a series of lectures now held at the University at Greensboro is named for him. The Baptist Student Union had a cottage on Forest Street, which had been donated by one of the nurses at the infirmary. Other groups were the Lutheran League, the Westminster Association, and the Wesley Foundation.[69]

ALUMNAE ASSOCIATION. At the first commencement, the ten graduates organized the Alumnae Fellowship. The motto which they chose, "Service," became the motto of the school, and appropriately so, for McIver taught that the college had "a duty to discharge, not only to those who study within its walls, but to that great body of people who will not enter this or any other school or college."[70] The first project of the new organization was to establish a loan fund, for many students found it difficult to finance their educations.

In 1903 the General Education Board offered to give $7,500 to the loan fund if the alumnae could match that sum in three years. They not only matched that amount, but in 1907, after merging with the Association of Former Students,[71] they undertook to raise $50,000 for the McIver Memorial Loan Fund. Etta Spier, Lewis Dull, and Jane Summerell, all alumnae, served as field secretaries, visiting sixty-eight

69. In 1966-1967 there are eleven organized religious groups. Five of these groups have full-time directors, of whom four are ordained ministers and the fifth is professionally trained. There are four student centers (Episcopal, Baptist, Methodist, and Presbyterian) in operation; the site for a fifth center has been purchased by the Lutheran Synod in North Carolina.

70. This quotation is from "Ideas for Which the College Stands," which appeared regularly in the catalogue.

71. The Association of Former Students was an organization of former students who were not graduates.

counties. Fifty-eight of these had local organizations which began collecting subscriptions and money by a variety of projects such as plays and booths at the county fair. Although that drive did not reach its goal, the McIver Loan Fund was $18,000 in 1967.[72]

One of the first acts of the Alumnae Association, incorporated by the General Assembly in 1910, was to purchase the Teague property because the college was unable to do so when the property was put up for sale. On that site they built a tea room, which was later bought by the college and incorporated into the new Curry Building.

Until 1912 news of the alumnae was included in the *State Normal Magazine*. In January of that year the first issue of the *Alumnae News* appeared. Published quarterly by the Alumnae Association, the magazine was offered at 25c a year. The first literary editor was Miss Julia Dameron, Latin instructor, and the first business manager was Miss Laura Coit, college secretary. In addition to the usual news items about the campus and the alumnae, the *Alumnae News* carried articles which illustrated the extent of the work of the alumnae: "From Hangchow, China," by Annie Chestnut Stuart; "Education in Cuba," by Mable Haynes; "Welfare Work in Philadelphia," by Alma Pittman; "A Letter from China," by Myrtle L. McCubbins; and "Student Activities at Smith College," by Janet Weil.

In 1919 the Board of Directors of the college, in co-operation with the Alumnae and Former Students Association, employed an alumnae secretary, whose responsibility was to arouse the interest of the alumnae in the college and to further the organization of county associations. The first secretary was Ethel Bollinger, a graduate of the Class of 1913, who had previously been in charge of the book store and the mail room. When she married Dr. James A. Keiger in 1922, Clara Booth Byrd took her place. Miss Byrd, who had also been graduated in 1913, served as assistant treasurer of the college. When she assumed the alumnae position, there was no office, only a desk in the Administration Building. She established a system of records, enlarged and improved the *Alumnae News*, organized local chapters, promoted alumnae seminars, and "sponsored and furthered the building of the Alumnae House (1937) to so great an extent that some would have said that but for her it would not have been built."[73]

72. In addition, there is an Alumnae Loan and Scholarship Fund of $37,000. Each year six incoming freshmen receive scholarships valued at $500, which may be renewed if conduct and scholarship are satisfactory.

73. Marjorie Mendenhall, "Clara Booth Byrd," *Alumnae News*, XXVII (Nov., 1939), 12. After her retirement in 1947, she organized the well-known Historical Book Club, which annually sponsors the Town Meeting on Books in Greensboro.

STATE NORMAL MAGAZINE. The *State Normal and Industrial Magazine* was first published on March 15, 1897. It was published quarterly from October to June by a board of editors elected from the Adelphian and Cornelian Literary societies under the direction of a managing editor chosen from the faculty. The Board of Directors of the college agreed that should there be any loss from the magazine the first year, they would sustain half of it, up to $50. The first managing editor, Miss Mary M. Petty, received a $50 raise for her work on the magazine.[74] The subscription rate was 50c a year or 15c for single copies.

The first board of editors was composed of three Cornelians: Mary Cheves West, Margaret McCaull, and Oeland Barnett, and three Adelphians: Mary Faison DeVane, Frances Eskridge, and Sudie Hanes. Miss Hanes was also the business manager.

The first issue contained articles by Dr. McIver, "Our Next Educational Advance" (local taxation); Dr. Joyner, "Iago, a Character Study"; Mr. Forney, "Sir Isaac Pittman"; Mary Faison DeVane, "The County Fair," a description of the program given for the legislators. The editorials discussed the change of the institution's name from "school" to "college," state appropriations, the legislature, the Cretan situation, and Alderman's inauguration as president of the University of North Carolina. Regular sections were "College News," "Alumnae Notes," "About Former Students," "In Lighter Vein" (poetry and jokes), and "Literary Notes" (authors and books).

The second issue was for commencement and included the Class Day essays: "The Duty of the Class of '97 to the State" by Bertha M. Donnelly, "The Jungle of the Guinea" by Harriet M. Berry, and "A Comparative Study of *Lycidas, Adonais,* and *In Memoriam*" by Bessie Lewis Whitaker. There was a play written especially for presentation at commencement by Robert Dick Douglas, prominent Greensboro attorney and, from 1906 to 1916, postmaster. All the speeches were given in full, including Walter Hines Page's "The Forgotten Man."

In the third issue, the first fiction appeared. "Kathryn Clemens' Thanksgiving" by Minna Curtis Bynum, was a sentimental piece about a poor, hard-working girl who was finally able to accept her rich lover's proposal of marriage. Illustrations were added in 1898.

In 1964 Miss Byrd received the Alumnae Service Award and in 1966 was elected president of Friends of the Walter Clinton Jackson Library.

74. Board of Directors, Proceedings, I (May 24, 1898), 295.

Florence O. Pannill and John J. Blair, later director of school grounds for North Carolina, drew sketches for a story by Minnie Halliburton.

For many years, the magazine had, in addition to the faculty and student contributions, articles by other people such as Dr. J. L. M. Curry, Colonel Julian S. Carr, Dr. George T. Winston, Dr. Claribel Cone, Dr. Miriam Bitting Kennedy, Charles L. Van Noppen, and Mrs. John Van Landingham. Mr. Van Noppen was a Greensboro publisher, noted for Ashe's *Biographical History of North Carolina*. Mrs. Van Landingham was active in the organization of the North Carolina Literary and Historical Association. Her address at the Normal in 1902, ''The Citizen Responsibilities of Southern Women,'' inspired the students to organize the Women's Association for the Betterment of Public School Houses in North Carolina.

The stories and poems are of slight interest, but the editorials give an interesting picture of student life. Comments on the rush to breakfast, the confusion in the halls between classes, the traffic jam in the post office, and the conduct in chapel seem to represent chronic problems. Some of the articles, however, show how very different life was in the earlier days. In 1911 Lila Melvin discussed the need for the addition of an extra hour to the Saturday night study period. In 1912 the request was made that study hour be on Friday night instead of Saturday. There were frequent articles on procrastination, rudeness, and the wasting of time. Although the contributors to the magazine were serious, not all the students were, for one was described thus: ''Seated on top of one of the front desks was a girl dangling her feet and singing a very comical song, to the amusement of several others gathered around her.''[75]

After the *Alumnae News* was started in 1912, the news of alumnae and former students and the commencement editions were omitted from the magazine. In 1914 the managing editor was replaced by an advisory faculty board and the students assumed more responsibility for the publication. In 1919, when the college name was changed, the magazine took a new name, *Coraddi*. The name was derived from the sponsoring societies: *Cor*nelian, *A*delphian, and *Di*kean. In the same year publication of the newspaper was begun, and the magazine dropped news items. For a time it retained the editorial section, but eventually it became solely a literary magazine. Gradually, too, the contributors were limited to students.

75. *State Normal Magazine*, XV (Dec., 1910), 178.

ATHLETIC ASSOCIATION. The Athletic Association had its beginning in 1898, when the juniors invited the other classes to participate in basketball and cricket matches. Lack of facilities hindered the development of the athletic program. Until 1922 there were only the tennis courts, where Mary Foust Hall now stands, the hockey field, now the site of the Science Building, outdoor basketball courts behind Kirkland, and the exercise room in the basement of South Spencer.

In 1909 Miss Bertha Bell, the director of physical culture, instituted the first Field Day. The events were basketball, hockey, jumping, ball throwing, tennis, baseball, and marching.

One of the favorite activities of the association was camping. Sometimes groups would hike two miles to Lindley Park with their tin cups and plates while Zeke carried the food in a wagon. Once dozens of girls were sick from drinking lemonade which had been left too long in galvanized containers. On another occasion 1,200 students cooked their suppers over campfires while they were entertained by a student band and song contests.

In 1929 the association purchased a camp, which they called a Hut-for-Fun. Five miles from the campus, just off the Pleasant Garden Road, the log cabin had a spacious living room with a wide fireplace, kitchen, bedroom, and a large loft for cots, providing room for fifteen or twenty girls. Students were asked to contribute their Meyer's Department Store trading stamps to help furnish the cabin, which was used for weekend trips.

MUSICAL GROUPS. In the fall of 1900 Charles J. Brockman organized the college orchestra, which played at the 1901 commencement. Known as the "Infant Orchestra," it had a repertoire of popular marches, waltzes, patriotic songs, a few concert overtures, and operatic selections, "not to mention a little ragtime occasionally."[76]

The glee club began work in 1901 under the direction of Clarence R. Brown and presented one complete operetta, "The Dress Rehearsal" by Louis Diehl. Sometimes called the College Singing Society and at other times the Choir, this group developed under Hermann H. Hoexter. After 1923 there were two groups, the Glee Club and the Choir.

WOMAN'S ASSOCIATION FOR THE BETTERMENT OF PUBLIC SCHOOL HOUSES. In 1902 Dr. McIver organized the Woman's Association for the Betterment of Public School Houses. Although this was a state organi-

76. *Decennial,* p. 122.

zation, many of the students belonged. After McIver's death, Mrs. McIver carried on the work as field secretary.

YEARBOOK. The *Decennial*, which was published by the Cornelian and Adelphian societies in 1902, had the format of a yearbook, but it was really a history of the first ten years at the college. The first yearbook sponsored by a class was in 1909 and was called the *Carolinian*. Dedicated to Dr. McIver, this first volume was a handsome edition with a green suede cover lined with watered silk. It contained individual pictures of faculty and seniors, group pictures of the other classes, the societies, and the athletic teams. The hockey players were shown in voluminous black bloomers and the tennis players in ankle-length white skirts. Other groups represented some of the counties of North Carolina, the District of Columbia, and the states of Georgia, South Carolina, New Jersey, Maryland, and Mississippi. The glee club, orchestra, and French Club were pictured as well as the casts of *A Midsummer's Night's Dream* and *She Stoops to Conquer*. The literary section included Tree Day exercises, parties, class histories, stories, poems, and jokes.

The design of the yearbook was similar through the years. When the newspaper was begun in 1919, it took the same name as the yearbook. At a mass meeting, the students decided to call the paper the *Carolinian* and the yearbook *Pine Needles*, the name under which it has been published since.

In 1912 and in 1916 there was no yearbook because all effort and money were devoted to the elaborate May Day programs. In 1919, because of the war, the students made scrapbooks in which they pasted pictures of the seniors and wrote character sketches. In other years themes were taken from Chaucer, Omar Khayyam, and Sandburg. Senior pictures sometimes were accompanied by a character sketch or horoscope as well as a list of achievements. Later yearbooks included more clubs, the last will and testament and prophecies for the senior class, and superlatives.

LANGUAGE CLUBS. The language clubs had a somewhat erratic history. Der Deutsche Verein, the German club, was organized in 1910, but it was not listed in the *Handbook* after 1913. However, club meetings and a German table in the dining hall were reported in the *Carolinian* in 1927.[77] The Fiftieth Anniversary yearbook described the group as "get-to-gethers rather than an organized club. Programs of German

77. *Carolinian*, Jan. 13, 1927.

music, commemorations of immortal persons, illustrated lectures and an annual unique 'Weihnachtsfeier' form the basis of these gatherings."[78]

The Latin Club, which was organized in 1913-1914, had as its purpose the study of Latin literature. Each class was to be in charge of a program and to present interesting background on the subject. The next year the name was changed to Classical Club. According to the *Handbooks*, the club was in operation until 1919. The 1920 *Pine Needles* carried a picture of a tombstone on the Classical Club page. Then the *Handbooks* included the club from 1923-1925, after which it apparently became inactive.[79]

The French Club was pictured in the *Decennial*, but it did not become active until twenty years later. Its sister organization, the Spanish Club, was organized in 1920. Both groups sought to promote interest in their language and sometimes presented plays for the student body. When the French Club gave *Le Bourgeois Gentilhomme*, Katherine Taylor played the fencing master.[80]

In 1926 both clubs changed their names. The French Club became Le Circle Français; the Spanish Club, El Circulo Espanol.

STUDENT GOVERNMENT ASSOCIATION. In the first year the students had established their own rules for evening study and "retirement hours," but the main responsibility for conduct was in the hands of the president and the faculty. McIver gave a warning to students who were "doing no good and were harmful because of idleness" yet were not guilty of any special wrong doing. If they improved, the case was closed. If not, they were refused readmission after the next vacation unless they made a special agreement to improve or to leave if there were any further cause for complaint. As a rule, only McIver and the student knew of the special pledge, and in no more than two or three cases was the pledge broken.

In February, 1901, Laura Sanford of Mocksville wrote in the *State Normal Magazine* that she was "proud and glad to say that 'the Honor System' alone [was] used in our college," that there were no rules except those of vital importance and most of those were made by the student body. She ended her article with the plea: "If the stu-

78. *Pine Needles*, 1942, p. 160.

79. The Classical Club was reorganized in 1938. *Pine Needles*, 1942, p. 151.

80. *Carolinian*, May 12, 1927. When Miss Taylor was graduated from the college in 1928, she received the Weil Fellowship and did graduate work at Radcliffe. She joined the French Department in 1929 and was appointed dean of women and later director of Student Services at the college.

dents do their duty, we need no rules. Let us not force the faculty to make them. Let us see how long we can live without them."

By 1910 some of the students were beginning to question the regulations, which included compulsory chapel attendance, walking period, and study hours at night. Only seniors left the campus during the week. Underclassmen, after passing inspection by the lady principal, were permitted to go to town during the day on Saturday. Male visitors were received only at certain times and then in Spencer parlor with a chaperone.[81]

Ten years after the student had praised the honor system at the college, another student wrote: "At present the government is entirely and absolutely in the hands of the Faculty. The rules of the institution are a burden which the student finds awaiting her upon registering."[82] She complained that the students did not know what they had contracted to do until they came to the college. For prospective teachers who would soon be governing others, this was not considered good training. In the same magazine another editorial reported on the success of student government at Bryn Mawr, Smith, and Wellesley. It advocated student government for the "present day girl—independent, resourceful, and self-reliant."[83] One of the class essays, written by Laura Barbara Weill, who also wrote the school song, was on "Self Government in Women's Colleges."[84]

In September of 1910 President Foust met with the members of the four classes to organize a Students' Council. Three members of the council were elected from each class, and the chief marshal, who was elected by the societies, served as president. The first officers were Frances Broadfoot, president; May Green, vice-president; and Mary Tennent, secretary.[85] Time was set aside at class meetings for a discussion of problems concerning the college as a whole, and suggestions were sent to the council. The aim of the organization was to serve as a means of communication between the administration and the student body and to detect and strengthen weakness in college life.

81. Lathrop, *Educate a Woman*, p. 44.

82. Janet Weil, "Advantages of Student Government at the Normal College," *State Normal Magazine*, XIV (May, 1910), 180.

83. *Ibid.*, p. 222.

84. Miss Weill, later Mrs. Julius Cone, became a distinguished alumna of the college, was for many years a member of the Board of Trustees of the Consolidated University, and in 1960 was the recipient of the first Alumnae Service Award.

85. Miss Tennent, a graduate of 1913, remained at the college and served as assistant registrar until 1956.

A point system was adopted in 1911 to distribute honors more evenly and to prevent some students from being overworked. A certain number of points was assigned to each office, and students were allowed to carry only a limited number.

In the fall of 1914 the Student Government Association was organized with two divisions, executive and legislative. The first executive board was composed of Gladys Avery, president; Ethel Thomas, vice-president; Evelyn Whitty, secretary; and Carrie Goforth, treasurer. In the legislative branch, the dormitories were divided into seven houses, over each of which a chairman presided. Under her there were a vice-chairman and proctors. The chairmen and proctors constituted the house committee.

Soon after it was organized, student government on the campus received the official sanction of the Board of Directors of the college. At the January meeting in 1915 the board passed a resolution that the "President and Faculty be empowered and authorized to inaugurate a system of student government in so far and to the extent that the President and Faculty think it wise and prudent."[86]

If the rules in the 1915-1916 *Handbook* are taken as an indication, one can assume that the Student Government Association made no radical changes. There was still a walking period from 4:30 to 5:15 every day except Saturday. During the week there was evening study from 7:00 to 9:45 and midday chapel from 12:40 to 1:00. Lights had to be turned out at 10:00 during the week and at 11:00 on Saturday night. On Sunday there was quiet period from 2:30 to 5:00 when students were required to remain in their own rooms and, hopefully, to rest or meditate. Students were allowed to use the telephone only with permission and could receive long distance calls only from their immediate family.[87] They were not to sit on the steps of the buildings or to walk on Spring Garden Street or Walker Avenue.

Students were not to leave the campus more than once a week without special permission from the lady principal and could not take a trip without the president's permission. Their trips to town were limited to Tuesday and Friday afternoons and Saturday morning, and they could not dine in restaurants, attend the theater or "moving picture shows," nor go to the depot without special permission. Students could receive visitors only in the parlor of Spencer Building,

86. Board of Directors, Proceedings, III (Jan. 1, 1915), 77.

87. *State Normal Magazine*, XII (Nov., 1907), 33. Sometimes such events occurred as the one referred to in this quotation: "Before a *Friend* turns *brother* to a girl and wishes to speak to her over the phone, he had better put the girl on to the racket. What is your opinion on the subject, 'Billy'?"

and young men were not received unless a girl's parents had sent permission to the lady principal. Even then they could not call on Saturday or Sunday nights or on Sunday afternoons. Students were allowed to shop on Walker Avenue and Spring Garden Street on Saturday afternoon within two blocks of the campus.

Violations of the rules were handled by the administration. In 1916 a freshman wrote a poem about a girl who had just received a summons to see the director of dormitories after lunch. She waited with much trepidation because her cousin had brought another boy to visit her and the boy had pretended to be her brother.[88]

A new constitution, adopted in 1921, organized the association into three groups: Senate, House of Representatives, and Advisory Committee. The Senate was composed of president, vice-president, secretary, and treasurer of the Student Government Association; chief marshal; fire chief; president of the YWCA; and representatives from the freshman and special classes. The House had seventy members: fifteen seniors, twenty juniors, fifteen sophomores, fifteen freshmen, two special students, and two town students. The vice-president of the Student Government Association was speaker of the house. The Advisory Committee was a joint committee of faculty and students. On it served the president of the college, the adviser of women, the director of dormitories, two members elected by the faculty from their number, the president and vice-president of the Student Government Association, and three members elected from the Senate. The Student Government Association was responsible for order in the dormitories and off campus, but only the administration had the power of expulsion or suspension.[89]

In 1921 the Community Budget was initiated, but it was not compulsory at first. In 1922 each student paid $12 for the support of the literary societies, the Athletic Association, the SGA, the YWCA, *Pine Needles, Coraddi,* and *Carolinian.*[90] In 1927 the fee had gone down to $7, and that year the YWCA received the largest amount of the money, over twice as much as any of the others.

The advent of the automobile brought rules concerning riding, and during this same period some of the other rules were relaxed. Freshmen and sophomores were required to have chaperones for evening engagements with young men and for riding with friends.

88. Nancy Yarborough, ''On the Reef of a Freshman's Woe,'' *State Normal Magazine,* XX (Jan., 1916), 140.
89. *Carolinian,* Sept. 17, 1921.
90. *Handbook,* 1922-1923.

Juniors and seniors were permitted to ride to and from a picture show or entertainment. ("It is understood a direct route to and from the college shall be taken.") Seniors might remain off campus until 10:00 P.M. any day except Saturday; juniors, one day each week. Students were allowed to receive young men, with permission from the residence hall counselor, any afternoon or night except Sunday when only out-of-town callers were received. Smoking was not permitted, and girls were not allowed to dance with men.[91] The girls were permitted to dance in the gymnasium from 7:00 to 7:30 P.M. A *Carolinian* editorial recommended that there be more opportunity for dancing and that a number of girls be on hand to see that the dancing was of the right kind. Since many of the students knew little of dancing before coming to college, they could not always tell which steps were "considered 'rough' in the sense that [they were] not allowed at good dances."[92]

Since automobiles were making travel easier, Thanksgiving and Easter vacations were added, and the students learned the significance of a weekend. In 1928 seniors were allowed four weekends away from the campus each semester. With permission from parents and counselor, juniors were allowed three, sophomores two, and freshmen one.

The student Senate handled the work later given to the Judicial Board. The *Carolinian* in 1926-1927 reported that 175 girls appeared before the Senate for offenses ranging from the minor to the most serious. The most frequently violated rules involved returning to campus at stipulated hours, going downtown on Saturday afternoon, and riding during the day. The most serious violations were riding at night, smoking, and cheating. These were in a minority. The first reference to cheating that appeared in the *Handbook* was in 1926-1927: "Any student found cheating in her work may be suspended or expelled from the College." No figures on expulsions are available. Dr. Foust, who was in charge of all expulsions, often made no records because he wanted to protect the girls' reputations.[93]

The enforcement of class attendance came under attack during the late twenties. The regulation stated that two unexcused absences were to be penalized as the teacher saw fit, the third was to be reported at once by the instructor, and the fourth was to bar a student from the examination in that course. Some students felt that since the rule was

91. *Handbook*, 1925-1926, p. 70.
92. *Carolinian*, Nov. 7, 1929.
93. Personal interview with Mrs. Julius I. Foust, August 25, 1964.

not always enforced, there was need for revision. When the same complaint was voiced two years later, a "cut" system for juniors and seniors whose work was satisfactory was recommended, but no action was taken for several years.

In 1929 an effort was made to improve the effectiveness of the Student Government Association by holding a leadership conference at Camp Yonahlossee, Blowing Rock. Thirty-five student officers attended with fifteen members of the administrative department, including Dr. Foust and Miss Lillian Killingsworth, counselor. Both students and faculty considered the conference extremely beneficial and recommended that it become a tradition.

THE JUNIOR SHOP. Although not an organization, the Junior Shop was for many years one of the most popular institutions in student life. In 1913 the juniors decided to help others and to raise money for their annual banquet both in the same venture. For several years they sold hot soup, hot chocolate, and sandwiches to the students at the training school, each item costing 5c. In 1918, during the influenza epidemic, they prepared meals for the patients, cooking them in the basement of the Curry Building and carrying them to Guilford Hall, which had been converted into a temporary infirmary.

After a few years the preparation of meals was discontinued because it required so much time, and the juniors placed a washstand in the post office, where they sold hairnets, pennants, film, and Sterno. Later the Junior Shop took over a small room of its own in the basement of the Administration Building, where candy, fruit, and sandwiches were also sold. Until the Soda Shop was opened in 1949, the Junior Shop was the favorite spot for the between-class Coke break.

DRAMATIC CLUB. The first significant dramatic venture at the Normal was a "State County Fair," presented November 30, 1894, under the direction of Mary Arrington of Nash County, Sethelle Boyd of Iredell, Daisy Waitt of Wake, and Ellen Barker of Buncombe. A series of skits and tableaux depicted distinctive features of several counties. With elaborate costumes and stage properties, groups of students presented outstanding historical personages, commercial products, or historical events that furthered the prestige of their native county. The girls from Rockingham County combined history and humor to win the prize. Two girls carried a cradle in which rested a sugar-cured ham. On the cradle was a sign, "Nursery of our Governors," and four other girls carried shields representing the four governors from their county. The prize was a framed picture of Pilot Mountain. Afterward the students had oysters and hot chocolate.[94]

This program was repeated for the Educational Committee of the General Assembly on February 12, 1897. The girls added a mock session of the legislature at which the Normal appropriation was increased to $100,000 with the appearance of a bottle of Old Nick Williams Whiskey.[95] The story is told that the Durham girls had sewn cigarettes to their costumes and after the program smoked them. News of such an act was hardly the type of publicity the college had planned.[96]

The entertainment for the Visiting Committee in 1899 included a skit in which Uncle Sam, played by E. J. Forney, instructed the Philippines, Hawaii, Puerto Rico, and Cuba in the "School of Freedom," teaching them to be as good as California, Texas, and Arizona.[97] This skit was, of course, prompted by the Spanish American War. The girls had been out to wave to the soldiers on the train as they went to Raleigh.

The societies were responsible for most of the dramatic activities. Some of the events they produced themselves; others they sponsored. One of the most publicized was the performance of *The Tempest*, which the Ben Greet Woodland Players gave in the outdoor theater in Peabody Park. Shakespeare's plays seemed popular, for *As You Like It, Romeo and Juliet*, and *Twelfth Night* were presented by the students. Girls still played boys' roles, but by 1911 they were allowed to wear trousers.

In 1912-1913 the Dramatic Club was organized. Since the societies were required to alternate in giving the annual public performance, the Dramatic Club sought to centralize their efforts and make it possible for girls really interested in dramatics to participate more often. Lizzie Roddick was general manager and Ione Grogan business manager of the new group. At commencement the club presented Booth Tarkington's *The American* in honor of alumnae and visitors. Miss Grogan's talent was not limited to the business angle, for she and Clara Booth Byrd took part in a play presented by the senior Latin Class, *The Mostellaria* by Plautus.[98]

94. Greensboro *Record*, Dec. 1, 1894.
95. *Ibid.*, Feb. 13, 1897.
96. Lathrop, *Educate a Woman*, p. 20.
97. *State Normal Magazine*, III (Feb., 1899), 421.
98. Miss Grogan was later a residence hall counselor at the college for many years, and so it is fitting that one of the new dormitories was named for her in 1963.

Although the Dramatic Club was somewhat active through the years, its real beginning came in 1921 when William Raymond Taylor joined the English Department. For thirty years he was director of drama at the college.[99]

In 1924 the Dramatic Association[100] reported a very successful year: five productions, all expenses paid, and money in the treasury. In the same year four men of the faculty, Benjamin B. Kendrick, Leonard B. Hurley, A. C. Hall, and W. R. Taylor, took singing parts in the play *Fashion*. A highlight of the evening was a dance, "Walking down Broadway," by Mr. Hurley and Helen Hall, one of the students. He was also a playwright. Two performances of his play *Blue Diamonds* were given at the college.[101]

In 1925 the association presented *Will-o'-the-Wisp* in a nationwide contest at Northwestern University and won second place. The students returned with "glowing tales of life in the big cities and experiences with cabarets, white bell hops, escalators, snow, and pickpockets."[102]

The Playlikers, as they were called at this time, carried their plays to Chapel Hill, to High Point, and to Pinehurst. They presented *Tarnish* while it was still on Broadway and gave a special production of it at the National Theater for the townspeople. Some of the other plays were *Craig's Wife, Of Arms and the Man, Dear Brutus,* Rostand's *Chanticleer,* Molnar's *The Swan,* and Dion Boucicault's *After Dark.*

Mr. and Mrs. Taylor for several years promoted further interest in the theater by taking a group of students to New York during the Christmas holidays. One year they saw eleven plays, among them Michael Arlen's *The Green Hat* with Katherine Cornell and *Hamlet* with Walter Hampden and Ethel Barrymore. The next year they saw *The Constant Wife,* with Ethel Barrymore, and eight other plays. They visited Chinatown, the Metropolitan Museum, the Aquarium, the

99. Taylor helped organize the Carolina Dramatic Association, of which he was the first president and the campus theater, opened in 1967, was named in his honor.

100. This club has had as many names as the college: the Dramatic Club, the Dramatic Association, the Playlikers, the Theater of the Woman's College of U. N. C., and the Theater of the University of North Carolina at Greensboro. Masqueraders was established to honor the outstanding students in drama.

101. Later Dr. Hurley became head of the English Department. Through the years his interest in students inspired and encouraged them. After his death a scholarship fund was established in his memory.

102. *Carolinian,* Jan. 10, 1925.

Statue of Liberty, and the Strand Roof Garden, where they heard Hal Kemp's orchestra.

The first student plays were presented in 1926. *The Quick and the Dead* by Andrina McIntyre was a tragedy laid in eastern Carolina. *Sims*, by Kate C. Hall, was a comedy. Since then the presentation of plays written by students has become a tradition.

CAROLINIAN. An effort to start a campus newspaper in 1918 proved unsuccessful. Adelaide Van Noppen of Greensboro wrote the War Industries Board for permission, but a wartime regulation prohibiting new papers forced a delay.[103]

The need for a paper had been recognized earlier. In 1914 an editorial in the *State Normal Magazine* had called for an official organ of the Student Government Association to provide opportunity for "expression of disagreement." When the idea arose again in Professor A. C. Hall's writing class, he agreed to help, and so the paper was born. The first issue of the *Carolinian*, which appeared on May 19 1919, covered the commencement news.

Florence Miller of Statesville was the first editor and Willie John Medlock of Charlotte, the first business manager. The paper carried news of the campus, editorials, alumnae news, intercollegiate notes, book reviews, and personals. In the beginning a four-page, four-column paper, it grew to six pages, six columns. In 1922 a *Summer Carolinian* was issued, but it was suspended after a few years. Dr. Ruth Strang of Columbia taught in the summer session of 1927 and started the *East Hall Daily*. It was so successful that she continued it in 1928.

The *Carolinian* staff belonged to the North Carolina Collegiate Press Association, and in 1921 Anne Cantrell of Winston-Salem was elected president and Emeline Goforth of Lenoir, general secretary. At that time ten colleges formed the association: Wake Forest, Davidson, University of North Carolina, Salem, Meredith, Elon, Guilford, Lenoir, Greensboro College, and North Carolina College for Women.

By the second year the staff acquired a room in the basement of the Students' Building, furnished with one desk, one table, a chair for each staff member, three packs of yellow paper, and some pencils. With this equipment they were prepared to be both conscience and voice of the students and faculty.

There were editorials condemning those girls who went to the

103. Letter from G. K. Ferguson, War Industries Board, Aug. 30, 1918, College Collection.

Greensboro Drug Store "to pick up" boys and those hatless students who wore their athletic sweaters to town. They attacked misbehavior in chapel, "bumming" rides to town, profanity, stealing, and cheating. Smoking regulations at other colleges were reported, perhaps in an effort to have the rule relaxed at the college. The controversy about compulsory chapel and class attendance made good copy for years.

The faculty came in for their share of the criticism. Keeping library books out indefinitely and breaking into lines were two of the most frequent complaints against them. One of the most outspoken indictments was in an editorial in 1926: "all the grossness and narrowness on the campus is not confined to the students. . . . But it is an accepted fact that some of our lords and ladies of learning are not above gossip, spite, smugness, Babbittry, and sheer stupidity."[104]

There were editorials, too, on evolution and academic freedom. Regular features such as "A Glimpse of Our Nation's Affairs" or "Did You Know?" kept students informed of current events. The *Carolinian* felt a responsibility for the minds as well as the manners of the students.

Always the *Carolinian* has provided the "opportunity for disagreement." More, it has recorded the life of the college so that one has only to turn to its pages in order to recapture the spirit of another time.

INTERNATIONAL RELATIONS CLUB. Under the direction of Miss Magnhilde Gullander, president, the social science students organized the International Relations Club in 1920. The first Board of Managers was composed of Ruth Vick of Seaboard, Mary Blair of Cape May, New Jersey, and Gladys Wells of Clinton. Membership was limited to juniors and seniors who had at least a grade of 2 (90-95) on their work in the department.[105] From their affiliation with the Institute of International Education, they received literature and plans for the study of conditions in Mexico, Russia, Japan, and the League of Nations. In addition to their regular programs they brought to the campus authorities on international topics. One such speaker was Baron L. A. Kroff, a Russian nobleman who discussed Bolshevism and conditions in Russia. Another was Dr. Ernst Jaeckh, a German

104. *Carolinian*, Oct. 7, 1926. In a faculty meeting years before, Dr. Foust had taken the faculty to task for talking so much in chapel. Faculty Council Minutes, III (Sept. 28, 1914), 11.

105. A 2 was the equivalent of a B. Numbers were used instead of letters until 1930.

statesman who had been with the delegation at Versailles. His topic was "The New Germany."

Another phase of the work of the International Relations Club was the organization of the Young Voters Club. This was open to all interested students, and through it they became affiliated with the League of Women Voters.

QUILL CLUB. Organized in the fall of 1920 by the editorial staffs of the *Carolinian* and the *Coraddi*, the Quill Club was one of the most select organizations on campus. Its membership was limited to twenty students interested in writing. New members were chosen on the basis of talent and interest. Mary Blair, *Coraddi* editor, was the first chairman, and Richard H. Thornton was the faculty adviser.

EDUCATION CLUB. Prospective teachers, in October, 1921, organized the Education Club. The first officers were Mabel Stamper of Leaksville, president; Muriel Barnes of Greensboro, vice-president; and Cleo Holleman of Cary, secretary-treasurer. The purposes were "to foster interest and pride in teaching as a profession, to become acquainted with educational problems and conditions in our state, and to enjoy social occasions together and become acquainted with one another and with the leaders of the state." At one meeting they had a debate on the topic: "Resolved: that corporal punishment is not as fashionable as the pure love method control in the public schools of the United States." At another they had a spelling match, in which the entire club missed "capuchian" [*sic*].[106] There were, of course, more serious occasions when state leaders in education spoke to the group.

TAU PI DELTA. In an effort to give recognition to campus leaders, the college organized an honor society in 1921. The eleven charter members were selected on the basis of college spirit, character, intellect, leadership, and special ability. The original members were Mary Sue Beam (Shelby), Matilda Lattimore (Shelby), Iola Parker (Rocky Mount), Virginia Terrell (Raleigh), Marie Bonitz (Wilmington), Martha Bradley (Gastonia), Anne Cantrell (Winston-Salem), Hazel Mizelle (Robersonville), Branson Price (Chapel Hill), Ruth Teachey (Reidsville), and Myrtle Warren (Gastonia). In 1923 the members decided to disband, believing that there was no need for the group since the "all-round type of college girl should be and was the rule instead of the exception" and that the existence of their club indi-

106. *Carolinian,* April 8, 1922.

cated otherwise. As a reminder of their short existence, they erected a stone in Peabody Park with a bronze marker bearing the letters Tau Pi Delta and the flame of service.

PHOENIX CLUB. An organization of students majoring in public school music, the Phoenix Club was formed in 1924. The first officers were Lola Harwood of Bryson City, president; Margaret Hartsell of Greensboro, vice-president; Eva Call of Mocksville, secretary; and Mary Jacocks of Tarboro, treasurer. Each year the group presented a program for the public. The purpose of the club was to stimulate professional interest in music education and to promote the love of music among the students at the college. The name was changed to Madrigal Club in 1927 and still later to the Music Education Club.

HOME ECONOMICS CLUB. An effort to establish a Home Economics Club was made in 1917, but the permanent organization came in 1925. The officers at that time were Inah Kirkman of Climax, president; Elizabeth French Boyd of Mooresville, vice-president; Bess Newton of Fayetteville, secretary; and Annie S. Henderson of Maysville, treasurer. The club stimulated interest in home economics, promoted an appreciation of homemaking, and provided an opportunity for social contacts.

SCIENCE CLUBS. Although the Science Club was a faculty organization, clubs were established for the students in botany, chemistry, zoology, and mathematics. They provided an opportunity to explore areas not included in the formal courses. Advanced students were eligible for membership. In addition to the regular programs there were field trips for the Zoology Club and camping trips to the mountains for the Botany Club. The Botany Club also sponsored an Arbor Day program. One year they planted 650 pine trees which had been given by the state Forestry Department. Other years they planted trees, shrubs, flowers, and other trees.

DOLPHIN CLUB. Open only to advanced swimmers, the Dolphin Club was organized to give these students an opportunity to become expert swimmers. The first officers were Rosalie Jacobi of Wilmington, president, and Katherine Hardeman of Greensboro, secretary-treasurer. The charter members were Martha Farrar of Greensboro, Sarah Foust of Greensboro, Helen Hodges of Kinston, Georgia McCaskill of Fayetteville, Mary Clara Tate of High Point, and Julia Wright of Ingold.

After passing a difficult examination for admission, members could earn emblems for their swimming. One of the highlights of the year was the water festival, in which the members performed original stunts. Later the Seal Club was organized for less advanced swimmers.

ORCHESUS CLUB. For those students who excelled in dance drama, the Orchesus Club[107] was organized in 1926. The first president was Nellie Irvin of Greensboro, who was also chief marshal. Frances Barber of Asheville was the first secretary, and Miss Helen Robinson, the first director. Specializing in interpretive dancing, both lyric and dramatic, the club furnished dancers for many college events and produced a dance drama for Field Day. Membership was so selective that, at one time, of the fifty-two students who competed, only five were elected to the club. Eleven others were given probationary membership.

DAY STUDENTS' ASSOCIATION. Although the town students had been represented in the Student Government Association for many years, they were not formally organized until the spring of 1929. The officers for the year 1929-1930 were Edith Harbour, president; Helen Felder, vice-president; Bernice Apple, secretary; and Dorothy Donnell, treasurer. A special room was provided for them in the basement of the Administration Building, where they could study, play cards, or relax.

HONOR SOCIETY. In preparation for a local chapter of Phi Beta Kappa, the college organized an Honor Society in 1930. Membership was limited to 5 per cent of the seniors and 2.5 per cent of the juniors. Students who had an average of 2 (90-95) with no grade lower than a 3 (80-90) for five semesters were considered. In the first year twenty girls were selected: Mabel Aderholt, Lexington; Nancy Baker, Charlotte; Elizabeth DuVernet, Greenville, South Carolina; Ellen Fletcher, Anderson, South Carolina; Louisa Hatch, Hamlet; Roberta Hayes, Grifton; Gladys Hicks, Rockingham; Mary Elizabeth Hoyle, Gastonia; Fleeta Martin, Dunn; Charlotte Purcell, Salisbury; Manie Robinson, Morven; Cecil Rogers, Statesville; Ruby Rosser, Jonesboro; Janie Secrest, Monroe; Helen Seifert, New Bern; Mary Boddie Smith, Chadbourn; Mary Jane Wharton, Greensboro; Frances White, Clayton; Margaret Ann Williams, Asheville; and Mary Lewis (a junior), Norfolk, Virginia. Dr. Helen Barton, who later became head of the mathematics department and served the college with distinction until

107. Also spelled ''Orchesis.''

her retirement, was chairman of the faculty committee to advise the group. The designation "Honor Society" continued to be used until Phi Beta Kappa was organized.

Many groups were organized that did not survive. One of these was the Consumer's League, a branch of the national organization which had as its purpose the betterment of labor conditions in the United States. There was the Hiking Club, which conducted an eight-mile hike on Wednesdays and seven-mile supper hikes on Saturdays. There were at least two clubs that studied current events, the Miscellany and the Current Topics Club. Others were the Opera Association, the Shakespeare Club, the Howell's Club, Ye Archery Club, and the Bird Club. All of these, at least for a time, filled a need for the students.

seven

The Alumnae

When the first graduates of the State Normal and Industrial School for Girls formed the Alumnae Association in 1893, they selected as their motto "Service," and as they received their diplomas, President McIver reminded them that North Carolina expected a return from her investment. This idea was perpetuated through the years, and in 1926 Dr. Foust reported to the Board of Directors:

> The college attempts to keep in mind always at least a few fundamental aims. The spirit of unselfish service should be one of the definite characteristics in the life of both the faculty and students. The young women who enjoy the larger opportunities and privileges afforded by college training should never lose sight of the fact that the state of North Carolina has provided these things for them that they may make better the life of the whole people of the state. This college is simply one of the instruments employed by the commonwealth to furnish sane and wholesome leadership to all its citizens. It is my firm conviction that the students who attend this institution have endeavored after leaving it to give something of their strength and happiness to those people who for one reason or another have been denied the privilege of a college education.[1]

The *State Normal Magazine* and the *Alumnae News* through the years have reported the activities of the alumnae, and an examination of these publications shows the variety of careers they followed. From the reports, a number have been selected to illustrate the diversity of occupations. Some of these women held their positions for a lifetime; others gave them up after a brief time for marriage or other careers. All of them, however, are a part of the story of the college, for the value of the institution is measured by its graduates and former students.

1. Julius I. Foust, "President's Report" in the *Report of the Board of Directors for the Years 1924-1926*, p. 28.

Education

Until 1930 the college catalogue stated the purpose thus: "The chief mission of the College has been and will continue to be the preparation of teachers." Consequently, it was only natural that most of the graduates gave their service in the field of education. Of the 717 young women who were graduated during the first twenty-two years, only 33 did not teach in the schools of North Carolina.[2] Most of the graduates in the succeeding years as well had some experience in the classroom.

Many of these young women gave up teaching for homemaking or for another career, but there were others who taught for many years. Rhea Featherston, 1900,[3] was a physical examiner and corrector of gymnastics in the public schools of California until her retirement in 1950. Mary Callum Wiley, 1894, taught in Winston-Salem for almost fifty years. Among others with periods of service of over forty years were Fannie McClees, 1899; Mary Wilson Brown, 1902; Irma Ellis, 1905; Emma McKinney, 1906; Florence Gray, 1907; Marguerite (Wiley) Bilbro, 1916; and Grace Frazier, 1920.

A smaller number of graduates went into college teaching. Barnette Miller, 1905, perhaps the first to receive the Ph.D. degree, taught at the American College for Girls in Constantinople and then at Wellesley. Margaret Horsfield, 1906, taught at the University of Kentucky; Edith Haight, 1915, at the University of Wyoming; Mary Poteat, 1919, at Duke University; and Ezda Deviney, 1919, at Florida State University, where a dormitory is named for her. Joyce Cooper, 1928, taught at the University of Florida, after being a supervising teacher at Curry School and a director of instruction in Olympia, Washington. Three were critic teachers at college training schools: Evelyn (Royall) Coward, 1904, at Western Carolina College; Dora Coates, 1912, at East Carolina College; and Corinne (Cook) Baker, 1929, at the State Teachers' College of Alabama. Among those who taught at their own college were Miriam McFadyen, 1900; Betty Aiken Land, 1903; Mary Fitzgerald, 1908; Jane Summerell, 1910;

2. Julius I. Foust, "The History of the Woman's College" (unpublished history, Chancellor's Office, The University of North Carolina at Greensboro), p. 29.

3. The date given after the name usually indicates the class to which the student belonged. In the early years, however, classes were not so clearly defined and the date indicates the last year the student attended the college. No distinction has been made here between graduates and non-graduates. For married women, the maiden name is given in parentheses. The past tense has been used throughout this account even though some of the alumnae are still active in the vocations listed.

Ione Grogan, 1913; Ruth Gunter, 1914; Annie (Beam) Funderburk, 1916; Elizabeth (Duffy) Bridgers, 1925; Elizabeth Hathaway, 1925; Josephine Hege, 1927; Katherine Taylor, 1928; and Elizabeth Avent, 1929.[4]

Clee Winstead, 1898, and Ivey Paylor, 1913, represent those who became school principals. Miss Winstead was principal of a school in Wilson, which was named in her honor. Miss Paylor was at the Johnson Street School in High Point.

Supervisors were also among the ranks of the graduates. Mary Arrington, 1895, one of the first rural supervisors, was the first woman to serve on the North Carolina State Board of Vocational Education. Mary Hyman, 1907, served as supervisor in Cumberland, Guilford, Halifax, Orange, and Cabarrus counties. Hattie S. Parrott, 1901, was with the State Board of Public Instruction for thirty years. Elizabeth Kelly, 1899, was a member of the staff of the state superintendent of public instruction, working in the field of adult illiteracy. She also directed the first school for training teachers in this program. She was the second woman to be elected president of the North Carolina Education Association. The first, Mary Owen Graham, was a member of the Normal faculty and later president of Peace Institute in Raleigh. Other graduates who served as president of the North Carolina Education Association were Annie M. Cherry, 1912; Leafy Spear, 1918; and Maie Sanders, 1924.

As new developments were made in education, alumnae often had a part. Emma Lewis (Speight) Morris, 1900, was the founder and volunteer director of the Night School for Adults in Salisbury. She was the first woman to serve on the Salisbury School Board and for twenty-seven years was chairman of the Rowan County Library Board. Two others who promoted adult education through the "Moonlight Schools" were Mattie Blackwood, 1913, and Hester Cox Struthers, 1894.

Margaret (Peirce) Orme, 1899, was a leader in "natural education." In Washington, D. C., she started a training school for teachers in this field and headed a school in which preschool children learned foreign languages, typing, spelling, and good manners through plays, games, and songs.

Maude F. Rogers, 1909, started the Cooperative Class at Durham High School in 1921. This class made it possible for students to continue their education even while earning a living.

4. Other graduates who were connected with the college are in the chapter on faculty. Others, who taught for shorter periods of time, are not included.

Educational television is represented by Iola Parker, 1923, and Mary (Polk) Gordon, 1926.

The field of guidance has drawn many of the graduates. Some, like Fannie Starr Mitchell, 1914, were deans of girls in high schools. Others were deans at colleges: Inez (Koonce) Stacy, 1907, of the University of North Carolina; Leah Boddie, 1912, of the New Jersey College for Women; and Katherine Sherrill, 1926, of Hood College. Anne (Fulton) Carter, 1921, and Dorothy Clement, 1923, returned to their alma mater as counselors. Miss Clement later went to the University of Arizona as assistant dean of women.

Librarians compose another important group in the field of education. Carrie L. Broughton, 1897, was state librarian in Raleigh. Georgia Hicks Faison, 1911, worked as a librarian at Randolph-Macon Woman's College, Yale University, and the University of North Carolina. Catharine (Jones) Pierce, 1911, was at Swarthmore and Duke. Annie Lee Yates, 1924, was at Florida State University, and Marjorie Hood, 1926, became head circulation librarian at the University of North Carolina at Greensboro. Mary Theresa (Peacock) Douglas, 1923, was state superintendent of school libraries in North Carolina. She wrote the *Teacher-Librarian's Handbook*, which was published by the American Library Association.

Business

Alumnae found their places in the business world, sometimes on their own and sometimes with their husbands. Genevieve Moore, 1916, was owner and manager of her own book store in High Point. Lena (Hartsell) Stradley, 1919, operated a tea room, and Rosalynd (Nix) Gilliatt, 1925, a florist shop. Ora (Miller) Pike, 1906, and Alma (Rightsell) Pinnix, 1919, both inherited businesses from their husbands. Mrs. Pike operated her husband's drug store before opening a corset shop specializing in surgical fittings. Mrs. Pinnix was president and general manager of a realty company which specialized in selling mill villages. Faith (Johnson) Bunn, 1924, had a hotel in Clinton with her husband. Grace Eaton, 1912, was in the insurance business in Washington, D.C. Emily S. Austin, 1901, was assistant secretary-treasurer of Carolina Telephone and Telegraph Company.

After teaching for a few years, Ann (Harrelson) Floyd, 1924, became a buyer for a department store in Greensboro. Catharine (Vernon) Carpenter, 1912, was personnel director for B. F. Compton and traveled over the country selecting company representatives. Cary (Batchelor) Kline, 1922, did personnel work for Macy's in New

York, and Marie (Bonitz) Darrin, 1922, was a buyer for Lord and Taylor's. Stella (Williams) Anderson, 1923, was advertising manager for a department store in Charlotte. After the death of her husband, she published five non-daily newspapers and was part owner and executive of five radio stations, all in western North Carolina.

As secretaries and office managers, others were successful. Florence (Smith) Cannon, 1898, the first woman employee of the Coca-Cola Company in Atlanta, Georgia, was later office manager for Joseph Whitehead Foundation, also in Atlanta. Lila Walsh, 1913, did office work for Pee Dee Mills for thirty-seven years. Virginia (Smith) Gibson, 1926, was stenographer for the Alabama State Department of Revenue.

With the federal government were Fodie (Buie) Kenyon, 1893, and Lillie V. Keathley, 1900. Mrs. Kenyon, who had been secretary to Dr. McIver, achieved the third highest position in the Appointments Division of the Department of Justice. Miss Keathley was with the Bureau of Insular Affairs working in Philadelphia and Puerto Rico.

There were others who were concerned with the business affairs of colleges. Those who remained at their own institution were Edna Forney, 1908, assistant treasurer; Mary Tennent, 1913, assistant registrar; Kathleen (Pettit) Hawkins, 1923, student aid officer; and Ruthe Shafer, 1931, cashier. Edith Lewis (Harris) Kirby, 1905, was secretary to the dean of Teacher's College, Temple University.

Law

Some of the most distinguished alumnae have been the lawyers. One of the first was Lucille Pugh, 1902, who received her law degree from New York University and tried her first case when she was twenty. She received national publicity as the first woman, at least in New York, to defend a murderer. Margaret (Berry) Street, 1912, received her law degree from the University in Chapel Hill and practiced law in Charlotte. Willie Mae (Stratford) Shore, 1914, also graduated from U.N.C. and ranked highest in the class appearing before the Supreme Court. Gladys (Wells) Ringer, 1921, who studied at the University of Michigan, was the first woman in North Carolina to receive the Doctor of Jurisprudence degree. Susie Sharp, 1928, another U.N.C. graduate, became a judge of Superior Court and associate justice of the North Carolina Supreme Court. When she was a student at N.C.C.W., she wrote a story for the *Coraddi* about the execution of a convicted murderer. Norma (Hardy) Britton, 1906, attended the Washington College of Law after her husband's death. When she received her degree in 1929, she tied with a fellow student for the medal given annually for the highest scholastic average.

Medicine

The medical doctors have composed another interesting group. One of the earliest was Lois (Boyd) Gaw, 1898, who was resident physician at N.C.C.W. and at Winthrop. Pattie Groves, 1914, served in that capacity at Mount Holyoke. Margaret (Castex) Sturgis, 1905, after receiving her M.D. from Woman's Medical College of Pennsylvania, was clinical professor of gynecology there and chief of gynecology and obstetrics at two hospitals in Philadelphia. Annie V. Scott, 1914, who paid her expenses at the Normal by selling subscriptions to *Current Opinion*, served as a medical missionary in China until the war made it necessary for her to return to the United States. She then joined the staff of the medical school in Chapel Hill, where she taught until her retirement in 1964. Lula Disosway, 1918, also served as a medical missionary in China. After 1920, more graduates studied medicine. One of these, Sarah Vance (Thompson) Alexander, 1926, specialized in psychiatry and became director of the Colorado Springs Child Guidance Clinic.

Other medical fields drew alumnae. Phoebe (Pegram) Baughan, 1897, and Isabel (Brown) Funke, 1899, were chiropractors. Lillian Hunt, 1914, was an occupational therapist. Beulah McKenzie, 1924, was a medical social worker in Chicago, and Katherine Lewis Barrier, 1930, was medical social consultant to the North Carolina Board of Health. Among those who became nurses were Lorna (Thigpen) David, 1925, who was educational director in the School for Nursing at the Baptist Memorial Hospital in Memphis, and Daphine Doster, 1927, who was public health nursing consultant in four states, Puerto Rico, and the Virgin Islands. Celestia Weeks, 1926, was a laboratory technician at Johns Hopkins Hospital, and Emily Cate, also of 1926, was director of health education for a YWCA. Sallie (Tucker) Mumford, 1922, was chief laboratory technician for the Greensboro Health Department. Sadie (McBrayer) McCain, 1916, was organizing president (1923) and first president (1924) of the Auxiliary to the North Carolina Medical Society.

Social Service

Many alumnae served through the Red Cross, the Young Women's Christian Association, and departments of welfare. Annie (Kizer)

Bost, 1903, was North Carolina commissioner of public welfare. After being a social worker for a large manufacturing company in Chicago, Annie E. Trotter, 1896, worked for the YWCA for twenty-five years. Also with the YWCA was Sallie Sumner, 1913, who was an executive secretary. Emily (Gregory) Thompson, 1897, worked at Jackson Training School in Concord and at the Children's Home in Winston-Salem before becoming girls' probation officer and assistant superintendent of public welfare in Forsyth County. Minnie Fields, 1902, was a welfare worker in a mill village in Greensboro, and Mary Jones, 1904, was a medical social worker with the American Red Cross. Louise Maddrey, 1917, was director of girls' work at a community house in New York. Helen (Chandley) Chalmers, 1923, was first case worker and then general secretary of the Greensboro Welfare Department, and Ruth Clinard, 1929, became executive director of the Greensboro chapter of the American Red Cross.

Home Economics

Even before the Department of Home Economics became as outstanding as it is today, alumnae of the college found employment as dietitians and county home demonstration agents. One of the earliest students, Laura Falls, 1896, reported from Dallas, Texas, in 1919 that she was a Red Cross dietitian, a member of a committee on Child Welfare, a visiting housekeeper for the United Charities of Dallas, a teacher of dietetics at City Hospital, a demonstrator for the State Food Administration, and a teacher of knitting for the Red Cross. Mabel Massey, 1899, was a county home demonstration agent, and Carrie Toomer, 1913, was a hospital dietitian. Alice (Sawyer) Cooper, 1915, was manager of a cafeteria operated by the Consumers' Cooperative Association of New York, which had 2,000 members. Sue Ramsey (Johnston) Ferguson, 1918, was "an itinerant teacher of foods and nutrition" sent out by the State Department of Vocational Education to work with clubs. Rebecca Cushing, 1920, was state supervisor of home economics, and Nell Kennett, 1928, was director of home demonstration agents for western North Carolina.

Agriculture

Few graduates turned to agriculture as a primary occupation, but Bessie Heath Daniel, 1905, who ran a farm in Pearson County, was described by the editor of her local paper as one who had meant most "to the general uplift of the farmer and the county in general." Elsie Brame Hunt, 1926, served as North Carolina Grange deputy and was the first woman to be on the North Carolina State Board of Health. Grace (Stone) Kennett, 1923, worked as a seed analyst for the North Carolina Department of Agriculture. Margaret (Hood) Caldwell, 1933, was twice elected master of the North Carolina State Grange. Only three other women in the United States have served as state master, and they were elected only once. There were others who, like Blanche (Hedgecock) Owen, 1924, looked on farming as a secondary occupation. After her husband's death, she taught school, operated a farm, reared her own child and two of her brother's, and helped organize a 4-H Club in Guilford County.

Writing

Newspaper work has called forth the talents of some of the alumnae. Minnie Littman, 1911, was a reporter for the New Bedford (Massachusetts) *Evening Standard,* and Gertrude Carraway, 1915, worked for papers in Smithfield and New Bern. Anne (Cantrell) White, 1922, was woman's editor for the Greensboro *Daily News,* and Nell (Craig) Strowd, 1923, filled that position for the Greensboro *Record.* Mrs. Strowd was later director of the News Bureau at the Woman's College. Frances (Gibson) Satterfield, 1928, a feature writer, published a biographical sketch of Charles Duncan McIver. Hazel Mizelle, 1922, worked for the Asheville *Times* and then edited her own paper, the Black Mountain *News.* Virginia (Terrell) Lathrop, 1923, author of *Educate a Woman,* had perhaps the most varied experience, having worked as a reporter in Raleigh, Greensboro, Asheville, New York, London, and Paris.

Rose (Batterham) Housekeeper, 1911, was one of the first graduates to have a book published, *Pleasure Piece.* Mildred (Harrington) Lynch was at one time an editorial assistant and feature writer on the staff of *American Magazine;* later she had stories published in *Good Housekeeping, Saturday Evening Post,* and several other magazines. She also published *My Own Story,* by Marie Dressler as told to Mildred Harrington. Jane (Groome) Love, 1913, wrote *Earth Child and Other Poems.* Marjorie Craig, 1919, also a poet, had a book of poems published posthumously, *The Known Way.* As a teacher, she inspired many young writers, among them Edythe Latham and Burke Davis. Mr. Davis dedicated his third novel, *Yorktown,* thus: "For Marjorie Craig, who first encouraged." Edith (Russell) Harrington, 1919, wrote over fifty pageants for her company, Harrington-Russell Festivals. Julia (Montgomery) Street, 1923, was the author of several books for young people. Julia (Blauvelt) McGrave, 1926, wrote poems for *Saturday Review, Poetry, Atlantic Monthly, Harper's,* and other magazines.

Art

Although art courses were limited at the college until after 1931, there were a few alumnae who pursued careers in this field. Bessie Battle, 1895, gave private lessons and painted china and greeting cards. Inez Croom, 1910, taught at the New York School of Interior Design and worked as a decorator with a company producing hand-painted wall paper. Margaret Rowlett, 1925, designed fabrics, gift cards, and wrapping paper. She was also the author of children's books, for which she did the illustrations. Brooks (Johnson) Silvette, 1926, after receiving her M.F.A. from Columbia, studied in Paris. Some of her paintings were exhibited at the Grand Palais. Ruth (Abbott) Clarke, 1931, had one-man shows in Greensboro, Raleigh, Reidsville, Winston-Salem, and Charlotte. At least two of the graduates were connected with museums. Margaret Gash, 1895, was with the Metropolitan Museum of Art, and Lucy Cherry Crisp, 1919, was executive director of the North Carolina Museum of Art and later of the Greenville W.P.A. Art Gallery. She also published a book of verse, *Spring Fever.* There were, of course, others who taught art in the public schools.

Music

Among the musicians was Alice Vaiden Williams, 1917, who did further study in New York. She was accompanist for performers such as Madame Nina Morgan and Lawrence Tibbett. Marie (Davenport) Harrill, 1922, played the organ at theaters in New York. Hermene (Warlick) Eichhorn, 1926, was a composer as well as organist and choir director. Louise (Gorham) Winstead, 1921, was one of the larger number who taught public school music.

Theater

The theater has attracted such graduates as Hattie Motzno, 1913, who was secretary of the Greenwich Village Theater. One of her duties was to select plays to be produced. Mary (Low) Burns, 1918, performed in vaudeville across the country. Margaret (George) Hosmer, 1918, and Edith (Russell) Harrington, 1919, established the Players Guild, a stock company in Asheville. Mrs. Hosmer performed with stock companies in Canada and Pennsylvania. Ellen (Rose) Miller, 1917, was once *premiere danseuse* at the Hippodrome in New

York. Phoebe (Baughan) Barr, 1927, taught dancing and performed with the Denishawn Dancers, also in New York.

Religious Work

Foreign mission work called many of the alumnae to serve around the world. Alma Pittman, 1902, was superintendent of nurses in a hospital in China. Also in China were Frances Burkhead, 1899; Lelia Tuttle, 1900; Annie (Chestnutt) Stuart, 1904; Lettie (Spainhour) Hamlett, 1905; Mary (Jarmon) Hearn, 1905; Mary (Bryson) Tipton, 1906; Grace (McCubbins) Crable, 1909; Helen (Howard) McFadyen, 1909; and Venetia Cox, 1912. Ida Hankins, 1903, served thirty-six years in Korea. Euline Smith, 1917, taught at the Carolina Institute in Seoul, Korea, and was an ordained minister of the Korean Methodist Church. Naomi Schell, 1911, was in Japan. Africa called Louise (Dixon) Crane, 1905; Mary Wood McKenzie, 1911; Cora Caudle, 1916; Lorena Kelly, 1925; and Nolie K. McDonald, 1926. Sadie Woodruff, 1914, went to Rangoon, Burma. Annie Lee Stafford, 1919, was principal of Moravian Junior High School in Nicaragua, and Hazel (Black) Farrior, 1913, served in Mexico, where she wrote a booklet, *Mexico, Land of Charm,* which was published by the Presbyterian Church of the United States.

Others found full-time religious work at home. Some, like Natalie Nunn, 1911, were pastor's assistants. Others have served as student secretaries to religious groups on college campuses. One of these was Cleo (Mitchell) Espy, 1924.

Miscellany

Some of the careers were less common. Daphne King Carraway, 1894, was a Chatauqua lecturer. Mary (Bayard) Wootten, 1894, became a photographer and was part owner of Wootten-Moulten Studios in Chapel Hill. Fay (Davenport) Harmond, 1912, was superintendent of public welfare in Gaston County, a job which required her to carry a gun. One of her classmates, Myrtle (Siler) Thompson, 1912, was the first woman sheriff in North Carolina, in Chatham County. Gladys (Avery) Tillett, 1915, was a leader in expanding opportunities for women through the Democratic party and was appointed United States representative on the United Nations Commission on the Status of Women. Ruby (Patterson) Chandler, 1917, was the first woman in North Carolina to hold a license as manager of a cotton warehouse. Mary Gwynn, 1916, was owner and manager of a camp for girls in western North Carolina. Ruth Johnston, 1914, was a "social expert and survey organizer." Her main duty was to direct surveys for organizations. Virginia Tucker, 1930, was an aerodynamicist with Northrop Aircraft in California. One who had different jobs was Harriet Berry, 1897. For several years she was executive secretary for the North Carolina Good Roads Association. Later she organized the Farmers' Credit Union and edited *Market News* for the North Carolina Department of Agriculture.

War Work

During World War I alumnae served at home and overseas. Among the nurses in France were Frances Hays, 1912; Mary (Greenfield) Watson, 1906; Maud Vinson Elliott, 1912; and Nannie Burnette, 1899. Mrs. Watson served with the hospital unit directed by Dr. Wesley Long, prominent physician and surgeon, after whom the community hospital in Greensboro is named. Annie A. Vaughn, 1911, received a medal from the British government in recognition of her services with the YMCA overseas. Martha Peden, 1903, served with the Red Cross as secretary to the chief of military affairs. She worked with refugees, nursed the wounded, and organized entertainment.

During World War II Mary Webb Nicholson, the first woman pilot in North Carolina, was killed in a crash landing while flying for the British Air Transport Auxiliary of the Royal Air Force. The first woman to receive the Legion of Merit was Westray (Battle) Long, 1919, who was a lieutenant colonel in the Women's Army Corps. Also active in World War II were Lorna (Thigpen) David, 1925; Katherine Taylor, 1928; Inez (Spainhour) Corbitt, 1930; Mabel F. LaBarr, 1930; and Mary Edith (Kimsey) Benedict, 1931. Dorothy Clement, 1923, served with the Red Cross in North Africa and Italy. There were, of course, many graduates of later years who joined the armed services.

Alumnae Service Award

In 1960 the Alumnae Association initiated the Alumnae Service Awards to give recognition to those members who had rendered outstanding service to the college. Those who have been thus honored are Emma Lewis (Speight) Morris, 1900; May (Lovelace) Tomlinson, 1907; Laura (Weill) Cone and Jane Summerell, 1910; Clara Booth Byrd, 1913; Sadie (McBrayer) McCain, 1916; Juanita (McDougald) Melchior, 1917; Virginia (Terrell) Lathrop, 1923; and Emily (Harris) Preyer, 1939.[5]

5. Although Mrs. Preyer attended the college after 1931, her name has been included so that the list might be complete.

Honorary Degrees

Recognition of the achievements of former students has come from the college itself. Twelve have been awarded honorary degrees: Mary Callum Wiley, 1894; Emma Lewis (Speight) Morris, 1900; Annie (Kizer) Bost, 1903; Dr. Margaret (Castex) Sturgis, 1905; Laura (Weill) Cone, 1910; Gertrude Sprague Carraway, 1915; Gladys (Avery) Tillett, 1915; Sadie (McBrayer) McCain, 1916; Virginia (Terrell) Lathrop, 1923; Judge Susie Sharp, 1928; Margaret (Hood) Caldwell, 1933; and Margaret Coit, 1941.[6]

Although these examples from the *State Normal Magazine* and the *Alumnae News* were selected to give a comprehensive view of the abilities and the fields of service of the alumnae of the college, the most common items in the journals are not represented. These tell the story of club activities and community service, of graduate study and summer travel. Most important, they tell the story of marriage, of children, and of grandchildren. It was this part of the story that Dr. McIver had in mind when he said, "Educate a man and you educate an individual; educate a woman and you educate a family."

6. Although Miss Coit attended the college after 1931, her name has been included so that the list might be complete. Margaret Coit, distinguished biographer, is a niece of Miss Laura Coit.

eight

Year of Consolidation: 1930-1931

The year 1930-1931 marked a turning point in the growth of the college. Governor O. Max Gardner had long cherished a dream of a great state university developed through the consolidation of the University of North Carolina, North Carolina College of Agriculture and Engineering, and the North Carolina College for Women. The serious economic conditions brought about by the Depression provided just cause for such a change, since it would eliminate duplication of services. Thus the General Assembly voted in 1931 to consolidate the three institutions and to provide for a commission to establish the program by which changes would be made.[1]

The idea of consolidation was not new. According to the Greensboro *Record*, September 5, 1904, it was first mentioned in a speech by Chief Justice Walter Clark at Chapel Hill. The proposal made at that time was similar to the plan which was eventually adopted. One president was to serve the three branches. On each campus the chief executive would be vice-president of the University of North Carolina and dean of administration of his institution. A Board of Trustees of one hundred members was to serve the consolidated university. It was stipulated that ten of these should be women, out of deference to the branch in Greensboro.

One of Dr. Foust's reasons for favoring consolidation was presented in his unpublished history of the college: "I did hope, and still hope that we may finally have co-education at Greensboro, Raleigh, and Chapel Hill. I was then and still am in favor of co-education, and I thought by working on equal terms with the University authorities

1. *Public Laws and Resolutions of the State of North Carolina passed by the General Assembly at its Session of 1931*, c. 202.

this might be attained for all three institutions and the College for Women be saved from unfair competition."[2]

Many changes lay ahead of the North Carolina College for Women, but a review of its last year as a separate institution shows that a good foundation had been laid for the university that it was to become.

Expenses

There was little to set this last year apart. Because of the Depression, which had caused a reduction in the faculty the year before, the enrollment dropped from 1,888 in 1929-1930 to 1,761, and in the second semester the number was 1,650.[3] A severe cut in the state appropriation forced an increase in student fees of $20. Expenses for free tuition[4] students amounted to $324 and for other North Carolina students $369. Out-of-state students paid $424.

Many of the girls sought work to help pay for their expenses. They found jobs on the campus in the dining rooms, laboratories, the library, the bookstore, at the switchboard, and in offices doing typing and clerical work. Others acted as agents for dry cleaners, sold Christmas cards and stationery, and delivered newspapers in the dormitories.

Although the Depression intensified the self-help movement, part-time work had been an accepted practice long before. In 1896 a student from Iredell County wrote to her hometown paper, "This is one place where work is honorable, and some might be surprised to find some of the poorest girls, and who are known to work for their expenses, taking the lead in school and holding the highest esteem."[5] Of the 179 students with jobs in 1931, 62 were listed on the honor roll.

Financial assistance for the students was available from scholarships and loan funds. During the year 1893-1894 there were five scholarships. These had been donated by the faculty, the Class of 1893, Dr. R. H. Stancill (a member of the first Board of Directors), Colonel E. G. Harrell (editor of the *North Carolina Teacher*), and Mrs. Charles D. McIver. The next year scholarships were added by the societies, and the first loan fund was established by Mrs. J. C.

2. Julius I. Foust, "The History of the Woman's College" (unpublished history, Chancellor's Office, The University of North Carolina at Greensboro), p. 173. This hope was not to be realized at the Woman's College until 1964, a year after it became the University of North Carolina at Greensboro.

3. "Vital Statistics," *Alumnae News*, XIX (April, 1931), 12. In 1933-1934 enrollment reached its lowest point, 1,266.

4. Free tuition was abolished in 1931 as a result of consolidation.

5. Statesville *Landmark*, Jan. 31, 1896.

Buxton of Winston-Salem, who gave the money her invalid son had saved during his brief lifetime.[6] Other scholarships and loan funds were established through the years, making possible the education of many girls. One such student was Antoinette Black, who borrowed $220 from the Alumnae Fund. After she was graduated in 1911, she began paying the money back, pasting each canceled note in her scrapbook as she received it. When she finished the payments on February 25, 1915, she wrote in the book, "It was very hard—but it pays." Her scrapbook is now in the College Collection.

In 1930 the loan funds totaled almost $60,000, and there were a few scholarships. One was the Sarah and Evelyn Bailey Scholarship, which had been established by Mr. and Mrs. T. B. Bailey in memory of their daughters who died in the typhoid epidemic of 1899. Some which have been continued were those given by the United Daughters of the Confederacy and by Judge John Gray Bynum. The Henry Weil Fellowship was given to an outstanding senior for graduate study. Since the girl selected had the highest scholastic average in her class, this award was a great honor. The recipients from 1924 to 1931 were Julia Ross (Asheboro), Margaret Bridgers (Tarboro), Kate Hall (Asheville), Josephine Hege (Rosemary), Katherine Taylor (Salisbury), Clara Guignard (Lincolnton), Mattie-Moore Taylor (Enfield), and Mary Jane Wharton (Greensboro).

The Student Body

Since Dr. McIver wanted his college to represent "every respectable class" and all sections of the state, he would have been proud of the scope of the student body in 1930-1931. Ashe and Graham were the only North Carolina counties that did not have representatives at the college. There were students from eighteen states, and one student was registered from China. In 1892 fathers of students had been classified in seventeen occupational groups; in 1930 the number had grown to seventy-six. Farmers and merchants headed the list in both years, but the proportion of merchants had increased. McIver would also have been pleased that 122 of the students were daughters of former students.

Admission Requirements

The standards by which the students were selected in 1930 were far more specific than those of the first year. All students were

6. *Second Annual Catalogue,* p. 48. This loan fund was later combined with others to form the Students' Loan Fund. *Thirty-ninth Annual Catalogue,* p. 49.

required to have three years of English, two and a half years of mathematics, and two years of history. Two years of a foreign language were required of all except those wishing to major in literature and languages, who were required to present three years of Latin and two years of a modern foreign language. Those majoring in science, physical education, and home economics had to have one year of science, and those in music, two years of music. Electives sufficient to complete fifteen units were to be chosen from a prescribed list. Specific requirements, such as subject matter and textbooks, were given for mathematics, history, Latin, French, German, Spanish, home economics, and music.

Enrollment by Departments

The following table will show the size of the departments in the fall of 1930.

	No. of Instructors	No. of Courses	No. of Sections	No. En-rolled	No. of Majors
Biology	9	15	33	763	31
Chemistry	5	7	14	243	12
Education	19	15	37	611	135*
English	14	25	68	1,797	95
German	1	3	6	119	
History and Political Science	8	12	34	1,059	50
Home Economics	7	14	19	462	77
Hygiene	3	3	18	531	
Latin	1	5	5	38	4
Library Science	1	5	5	132	51
Mathematics	3	8	13	174	14
Music	12	21	28	577	33
Physical Education	8	17	60	1,797	26
Physics	2	4	6	130	2
Psychology	4	5	20	511	
Romance Languages	11	22	51	1,040	45
Sociology and Economics	3	8	12	275	18**

* This number includes only those majoring in primary and elementary education.

** Mary Taylor Moore, ''Report of the Registrar,'' in the *President's Report to the Board of Directors, 1928-1930*, p. 26. Of the forty-five majors in Romance languages, forty were in French. There were six majors in economics, and twelve in sociology.

There were 281 graduates in 1931. Although several master's degrees had been awarded in preceding years, there were no candidates at this time. The following degrees were conferred: Bachelor of Arts, 215; Bachelor of Science in Home Economics, 38; Bachelor of Science in Music, 17; and Bachelor of Science in Physical Education, 11.[7]

Student Personnel Services

When college opened in the fall of 1930, the new students came early for Freshman Week, an orientation period initiated in 1928. After aptitude tests and placement tests in English and foreign languages were given, students registered and bought their books. During the week there were lectures on such subjects as "How to Study," "How to Use the Library," "History and Tradition of the College," and "Citizenship in the College Community." Some of the juniors came to advise the freshmen and to plan entertainment.

The Department of Student Life met weekly to discuss student problems. This organization grew out of the Council of Faculty and Students on Non-Academic Activities, which had been organized in 1918. The faculty members of the department were the president, the dean of women, the college physician, counselors, the alumnae secretary, the YWCA secretary, the vocational director, the placement secretary, the dietitian, and the supervisor of dormitories. Students were the president and vice-president of the Student Government Association, the presidents of the YWCA, the Athletic Association, and the senior class, and the editor of the *Carolinian.*

President Foust had worked steadily during the years to develop a strong staff in student affairs. In the beginning, the president, the college physician, and the lady principal were primarily responsible. McIver and Foust handled serious discipline problems, Dr. Gove was responsible for the health of the students, and Miss Kirkland and later Miss Emma King supervised social activities. Faculty members lived in the dormitories. Later these were replaced by counselors who were primarily responsible for the conduct of the students. When the freshmen were placed in a separate hall in 1926, Miss Jamison was appointed adviser to freshmen.

Miss Jane T. Miller came in 1912 as the first general secretary for the Young Women's Christian Association. In 1913 Miss Frances Womble, an alumna, was employed as high school visitor. Her duty was to acquaint high school students with the college.

Mrs. Chase Going Woodhouse was appointed vocational director in 1928. There had been a placement service for years through the Commercial Department and the School of Education, but Mrs.

7. Mary Taylor Moore, "Report of the Registrar," in *President's Report to the Board of Directors, 1930-1932.*

Woodhouse's duties included the investigation of job opportunities and the guidance of students as well as placement. She was also in charge of the Institute of Women's Professional Relations, which published "Occupations for College Women," an annotated bibliography of 1,184 articles and books; "Fellowships and Other Aid for Advanced Work"; and "Women and the Ph.D."

In 1929 Mrs. Frone Brooks Hughes came as appointment secretary, her main responsibility being the placing of graduates.

An Academic Board was appointed in 1929 to consider failures. It was the duty of this committee to decide which students should be asked to leave and which should be placed on probation.

Lecture-Entertainment Series

The Depression did not curtail the lectures and concerts. The Civic Music programs included Alexander Brailowsky, Dusolina Gianni, the English Singers, the Minneapolis Symphony, and the Gordon String Quartette.

The Lecture Series brought twelve speakers, many of whom were outstanding: Dr. Everett Dean Martin, American educator and author; Miss Agnes McPhail, first woman member of the Canadian Parliament; Samuel Gaillard Stoney, Southern writer and speaker; John Herman Randall, author and professor of philosophy at Columbia University; Sir Hubert Wilkins, Australian polar explorer and aviator; Ronny Johansson, Swedish dancer; Miss Frances Perkins, head of the Department of Labor of New York, later U. S. secretary of labor; Salvador de Madariaga y Rojo, Spanish writer and diplomat; Louis Untermeyer, poet, critic, anthologist; Lowell Thomas, author and radio news commentator; Dr. Howard Lee McBain, author and professor of political science at Columbia University; and Dr. Fred Louis Pattee, noted authority on American literature.

Another cultural event was the appearance of the Ben Greet Players. Under the direction of Sir Philip Ben Greet, they presented *Hamlet* and *Twelfth Night* in Aycock Auditorium.

Student Organizations

In 1930 the Student Government Association held the preschool conference at Silver Pines Camp, Roaring Gap. Mary Jane Wharton of Greensboro was president. The constitution was revised that year, making three divisions of government instead of two. The executive branch remained the same, but the Legislature replaced the Senate.

The judicial function of the Senate was taken over by the Judicial Board.[8]

The rules still forbade smoking,[9] and at only one dance a year were men permitted. Freshmen and sophomores were required to have chaperones for evening engagements with men, but seniors were allowed to attend a Saturday night movie with an escort or in groups of three. On every night except Saturday all students were required to be in their rooms at 10:30 and freshmen and sophomores to have their lights out.[10]

The number of organizations had grown to over two dozen. There was an organization for almost every department, and some for special interest groups. The major ones were the Quill Club, Madrigal Club, Speakers Club, Zoology Field Club, El Circulo Espanol, Dolphin Club, the newly organized Seal Club, Young Women's Christian Association, Home Economics Club, Journalism Club, Botany Club, Le Circle Français, Mathematics Club, Archery Club, Orchesus Club, Der Deutsche Verein, Chemistry Club, Orchestra, Education Club, International Relations Club, Masqueraders, Playlikers, Physics Club, Young Voters Club, Athletic Association, and the four societies.

Stunt Night centered around well-known national advertisements. The senior class skit was called "Good to the Last Drop," and the Athletic Association called theirs "Body by Fisher." The *Carolinian* choice, "Even Your Best Friend Won't Tell You," was somewhat cryptic.[11] Freshmen were entertained by their sister class, the juniors, with a secret Green and White Ceremony. Afterward there was a weiner roast and the Junior Serenade. On another occasion the YWCA gave a tea for the freshmen.

The YWCA held the annual Lantern Festival in Peabody Park on October 4. The work of the organization was carried out on a dormitory plan. A vesper service was held in each dormitory on Sunday evening, and there was a general meeting once a month.[12] Mary Delia Rankin of Mount Holly was president.

Founder's Day was a holiday, featuring a speech by Dr. Beverly Tucker, professor of neurology at Richmond Medical College, who spoke on Leonardo da Vinci.[13]

8. *Carolinian*, Sept. 25, 1930.

9. This ban was lifted in 1932 to permit girls to smoke in their rooms.

10. Student Government Association Constitution and Regulations, 1930-1931, in *Students' Handbook*.

11. *Alumnae News*, XIX (Nov., 1930), 22.

12. *Ibid.*

13. *Carolinian*, Oct. 2, 1930. The observation of Founder's Day as a holiday was abolished within a few years.

The four literary societies had become social in nature since their earlier functions had been taken over by specialized groups. They now sponsored parties, dances, sports day, receptions, and bridge parties with gentlemen guests. They continued initiation ceremonies each fall. The new students in 1930 were told to have umbrellas and stockings to match, to wear bright hair bows, and to carry towels for shawls. Of course, they sang the laundry list and bowed to upper classmen.

In October, Student Government Week was observed by the North Carolina Federation of Students. The main event of the week at the college was an address by Edward R. Murrow, a Guilford County native, who was president of the National Student Federation of America.

Playliker productions included *The Fool* by Channing Pollack, *Torches* by George Kelly, *Holiday* by Philip Barry, *Quality Street* by James Barrie, and *The Maid Who Wouldn't Be Proper*, which was directed by a student, Ruth Abbott of Greensboro.

The Speakers Club sponsored debating teams and was responsible for the first intercollegiate debate ever participated in by the college. The N.C.C.W. debaters split teams with the University of North Carolina and debated the topic of compulsory unemployment insurance. The debaters were Eugenia Talley of Randleman, Margaret Bane of Reidsville, Evelyn Underwood of Waynesville, Rosalind Trent of Leaksville, C. A. Shreve, C. D. Wardlaw, W. W. Speight, and F. C. Wardlaw.

The *Coraddi*, now a literary magazine, was composed mostly of poetry with a few stories and sketches. There were also editorials, book reviews, comments on other college magazines, and some light verse. Catherine Harris of Elkin was editor and May Swan of Stedman business manager. Since the students had expressed a desire for illustrations, the first art editor, Florence Barefoot of Wilmington, was appointed. There had also been criticism that the magazine was too sophisticated. The staff interpreted this as an indication that the students needed a magazine that would provide "both satisfaction and cultivation."

Meanwhile the *Carolinian*, under the direction of Betty Brown[14] of Greensboro as editor and Frances White of Clayton as business manager, was raising money for needy families at Christmas, debating

14. Betty Brown, later Mrs. Carlton Jester, Jr., was alumnae secretary at the Woman's College from 1947 to 1955. She was succeeded by Barbara Parrish, Class of 1948.

"Should Women Tolerate Drunkenness?" and winning first place at the North Carolina Collegiate Press Association. There were the usual complaints about conduct in chapel and girls who "bummed" rides to town.

Mabel Tate of High Point was editor of the *Pine Needles* and Sue Trenholm of Rocky Mount was business manager. The yearbook was dedicated to Dr. Gove, and the theme was taken from *The White Doe*, a legend about Virginia Dare written by Mrs. Sallie Southall Cotten, for whom Cotten Hall was named.

The biggest event for Le Circle Français was the production of a play written by M. René Hardré, *Monsieur Dumallet Vient a Paris*, in which Miss Katherine Taylor played a part.[15] In the same year another member of the French department, Miss Jessie T. Laird, was awarded the Palmes Academique by the French government in recognition of her work with war refugees.

There were the traditional observances: the Halloween Party, the Sophomore Christmas Pageant, the Senior Unmusical, Arbor Day, Sports Day, and May Day. The May Queen of 1931 was Esther Shreve of Moorestown, New Jersey, and her attendants were Mary Jane Wharton of Greensboro and Eliza Hatcher of Dunn. The pageant, telling the history of May Day, was directed by Kathryn Mauer of Linden, New Jersey. The climax of the work of the Chorus and Glee Club was their production of the *Messiah*.

Banquets were held by the staffs of the *Carolinian*, the *Coraddi*, and *Pine Needles*, and by the Dolphin Club and the Athletic Association. There were parties for the faculty, for the seniors, for the juniors, and for the students on the Honor Roll. At the Junior-Senior Prom, the couples danced to the music of Jelly Leftwich and his Duke Blue Devils.[16]

Commencement

Commencement festivities began on Friday night with Park Night, followed by a reception of parents, seniors, and alumnae in Anna Howard Shaw Hall. Saturday's activities included Alumnae Day, Class Day, reunion suppers, and a performance of *Quality Street*. The baccalaureate sermon was given on Sunday morning by Dr. Franklin S. Hickman of Duke, and in the afternoon there was an

15. M. Hardré, who served the college as professor of Romance languages for thirty-three years, was one of the best-loved and most highly respected members of the faculty.
16. *Carolinian*, April 23, 1931.

organ recital by Mr. George M. Thompson. The principal speaker for the commencement exercises on Monday was Mr. Deets Pickett, director of the Board of Temperance, from Washington, D. C. For the first time since 1894 the graduates did not receive Bibles, perhaps because of the Depression. Degrees were awarded to 281 graduates.

After consolidation was implemented in 1932, the name of the college was changed to the Woman's College of the University of North Carolina. As such it expanded its offerings while maintaining the same standards of quality and service for which it had always been known. In 1963 the General Assembly, recognizing the expansion of the institution, changed the name to The University of North Carolina at Greensboro. In 1964 it become coeducational, thus broadening its role in the state system of education.

From the beginning, "Service" has been the motto of the institution. Seventy-five years after the founding, the catalogue still announces that "it desires to be of the greatest possible service to the people of North Carolina." The record of the past indicates that in the future The University of North Carolina at Greensboro will become an even more vital force in the state. "Of a good beginning cometh a good end."

BIBLIOGRAPHY

A. BOOKS

Arnett, Ethel Stephens. *Greensboro, North Carolina.* Chapel Hill: The University of North Carolina Press, 1955.

Camp, Cordelia (ed.). *Some Pioneer Women Teachers of North Carolina.* Delta Kappa Gamma Society, North Carolina State Organization, 1955.

Forney, E. J., Fodie Buie, and Emily Semple Austin. *Leaves from the Stenographers' Notebooks.* Greensboro: Harrison Printing Co., n.d.

Holder, Rose Howell. *McIver of North Carolina.* Chapel Hill: The University of North Carolina Press, 1957.

Knight, Edgar W. *Public School Education in North Carolina.* New York: Houghton Mifflin Company, 1916.

Lathrop, Virginia Terrell. *Educate a Woman.* Chapel Hill: The University of North Carolina Press, 1942.

Pearson, Thomas Gilbert. *Adventures in Bird Protection.* New York: D. Appleton-Century Company, 1937.

Russell, Phillips. *The Woman Who Rang the Bell.* Chapel Hill: The University of North Carolina Press, 1949.

Scarborough, John C. *Biennial Report of the Superintendent of Public Instruction.* Raleigh: Ashe and Gatling, 1883.

Smith, William C. *Mary Settle Sharpe.* Philadelphia: Stackhouse, n.d.

Turrentine, Samuel Bryant. *A Romance of Education.* Greensboro, N.C.: Piedmont Press, 1946.

Wilson, Louis R. *The University of North Carolina under Consolidation, 1931-1963: History and Appraisal.* Chapel Hill: The University of North Carolina Consolidated Office, 1964.

B. PERIODICALS

Alumnae News (University of North Carolina at Greensboro), Vol. I (January, 1912)—Vol. XXXIX (May, 1951).

Coraddi (University of North Carolina at Greensboro, student literary magazine, continuation of *State Normal Magazine*), Vol. XXIV (October, 1919)—Vol. XXXV (May, 1931).

Shuler, Marjorie, "A Friendly Parallel," *Woman's Home Companion,* LI (August, 1924), 20.

State Normal Magazine (student literary magazine, later named
Coraddi), Vol. I (1897)—Vol. XXIII (1919).

C. NEWSPAPERS

Carolinian (published by the students of the University of North
Carolina at Greensboro), May, 1919-June, 1932.
All other newspapers cited were represented by clippings in the
Woman's College Scrapbooks, Vol. I (1891-1893)—Vol. XXXVII
(1929-1931). This collection was begun by Dr. J. M. Spainhour,
charter member of the Board of Directors. After his death it was
continued by the college.

D. PERSONAL INTERVIEWS

Dusenbury, Margaret (Winder), November 17, 1964.
Foust, Mrs. Julius I., August 25, 1964.
Gunter, Ruth, August 19, 1964.
Gwynn, J. Minor, December 17, 1963.
Hathaway, Elizabeth, November 17, 1964.
McKinney, Emma, November 8 and 17, 1964.
Patterson, Mrs. F. N., Sr., December 28, 1963.
Shamburger, Anne, September 29, 1964.
Summerell, Jane, August 21, 1964.
York, Mary, February 2, 1965.

E. PUBLICATIONS AND DOCUMENTS OF THE UNIVERSITY
OF NORTH CAROLINA AT GREENSBORO

Annual Catalogue. Vol. I (1892-1893)—Vol. LV (1931-1932).
Board of Directors. *Annual Report.* 1892-1930; 1930-1932.
———. Proceedings, 1891-1933. 4 vols.
Brown, Wade R. "Reports of the Dean of the School of Music" in
Report of the Board of Directors, 1892-1930.
Building Committee. Minutes, 1922-1933.
Carolinian (yearbook). 1909, 1910, 1911, 1913, 1914, 1915, 1917.
Cook, John H. "Reports of the Dean of the School of Education" in
Report of the Board of Directors, 1892-1930.
———. "Reports of the Director of Summer Session" in *Report of
the Board of Directors, 1892-1930.*
Decennial (published by the Adelphian and Cornelian Literary
societies of the State Normal and Industrial College). 1902.
Executive Committee of the Board of Directors. Minutes, 1913-1918.
2 vols.
Faculty Cabinet. Minutes, 1922-1930.
Faculty Council. Minutes, 1898-1932. 5 vols.
Faculty File in the College Collection, Walter Clinton Jackson Li-

brary, University of North Carolina at Greensboro. Alphabetical file containing clippings and memorials.

Forney, E. J. "Reports of the Treasurer" in *Report of the Board of Directors, 1892-1930.*

Foust, Julius I. "Reports of the President" in *Report of the Board of Directors, 1892-1930; 1930-1932.*

Livers, W. H. "Reports of the Director of Extension" in *Report of the Board of Directors, 1892-1930.*

McIver, Charles Duncan. "Reports of the President" in *Report of the Board of Directors, 1892-1930.*

Moore, Mary Taylor. "Reports of the Registrar" in *Report of the Board of Directors, 1892-1930.*

Pine Needles (yearbook). 1920-1942.

"Prospectus of the Normal and Industrial School of North Carolina, 1892-'93" in *Report of the Board of Directors, 1892-1930.*

Shaffer, Blanche E. "Reports of the Dean of the School of Home Economics" in *Report of the Board of Directors, 1892-1930.*

Shaw, Charles B. "Reports of the Director of Extension" in *Report of the Board of Directors, 1892-1930.*

——. "Reports of the Librarian" in *Report of the Board of Directors, 1892-1930.*

Smith, William C. "Reports of the Dean of the College of Liberal Arts and Sciences" in *Report of the Board of Directors, 1892-1930.*

Stone, Charles H. "Reports of the Librarian" in *Report of the Board of Directors, 1892-1930.*

Students' Handbooks. 1897-1932. Issued by the Young Women's Christian Association and by the Student Government Association.

F. MISCELLANEOUS

Black, Antoinette. Scrapbook. Now in the Walter Clinton Jackson Library, The University of North Carolina at Greensboro.

Foust, Julius I. "The History of the Woman's College." Unpublished history, Chancellor's Office, The University of North Carolina at Greensboro.

Holder, Elizabeth Jerome. "A History of the Library of the Woman's College of the University of North Carolina." Unpublished M.A. thesis, School of Library Science, The University of North Carolina at Chapel Hill, 1955.

Holt, Thomas M. *Dedication Address by The Honorable Thomas M. Holt at the State Normal and Industrial School. Greensboro, N.C., May 23, 1893.* Greensboro, N.C.: Reece and Elam, Power Printers, 1893.

Laws and Resolutions Passed by the General Assembly at its Session of 1891, c. 139, ss. 1-4.

Lee, Bertha M. Scrapbook. Now in the Davie County Library, Mocksville, N.C.

North Carolina Teachers' Assembly. *A Memorial to the General Assembly of North Carolina from the State Teachers' Assembly, praying the establishment of a North Carolina Normal College for training the Men and Women of the State Who Are Preparing to Teach together with the proposed "Act to Establish a Normal College."* 1886.

————. *Memorial in Behalf of the North Carolina Teachers' Training School.* N.p., 1886.

O'Neill, Marion. "A History of the Physical Education Department at the Woman's College of the University of North Carolina." Unpublished M.A. thesis, Department of Physical Education, Woman's College of the University of North Carolina, 1955.

Proceedings of the Fourth Annual Session of the North Carolina Farmers' State Alliance held in the city of Asheville, N.C.— August 12, 13, 14, and 15, 1890. Raleigh, N.C.: Edwards and Broughton Co., 1890.

Public Laws and Resolutions of the State of North Carolina Passed by the General Assembly at its Session of 1897, c. 230, and *1931,* c. 202.

Report of the Commissioner of Education for the Year 1890-'91. Washington: Government Printing Office, 1894.

INDEX

A

Abbott, Alice, 65

Abbott, Ruth, 176. *See also* Clarke, Mrs. Ruth A.

Adelphian Society, organized, 19. *See also* Literary societies

Ader, Ada, 124

Aderholt, Mabel, 155

Administration Building. *See* Main Building

Albright, Myra Alderman, biographical sketch, 49 (photograph facing p. 118)

Alderman, Edwin A., appears before General Assembly, 6; selected professor of English and history at Normal, 8; develops curriculum, 21; biographical sketch, 31-32; mentioned, 4, 11, 30, 78 (photograph facing p. 38)

Alethian Society, 135

Alexander, Dr. Annie Laurie, 33

Alexander, Dr. Sarah V. Thompson, 162

Allen, Judge Florence E., 119

Alumnae Association, 87, 137-38

Alumnae Tea Room, 87, 90

Anderson, Mrs. Stella Williams, 161

Andrews, E. Benjamin, 18

Angle, Mary Ruth, 65

Anthony, Lucy B., 130

Apple, Bernice, 155

Applewhite, Mary K., 21, 114

Armstrong, Mrs. Mary Foust, 92

Arnet, Dr. Alex Matthews, 55, 65

Arrington, Mary, 19, 148, 159

Athletic Association, 141, 175

Atkisson, Mrs. Claire Henley, biographical sketch, 64-65

Austin, Eliza, 17

Austin, Emily Semple, 17, 160

Avent, Elizabeth, 159

Avery, Edith, 129

Avery, Gladys, 145. *See also* Tillett, Mrs. Gladys A.

Aycock, B. F., 7, 8

Aycock, Charles B., 18, 74, 77, 90

Aycock Auditorium, 90

B

Babbitt, Pattie, 124

Bagby, Gertrude, 114

Bailey, Dr. C. T., 26

Bailey, Evelyn, 75, 124

Bailey, Sarah, 75, 124

Bailey, Thomas B., 75, 85

Bailey Hall, 85

Bailey Memorial Room, 75

Bailey Scholarship, 171

Baker, Mrs. Corinne Cook, 158

Baker, Nancy, 155

Balcomb, E. E., 103

Bane, Margaret, 176

Baptist Student Union, 137

Barber, Frances, 155

Barefoot, Florence, 176

Barker, Ellen, 148

Barn, 82

Barnes, Muriel, 153

Barnet, Oeland, 139 (photograph facing p. 39)

Barney, Winfield S., biographical sketch, 62; mentioned, 53, 103

Barr, Mrs. Phoebe Baughan, 166. *See also* Phoebe Baughan

Barrier, Katherine L., 162

Barrow, Elva, biographical sketch, 64

Barton, Helen, 65, 155

Batterham, Mrs. Rose, 164

Battle, Bessie, 165

Baughan, Phoebe (photograph facing p. 55)

Baughan, Mrs. Phoebe Pegram, 162. *See also* Pegram, Phoebe

Baynes, Effie (photograph facing p. 119)

Beall, Dr. W. P., 124

Beam, Annie, 129. *See also* Funderburk, Mrs. Annie B.

Beam, Mary Sue, 153

Beard, Charles A., 102